Nonlinear Contingency

Nonlinear Contingency Analysis is a guide to treating clinically complex behavior problems such as delusions and hallucinations. It's also a framework for treating behavior problems, one that explores solutions based on the creation of new or alternative consequential contingencies rather than the elimination or deceleration of old or problematic thoughts, feelings, or behaviors.

Chapters present strategies, analytical tools, and interventions that clinicians can use in session to think about clients' problems using decision theory, experimental analysis of behavior, and clinical research and practice.

By treating thoughts and emotions not as causes of behavior but as indicators of the environmental conditions that are responsible for them, patients can use that knowledge to make changes that not only result in changes in behavior, but in the thoughts and feelings themselves.

T. V. Joe Layng, PhD, partner at Generategy, LLC.

Paul Thomas Andronis, PhD, Professor Emeritus of psychological sciences at Northern Michigan University.

R. Trent Codd III, EdS, executive director at the Cognitive-Behavioral Therapy Center of Western North Carolina.

Awab Abdel-Jalil, MS, Constructional Coach at Eastern Florida Autism Center/Great Leaps Academy and graduate student in clinical behavioral psychology.

Nonlinear Contingency Analysis

Going Beyond Cognition and Behavior in Clinical Practice

T. V. Joe Layng, Paul Thomas Andronis, R. Trent Codd III and Awab Abdel-Jalil

Routledge
Taylor & Francis Group

NEW YORK AND LONDON

First published 2022
by Routledge
605 Third Avenue, New York, NY 10158

and by Routledge
2 Park Square, Milton Park, Abingdon, Oxon, OX14 4RN

Routledge is an imprint of the Taylor & Francis Group, an informa business

Library of Congress Cataloging-in-Publication Data
Names: Layng, T. V. Joe, author.
Title: Nonlinear contingency analysis : going beyond cognition and behavior in clinical practice / T.V. Joe Layng, PhD, Paul Thomas Andronis, PhD, R. Trent Codd III, Ed S, Awab Abdel-Jalil, MS.
Identifiers: LCCN 2021019974 (print) | LCCN 2021019975 (ebook) | ISBN 9780367689537 (hardback) | ISBN 9780367689506 (paperback) | ISBN 9781003141365 (ebook)
Subjects: LCSH: Cognition disorders—Treatment. | Behavior therapy. | Behavioral assessment.
Classification: LCC RC553.C64 L39 2022 (print) | LCC RC553.C64 (ebook) | DDC 616.89/142—dc23
LC record available at https://lccn.loc.gov/2021019974
LC ebook record available at https://lccn.loc.gov/2021019975

ISBN: 978-0-367-68953-7 (hbk)
ISBN: 978-0-367-68950-6 (pbk)
ISBN: 978-1-003-14136-5 (ebk)

DOI: 10.4324/9781003141365

Typeset in Sabon
by Apex CoVantage, LLC

This book is dedicated to the memory of Israel
Goldiamond, late professor of behavioral sciences
(biopsychology), psychiatry, medicine (nutrition),
and in the College, the University of Chicago, whose
work serves as the foundation of the approach
found in the book. Izzy was a true scholar well
ahead of his time; his impact will continue to be felt
for many years to come.

Contents

About the Authors

T. V. Joe Layng, PhD, has over 50 years of experience in the experimental and applied analysis of behavior. Joe earned a PhD in behavioral science (biopsychology) at the University of Chicago. At Chicago, he investigated animal models of psychopathology, specifically the recurrence of pathological patterns (head-banging) as a function of normal behavioral processes. While at Chicago he contributed to the discovery and characterization of the behavioral process known as contingency adduction. Joe has extensive clinical behavior analysis experience with a focus on ambulatory schizophrenia, especially the systemic as well as topical treatment of delusional speech and hallucinatory behavior. He has also worked extensively on the design of learning environments. Joe co-founded the educational software firm Headsprout. There he was chief architect and led the scientific team that developed the technology that forms the basis of the award-winning, patented *Early Reading* and *Reading Comprehension* online programs. He has published over 50 articles or chapters, a wide array of software programs, and a self-instruction book introducing Signal Detection Theory. Joe is currently a partner at Generategy, LLC; a Fellow of the Association for Behavior Analysis International; and Chair, Board of Trustees, The Chicago School of Professional Psychology.

Paul Thomas Andronis, PhD, is a specialist in experimental and applied behavior analysis who served for thirty-one years as Professor of Psychological Sciences and Coordinator of Northern Michigan University's Behavior Analysis option, and taught courses in this and other areas of behavioral sciences. His research on some sources of novel patterns of behavior, and on animal behavior processes, guide his interests in widespread applications of behavioral technology to important social, clinical, and personal behavior problems. Paul performed the experimental investigation that led to the discovery of contingency adduction. He earned his PhD in biopsychology at the University of Chicago, completed a three-year USPHS Postdoctoral Fellowship in Psychiatry there, and subsequently was appointed Assistant Professor of Clinical Psychiatry in the Department of Psychiatry (Section on Behavioral Medicine), and Instructor in the Committee on Biopsychology, and in the College of the University of Chicago.

R. Trent Codd III, EdS, BCBA, is Vice President of Clinical Operations—North Carolina for Refresh Mental Health. He treats a broad range of clinical concerns but has particular interest and specialization in the treatment of disorders of over-control and Obsessive-Compulsive Disorder. In addition to delivering clinical behavior analytic services, he is active in training delivery, supervision, and practice-based research. He is editor or co-author of four books.

Awab Abdel-Jalil, MS, began his study of behavior analysis as an undergraduate at the University of North Texas and carried his passion for the science into the graduate program. On the graduate level, he was introduced to the work of Dr. Israel Goldiamond in Dr. Jesús Rosales-Ruiz's Constructional Life Design lab. In lab, he participated in streamlining and carrying out constructional programs for first-generation students and students from low-income families. Awab has presented on the constructional approach and other topics at the Association for Behavior Analysis International. He also conducted basic human operant research on resurgence, contingency adduction, stimulus control, and schedules of reinforcement using the Portable Operant Research and Teaching Laboratory (PORTL). He currently works as the Constructional Coach at Eastern Florida Autism Center/Great Leaps Academy.

Acknowledgments

All the authors want to acknowledge and express our profound gratitude to Israel Goldiamond. For some of us it is his genius, work, and many papers that inspired us. For Joe and Paul, he was also a teacher, mentor, and friend. His insight, perseverance, and humor in the face of obstacles that would have ended many careers, will always stand as a model of what a true commitment to scholarship should be. We thank all our colleagues and friends who took the time to read and comment on sections of this book as they were written. A special thanks goes to Susan Friedman, Adrienne Fitzer, Leah Herzog, and especially Russell Layng, who was instrumental in fine tuning the final text. We also greatly appreciate the work of Mary Andronis and Johanna Andronis on creating our index.

Paul Thomas Andronis and T. V. Joe Layng are extremely grateful for the support of our families, Lynn Andronis, and Joanne Robbins who made all our work possible. Joe would also like to thank Zachary Layng for always being willing to be his sounding board, Prentiss Jackson for the introduction to "Izzy," and his friendship and insights over the years and Susan M. Markle and Phillip W. Tiemann for providing the essential repertoires that enabled Joe to take full advantage of his time with Izzy.

R. Trent Codd III wishes to thank James B. Appel, PhD for first introducing him to behaviorism and Marc N. Branch, PhD for deepening his interest and knowledge of behavior analysis. He also wishes to thank Ginger, Isabella, and Caroline for their love and support.

Awab Abdel-Jalil wants to thank Dr. Jesús Rosales-Ruiz for introducing him to the constructional approach and the work of Dr. Israel Goldiamond. Much was learned from doing a master's thesis with Dr. Rosales-Ruiz, and from his classes, labs, and every interaction he's had with him. He also introduced him to Drs. T. V. Joe Layng and Paul Thomas Andronis. That introduction opened so many doors for him, including the opportunity to contribute to this book. They both extended what Dr. Rosales-Ruiz taught him and are great mentors, teachers, and friends. He wants to also thank his friends from graduate school. Their support and encouragement has always meant so much (along with Dr. Traci Cihon). Finally, he thanks his family for all their love and support—especially his parents, Muneeb and Hiam.

Our Purpose

> I am hearing our Lord and demons. On the bus, a man took out his wallet and began flashing his money. I started to nudge my girlfriend to say, "It sure would be nice to have all that money!" Before I could nudge her or say it, I heard a voice in my heart say, "Meet me when we get off the bus and you can have it." My voice in my mind was saying, "This is crazy; Lord, please stop this from happening." But again the voice in my heart took my voice and said, "OK," while I almost yelled out, "Lord, OK nothing! It's not OK!" Then the man put the money back in his wallet.

How might we approach helping the young woman who wrote this? We might prescribe medications, but in this case medical issues precluded that option. We could ignore her talking about her hallucinations and pay close attention when she talks of other things. Perhaps we can help her control her thoughts and feelings or help her simply to accept them and try to find value in other activities.

What all of these approaches have in common is that they are based on a traditional *linear analysis*. That is, the focus is on the disturbing behavior itself and perhaps its immediate (or at times delayed) consequences, often characterized as some type of escape or avoidance. Where the disturbing behavior appears not to have discernible consequences, the focus may be on some form of defective "rule-governed" behavior or maladaptive thoughts. Another approach, however, is possible—one that takes us beyond a focus on behavior, cognition, or defective verbal relations.

For over three decades, Goldiamond and his students worked to formulate a new approach to clinical treatment. What made this approach unique was its application of a *nonlinear contingency analysis* derived from the experimental analysis of behavior, decision theory, and clinical research and practice, which in turn led to often-surprising systemic clinical interventions that did not in fact directly target the presenting complaint. This approach goes beyond simply examining and treating

DOI: 10.4324/9781003141365-1

disturbing behavior, thoughts, or feelings and considers the larger context in which the pattern occurs. Seldom is "behavior," "cognition," or "emotion" the focus of the intervention. Instead, the emphasis is on the *nonlinear* consequential contingencies of which behavior, cognition, and emotion are considered to be a function. And, as we shall find, this is true for the "hallucinations" described in the opening quote.

We will explore what we mean by a nonlinear contingency analysis and its application to understanding disturbing behavior. We will not use the terms *dysfunctional, maladaptive, irrational,* and so on, for as we will discover a nonlinear analysis demonstrates that all of the behavior so labeled is indeed sensible. It may be costly; it may hurt; but in the end, it is the rational outcome of life's requirements.

The approach is consequential, meaning it examines the contingent consequences of one's actions. It also examines the consequences of not engaging in the disturbing behavior and the consequences attached to any available alternative behaviors. Behaviors, thoughts, and feelings are to be understood in this broader context. The joint effect of all of these *contingencies* is what we mean by *nonlinear.* We will find it insufficient to consider only the consequences of disturbing behavior.

The research history of Goldiamond's nonlinear contingency analysis, including its nonclinical roots, was described by T. V. Joe Layng in 2009,[1] yet this advanced approach remains virtually unknown. This book's purpose is threefold: 1) to (re)introduce the results of Goldiamond's extensive clinical work and the research in nonlinear contingency analysis conducted by him, his colleagues, and his students[2] and its more recent extensions; 2) to suggest that therapists and their patients/clients[3] could derive great value from its application; and 3) to assert that the procedures described may provide a fertile ground for further clinical research.

The research approach employed has been described as "control-analysis" investigation.[4] That is, relations are discovered as the investigator adjusts the procedures to gain experimental control. In the case of clinical intervention this means helping a patient achieve therapeutic outcomes, which, based on data may require changes during the treatment intervention.

A long-term clinical research program began in the 1960s with three investigators from three different disciplines: a behavior (contingency) analyst, Israel Goldiamond; a psychoanalyst, Jarl Dyrud; and a social psychiatrist, Miles Miller.[5] While one professional worked with a patient, the other two observed. After the sessions they would discuss what they saw and examine the record of the session. Each would describe the interaction from their perspective and suggest changes in the interactions. Goldiamond and the others would perform a behavioral contingency analysis of the observations and the recommended changes, with the intervention adjusted until patient progress was reliably obtained. The primary goal was to understand how verbal behavior changes in a session could result in behavior changes outside the session. Such transfer was thoroughly analyzed and described. Certain practices from psychoanalytic therapy were analyzed in terms of what technically was described as "stimulus control," which included abstraction and metaphorical extension. Research co-investigator psychoanalyst Jarl Dyrud later wrote, "Our assumption is that even seemingly erratic behavior is in fact consequential, often at a level below awareness, and that the elucidation of its consequences is our major vehicle for treatment (making the unconscious conscious). For this reason, I am confident that behavior analysis along Skinnerian lines can be helpful to us."[6]

Goldiamond and Dyrud[7] describe their approach this way:

> Our test for the efficacy of psychotherapy was not to compare it with some control group. Rather, we were concerned with a fine-grain analysis within sessions. Our task was to ascertain if we could observe functional relations within sessions between the behavior or procedures of the therapist, the independent variable, and the behavior of the patient, the dependent variable. If such functional relations could be found, the next question was whether they could be related to changes in referent behaviors outside the session. Within a context of control rather than prediction, the procedure would involve attempting to produce, in accord with the stipulated functional relations, programmed changes in the dependent variable by changing the values of the independent variable. This we would regard as an extension of the control-procedural-single organism strategy of operant research. The cumulative records provide for fine-grain analysis of ongoing events within experimental sessions, in contrast to the end-session comparison of total or before/after scores obtained using the predictive-statistical-group strategy.

This experimental investigation continued over a period of years with many patients and established the underlying strategies that would later evolve into Goldiamond's constructional approach and nonlinear contingency analysis. This approach to clinical investigation is not typical of most clinical research, which relies on testing different theories of intervention in group comparison studies, or with pre-tests and post-tests comprising a standard questionnaire or survey. The goal here was an ever-adjusting procedure, based upon ongoing patient data, that resulted in behavior change specific to the individual.

Goldiamond planned that in his retirement he would publish the most recent results of years of the control-analysis clinical research of which he was a pioneer and a master. Sadly, when he passed away in 1995, hundreds of patient files were destroyed in accord with university policy, and, unfortunately for clinicians, his plans were never realized. We hope that one outcome of this book is that a new generation will take up the research challenge.

Goldiamond's approach is rigorous and complex. It cannot be mastered in a weekend bootcamp or through a series of workshops. Most who participated in the development of the approach were well trained in the experimental analysis of behavior. They frequently drew upon such a background when they treated patients. Accordingly, one would often encounter references to "ratio-strain," "adjunctive behavior," "shaping," or "stimulus control" in clinical reports. The approach also draws upon extensive experimental work in decision theory, game theory, and other investigations into what may be considered choice. Nonetheless, others without an extensive experimental laboratory background have found the approach quite useful.[8]

The approach, analysis, and interventions can be powerful and life-changing for those who experience them, whether clinicians or patients. At times the effects are immediate and breathtaking; at other times it seems like a long uphill climb. And therein lies one of its salient features: there are no magical procedures, no simple recipes such as "if this diagnosis, do that." Nor is there an overriding theory of "pathological" behavior, thinking, or emotions; patients are not considered to be engaging in maladaptive or pathological behavior. Instead, each case is treated as a sensible outcome of each individual's personal interaction with the environment, in particular the consequential contingencies that shaped and maintain the pattern. As observed by noted clinical social worker Eileen Gambrill[9]:

> Appeal to thoughts and feelings are incomplete accounts which, when viewed as complete, hinder change. Somehow, we must show this over and over by memorable accounts of lost opportunities to help clients by accepting incomplete accounts. Only by a contextual analysis of problems is the heroic nature of clients revealed. Behaviors that appear bizarre are usually creative (but costly) solutions to life's challenges.
>
> (Goldiamond, 1974)

At no time are surveys, mental tests, or introspective indices of any sort used as "dependent variables." The only outcomes that matter are whether or not the patients achieve the (precisely defined and measured) behavioral outcomes they are after. In Goldiamond's formulation, the diagnosis or the setting do not matter. The same procedures are applicable in both inpatient and outpatient environments. The individuals Goldiamond and his students served comprised those found in typical inpatient and outpatient settings and included conditions described as catatonic states, acute psychotic episodes, the chronic multi-problem patient, all forms of anxiety, borderline personality disorder, depression, obsessive-compulsive disorder, etc. Some simply wanted to improve their day-to-day lives. Individuals where organic involvement was at the core (as with stroke, injury, cognitive decline, or disease) were not excluded.[10] The nonlinear analysis and interventions were not restricted to individual patients and were applied at scale across a range of environments including businesses, hospitals, and schools.

Three key features comprise Goldiamond's nonlinear contingency analysis: 1) a constructional, rather than pathological approach; 2) nonlinear, rather than linear analysis; and 3) systemic as well as topical interventions. As we will see in the following chapters, in practice all combine into a single vision. We will conclude with a case study involving the woman whose quote began this chapter that exemplifies much of this vision.

We have made several references to the term *contingency*. The term frequently occurs in discussions within behavior analysis. Seldom however is an explicit definition provided. We shall explore the concept in detail in Chapter 3, but in preparation for that we will first provide a brief overview of some of the fundamental concepts behind a consequential contingency analysis.

Notes

1 (Layng, 2009)
2 Andronis, Layng, & Goldiamond, 1997; Flanagan, Goldiamond, Azrin, 1958, 1959; Gimenez, Layng, & Andronis, 2003; Goldiamond, 1962, 1964, 1965a, 1965b, 1965c, 1969, 1970, 1974, 1975a, 1975b, 1975c, 1976a, 1976b, 1976c, 1977, 1978, 1979a, 1979b, 1984; Goldiamond & Dyrud, 1968; Goldiamond, Dyrud, & Miller, 1965; Goldiamond & Schwartz, 1975; Issacs, Thomas, & Goldiamond, 1960; Layng, 2006, 2017; Layng & Andronis, 1984; Layng, Merley, Cohen, Andronis, & Layng, 1976; Layng, Andronis, & Goldiamond, 1999; Merley & Layng, 1976; Schwartz & Goldiamond, 1975; Travis, 1982; Whitehead, Renault, & Goldiamond, 1976
3 At times the term *patient* will be used, and at other times *client* will be used in the following chapters.
4 Goldiamond & Thompson, 1967/2002
5 See Goldiamond et al., 1965; Goldiamond & Dyrud, 1968
6 Dyrud, 1971, p. 302
7 Goldiamond & Dyrud, 1968, p. 60
8 See for example, Gambrill, 2012; Schwartz & Goldiamond, 1975
9 2015, p. 132
10 See for example, Drossel & Traham, 2015; Goldiamond, 1974, 1979a; Layng & Andronis, 1984

2

Fundamentals of Consequential Contingency Analysis

The explanatory model favored here may be described as *radically behavioral*. This term is meant to convey not a restriction to publicly accessible behavior by individuals or a disregard for private experience, but that the analysis goes to the *root* causes of both public and private experience. It includes matters that go beyond the often superficial portrayal of behavioral approaches rendered in more mentalistic psychology texts. Hence, there are sections of this and later chapters that introduce readers to the role of emotions and emotional behavior, verbal behavior, and reports of "private events" (like thoughts and feelings) in the practical assessment and analysis of behavior problems. The current narrative is not meant to be an exhaustive review of specific methods of analysis, though some of these methods are covered in detail. It is, instead, a description of a particular approach to behavioral contingency analysis that articulates with common practices in a range of areas in psychology and psychiatry and can lead to more effective uses of behavioral principles in analyzing and ameliorating human suffering from behavior problems.

Consequential contingency analysis is not simply about observing and recording behavior alone. It involves a comprehensive examination of the context in which behavior occurs; that is, it investigates the relations among many environmental factors that can account for particular behavior occurring at given times and places. We say this to dispel the all-too-common and misleading assertion that behavioral approaches are superficial and interested only in "performance" on the surface of an inner world that requires a mentalistic analysis of more important psychodynamic forces that underlie behavior. This latter view portrays behavioral assessment as a mere descriptive cataloguing of actions by individuals (often in unnecessary and somewhat tiresome detail). But to borrow the thoughts of noted biologist Ernst Mayr, behavioral assessment is *not* mere postage stamp collecting.

First and foremost, behavioral contingency analysis is comprehensive. It entails the extensive collection of detailed data about behavior, preferably while it is occurring in its natural ecology. This includes precise

DOI: 10.4324/9781003141365-2

definition, careful classification, and direct observation of behavior and the subsequent analysis of data that describe the relations between behavior and its defining circumstances. The analysis is conducted within a theoretical model that pinpoints the specific behaviors that interest us and places them in an explicit causal framework based on over a century of painstaking empirical research on the environmental guidance of behavior. The ecological variables considered in this analysis include the following: 1) the contingent *consequences* of behavior (both those that increase or maintain the likelihood of the behavior's occurrence and others that make the behavior less likely to occur); 2) rules that define how those consequences will occur in relation to the frequency, rate, or timing of the behavior (technically referred to as *schedules* of consequences); 3) characteristics of the setting in whose presence the behavior results in those consequences technically referred to as *discriminative stimuli* (under whose control the behavior occurs); *instructional, abstractional,* and *dimensional* stimuli (these affect how and to what aspects of the discriminative stimuli the organism responds); as well as *stimulus props* (background stimuli that are present but not formally part of the defining contingency requirements and that can disrupt the behavioral relation if they change); 4) *potentiating variables* that make various elements in the contingency relation potent or effective (these can include so-called motivational factors, alternative contingencies available to the individual, other behaviors in the person's repertoire that may facilitate acquiring new ones, and so on); 5) patterns of ancillary or adjunctive behavior that are reliably induced by the contingency but are not necessarily required by it (in the literature, referred to as "schedule-induced behavior," but here labeled *contingency-induced patterns*); the individual's *history* in relation to the contingency at hand (or the *program* that led to the current behavior of interest); and 6) the other *alternative contingencies* to which the organism is exposed at the time the targeted behavior occurs. During assessment, the behavior's ecology is parsed into these classes of variables and analyzed in terms of their potential effects on the behavior. Particulars about both the physical and social environments are included. We will examine this causal model in more detail in subsequent chapters.

Aspects of the physical environment may facilitate or obstruct behavior in various ways. For example, a student will be more likely to attend to a critical term or phrase in a textbook if it is *italicized*, underlined, or
• bulleted. Similarly, consumers will notice advertising materials with bright colors and pleasant or unusual images more readily than they will black-and-white copy with mundane pictures. A worker is likely to be more productive in a well-organized setting with the appropriate tools or materials on hand, in good repair, and adequately supplied. Likewise, students might write more effectively if they have writing materials (pen and paper, or a laptop computer with a good word processor), as well as

a dictionary, thesaurus, style manual, or other reference materials physically close at hand. Some students are accustomed to loud music in the background while they study, while others require a quiet room. Turning off the telephone frees people from distracting calls while they pay bills, play with their children, or drive on crowded expressways. Conversely, construction noises entering a classroom from the street, or excessive summer heat, may make it difficult for a child to become engaged with instructionally important materials. Rearranged bedroom furniture may throw a child with autism into tantrums. A worn-out or excessively firm toothbrush may compromise a child's routine oral hygiene.

Elements of the social environment can play similar multiple roles in relation to behavior. Children learn quickly to ask one parent but not the other for snacks between meals. People will reveal personal problems to some friends but often not to others (or to casual acquaintances). Psychiatric patients may speak delusionally when certain people enter their rooms in the halfway house, but not when others do. Grandparents may circumvent parents' attempts to impose rules on their children by delivering unconditional favors or privileges in those very areas the parents seek to control (e.g., letting Billy have a bowl of ice cream an hour before dinner). The content and tone of a conversation at a party can change dramatically when a priest, pastor, rabbi, or imam enters into it. A piano student who can play an entire sonata without error from memory while practicing alone at home may stumble badly when performing in a recital at the local auditorium before an audience. Children are sometimes wary around strangers, though they may be outgoing and sociable among friends of the family. The presence of other people can enter into the contingencies that influence behavior in a number of ways and may serve the same function in a behavioral model as elements of the inanimate physical environment.

In addition to physical and social ecology, characteristics we attribute to individuals themselves can strongly influence how their behavior is connected to the various environmental factors assessed. In this sense, behavioral contingency analysis must include a direct inspection of certain characteristics of the organism as well as the environment. For example, children with reading difficulties may have problems with their eyesight or hearing; they may be distracted from their lessons by persistent hunger or by fear of violence in their schools and neighborhoods; they may lack proper motivating circumstances; or they may simply have had ineffective instruction at certain basic skills. Whatever the "causes" of their reading difficulties, any remedy must begin with a thoroughgoing assessment of the specific difficulties of each child. Likewise, psychiatric "symptoms" may result in part from hormonal or neurotransmitter imbalances, pituitary or adrenal tumors, genetic factors, traumatic brain injury, or from historical or experiential factors to which the person's individual adjustment has been troublesome. Because these difficulties may be different for each person, we must address them individually and take into account the specifics of each individual person and situation before, during, and after any attempts at remediation.

It is noteworthy here to say that "modern" psychological practice has focused most strongly on characteristics of the individual, through the measurement of "psychological factors" (internal, structural features of mental functioning) or by soliciting physical examinations that seek to reveal physiological causes of behavioral difficulties. Because of the rise in the importance psychologists place on the latter approach, we will discuss this briefly and place it in the context of behavioral assessment.

Medical approaches attempt to diagnose a wide variety of organic factors (physical characteristics of the people themselves) that are thought to result in or contribute to certain behavior problems, like the sudden onset of delusional speech and hallucinatory behavior, mood swings, violent temper outbursts, and tics or ritual and repetitive motor patterns. Accordingly, medicine offers primarily biological remedies, including pharmacological, surgical, and prosthetic means of treating identified problems. There are several important *assumptions* underlying most of these medical models, namely, that: 1) many if not all behavior problems are caused by *organic variables* (most likely structural problems in the nervous system); 2) these variables then result in some type of *biological dysfunction* or *disease process*; and 3) treatment should therefore be addressed toward restoring *"normal" organic activity*. This is readily apparent in media advertising that tells potential customers that their depression, anxiety, sleeplessness, restless legs, as well as a variety of other maladies, are caused by chemical imbalances among certain neurotransmitters in the brain—the remedy, of course, is to take specific medications that will restore the chemical balance associated with proper functioning in the current problem areas.

There are many familiar kinds of physical examination methods that are brought into play when we suspect organic causes of behavior problems, among them diagnostic blood and genetic assays, electroencephalography, a variety of brain imaging technologies like PET and CAT scans, fMRI, pneumoencephalography, evoked potential studies, and so on.

Traditionally, psychologists have contributed what, relative to these medical approaches at least, are considered ancillary diagnostic tools in the form of various psychometric tests, typically "paper-and-pencil" inventories that are said to reveal psychological "traits" or personality characteristics of the individuals being examined. The Minnesota Multiphasic Personality Inventory (MMPI), Beck Depression Inventory, and Taylor Manifest Anxiety Scale are but a few examples. In many hospital settings, the MMPI has become what some have called a "psychological CAT-scan," used routinely as a major source of diagnostic psychological information about patients with a variety of medical issues, from typical psychiatric conditions to their mental fitness to undergo surgery, chemotherapy, or other invasive and distressing medical procedures. Such approaches are vaganotic in the sense that they compare patients' current responses to questionnaire items against statistically normed samples from standard populations defined within a distinctly medical model of psychology. The particulars provided by such traditional psychological tests are sometimes supplemented by facts gleaned from examination of past treatment or employment records, as well as additional information recalled by the patients themselves or by other informants who are familiar with the patients. Nevertheless, these kinds of statistical psychological assessments can often be completed in just a couple of hours, which is their main appeal in a healthcare system critically concerned with economy of effort. Accordingly, even with the known problems with questionnaires (see Chapter 10) direct observations of actual behavior are scarce in these settings, largely because of costs associated with the requirement for additional specially trained staff engaging in long hours observing behavior, if the behavior of interest occurs at all under those circumstances.

Many psychologists have fundamentally accepted the medical assumptions both about putative organic origins of behavior problems and that these problems represent dysfunction, maladaptation, or disease processes. Note here that, in the not-too-distant past, psychologists who administered and evaluated psychological tests were called "psychometricians," which meant simply that they measured certain psychological traits or characteristics of people. This label has been replaced recently by a more fashionable term, *neuropsychologist*, which implies they are really measuring characteristics of the nervous system (or at least its downstream effects on behavior). Moreover, clinical psychologists also overwhelmingly subscribe to the taxonomy of behavior problems embodied in the American Medical Association's *Diagnostic and Statistical Manual of Mental Disorders (DSM)*. This is driven at least in part by third-party payment considerations (most insurance companies will not reimburse psychologists for services if a proper *DSM* diagnosis of the patient is not specified in the paperwork) but also by the very nature of clinical psychology which, at its roots, views most behavior problems as representing some form of mental dysfunction, maladaptation, personality disorder, irrationality, mental disorder, or mental illness. These biomedical assumptions inform both the tenor and the procedures clinical psychologists bring to bear on behavior problems. Witness the recent political pressure brought to bear by certain professional organizations to extend drug-prescribing rights to psychologists as well as physicians.

Behavioral contingency analysis can contribute a different, though equally precise and potentially more useful, description of current and historical ecological factors to help explain and guide the treatment of given behavior problems, even those considered to be the outcomes of disease processes. All the same, behavioral approaches make certain assumptions about behavior problems, orthogonal to those accepted by other fields of psychology—and as in these other areas, such assumptions guide behavioral practitioners in their treatment choices, but often in decidedly different directions. Perhaps the most fundamental and distinctive of these assumptions is that behavior, and the contingencies of which it is a function, is a subject worthy of consideration in its own right, not as an epiphenomenon of some unknown process at another level of analysis (e.g., neurophysiological or psychodynamic) but as a function of current and historical variables in the environment objectively linked to what the organism does. Another such assumption that flows from the first is that, by changing the environment in a prescribed manner, an individual's problem behavior will change in ways the larger community finds acceptable. These assumptions guide behavioral treatment approaches, but they have also caused some mischief, and we will take them up in order.

First, as noted earlier, the mentalistic style of much of psychology views behavior as merely an outward representation (a "performance") of players onstage in an inner world that really explains individuals' actions. The term *performance* is used deliberately as a pejorative (demeaning) term meant to devalue behavioral approaches, shifting attention away from the overt (or publicly accessible) actions that comprise behavior and toward a more covert (publicly inaccessible) set of factors that are available to us mainly through psychometric tests and currently popular psychological theories. The focus on objective measures of outward behavior and environmental variables seems to confirm that behavioral approaches are little concerned with the inner lives of individuals, hence the assertions that such approaches do not account for feelings, thoughts, and so on that make psychology so interesting to us in the first place. But that view is mistaken. Behavioral contingency analysis includes asking people what they think and feel, as well as what they do under various circumstances. The difference here is that what people say about their thoughts and feelings is regarded as verbal behavior, and as such, it can be analyzed within the same explicit framework as other behavior. "Mentalistic" psychology assigns thoughts and feelings the status of causing overt behavior. Behavioral approaches regard how people disclose these thoughts and feelings as additional behavior to be explained. Moreover, private emotions can be brought into play during treatment, as a basis for patients or clients to learn about the contingencies that often govern their actions.

A second set of assumptions concerns the "meaning" of behavior. We attribute meaning to behavior in a number of ways that result in categories and labels that imply causes. Behavior may appear simply different from what is expected or different from the way others typically behave under the same circumstances, and so we label it "abnormal," at least in the statistical sense; it may be labeled "inappropriate" if the behavior itself is "normal" but occurs under unconventional circumstances; or it may be considered "irrational" because it is not what we ourselves would do or what we think the individual *should* do under the prevailing circumstances. If the behavior causes distress, either to the individual or to other people, we say it is "antisocial," "maladaptive," "pathological," "disturbed," "dysfunctional," "problem behavior," and so on. But these are value-laden labels that may mislead us from the effective causes of the behavior, and as a result, guide us to intervene in ways that are ineffective, or perhaps worse, are not in the individual's best interests. At best, labels for behavior can serve as a kind of shorthand for describing complex actions that need to be addressed.

In applied settings (places like the clinic, classroom, workplace, or home environment, where we are concerned directly with practical problems), we first identify behavior we are interested in, and then list a wide range of variables (and their interrelations) that might account for the occurrence of that behavior. This is the *assessment* part of the story. In outline, it requires:

1. defining the behavior that is the target of our attention—including details about its form, frequency and rate, intensity, duration, and other characteristics we attribute specifically to that behavior;
2. observing and recording instances of the behavior, using methods that provide accurate and valid data about when and where it occurs, how often, and what its consequences are; and
3. a statement of accomplishments (the products of behavior).

From our listed items, we select the ones we think are most likely to be at work, and we design procedures around them that may be useful in remedying the behavior problems presented to us at the outset. Once we have implemented those procedures, we evaluate the results to reveal to us whether our account is true. The real test of our analysis is whether or not the behavior problem is successfully resolved by our intervention procedures. When we undertake this kind of assessment of behavior in the more controllable confines of the laboratory, we refer to the process as "the experimental analysis of behavior." In reality, the variables that constitute the analysis in applied settings have grown directly out of the arduous, comprehensive, and systematic work of laboratory researchers for nearly a century or more.

Behavior takes place under circumstances that include a formidable array of variables in the physical and social environment of the organism, as well as dynamic relations between behavior and those variables, and complex interactions among the variables themselves. This context is also historical—behavior is influenced not only by the current environment in which it occurs, but by past conditions as well. In other words, individuals are changed by their pasts, and those changes become part of the individuals' makeup. In the next chapter we will consider a formal model that has grown out of this long laboratory tradition that describes the central concept of our analysis: the consequential contingency. It is our Rosetta Stone for understanding and making sense of complex human behavior. Appendix D provides a more detailed overview of behavioral contingency analysis for those who would like deeper dive into the fundamentals of the science.

3

What Is a Consequential Contingency?

When we ask people to explain why they do certain things, make particular decisions, or why they excel in specific academic areas, they usually use such terms as *thoughts*, *expectations*, *feelings* and refer to special cognitive or intellectual abilities. A political candidate hides expensive gifts from an oversight committee and, when caught, says it was because he was preoccupied and simply thought his staff had reported the gifts. A child diagnosed with autism becomes frantic whenever she sees clowns. Her parents say it is because she associates them with a birthday party she once attended where a clown had frightened her badly by popping balloons. Why did the boy hit his sister? He tells his father that it was because she made him angry when she took his favorite toy. The girl's parents say she does well in certain subjects because she is gifted in those areas. In these several examples, thoughts, expectations, feelings, and cognitive or innate qualities are offered to explain observed behavior. Thinking about one thing precludes thinking about something else. A child expects another fright when a fearful object appears. Anger triggers aggressive behavior. High achievement in math comes from a deep intuitive understanding of numbers.

The main benefit of providing these kinds of explanations is that they usually satisfy people who demand that we explain our or other's actions—they usually get those people off our backs. But how useful are these explanations for suggesting what we might actually do to alter either our own or other people's behavior? How do we actually go about changing thoughts or feelings that take place in a person's mind or brain? When someone is not particularly gifted in an academic area, what specifically can we do to help him or her understand the material better? These mentalistically-framed questions are meant to provide pragmatic solutions concerned with the actions we might take to change behavior effectively. They are as important as the real problems they address. And they are only as useful as the concrete procedures they lead us to employ in order to change the ways we act, think, feel, expect, and so on.

DOI: 10.4324/9781003141365-3

An alternative to such explanations is to begin by asking what Goldiamond and Thompson[1] called "the basic behavioral question." That is to say, we can ask questions like, "What specific actions by Ramona lead us to say she is intelligent?" or "What does Frank do that tells us he has insight?" What other actions by these individuals might lead us to say they think irrationally, or fear something, or have mistaken thoughts? What behavior leads us to say one person really understands something, but another does not, or one student is organized, but another is not?

The traditional labels for these kinds of covert actions or complex mental qualities often serve as explanations. What would be more useful is to view them as shorthand for describing diverse classes of behavior from whose occurrence the mental activities or qualities are inferred. More important, asking the basic behavioral question can help us actually identify the numerous overt actions that make up these complex and often obscure repertoires, in ways that can be measured, counted, timed, and linked to particular ecological and historical circumstances.

Good study habits, appropriate social skills, effective community or communication skills, focused attention, and good organization skills, among many others, are class labels that may be applied to wide ranges of relatively complex behavior. For example, good organization can include routinely keeping lists of things to be done, assigning priorities to items listed, gathering all necessary materials to have on hand when taking on given tasks, checking off completed items, updating the list periodically, and so on. There is no need to label them as "executive functioning" skills.

All of these descriptions of actual behaviors can be counted, timed, placed in their respective contexts, and addressed in their own rights. They tell us what actual behaviors lead us to say a person thinks, feels, or expects something—the "basic behavioral question"—and allow us then to assess what variables are observably related to those behaviors. We must still account for what we mean when we say people think, feel, expect, and so on, but we may do so by linking the relevant behaviors, thoughts, and feelings to those circumstances that are functionally related to their occurrence.

Definition of Behavior

Commonly, people say behavior is whatever the organism does, or whatever a person says or does. For purposes of a more useful technical analysis, we will instead define behavior as *a change in the relation between an organism and its environment as measured by an investigator*. The investigator can be a scientist, clinician, teacher, and so on. These relations include physical movement by means of "voluntary" muscle contractions, glandular secretions, and various other physiological activities.

This definition obviously covers different kinds of locomotion (walking, running, creeping, and crawling), grasping and handling physical objects (like holding a pencil and moving its tip across a sheet of paper to leave marks we call writing, throwing a ball, eating with utensils, using a mouse and computer keyboard, etc.), maintaining certain body or facial postures (so-called body language, poses, and "facial expressions" related to emotional states), controlling bowel movements and bladder release, and so on. We can also include: 1) speaking (vocal behavior), which involves coordinated muscle contractions of our diaphragms, lips, tongues, jaws, throats, and so on, that produce specific and complex changes in air pressure that a listener experiences as meaningful sounds; 2) the release of hormone cascades that influence our bodies in numerous important ways (as when the "fight-or-flight" system kicks in when we are afraid of or just interested in something that happens suddenly around us); and 3) the myriad physiological activities of our central nervous system that are correlated in complex (and as yet poorly understood) ways with our more overt behavior—the kinds of biological events that neuroscientists study, like evoked potentials, the release of specific neurotransmitters, complex firing patterns in neuron arrays, interactions between brain areas, and so on, that take place when an organism behaves. In this latter case, we can envision a physicochemical description of those largely unobserved activities that are confined to the nervous system as adding to a modern neurobiological account of complex behavior.

With this said, the reader should note that behavior analysis cannot be simply about behavior alone, because behavior always occurs in a context whose details crucially influence its form, timing, "meaning," and whether or not the behavior even occurs. Without pencil and paper, the complex movements of a person's hand and fingers cannot really be called "writing." Tapping the fingers of both hands in a coordinated complex rhythmic pattern on an empty tabletop cannot be called "typing" or "playing the piano." Reaching one's arm out into the air and moving the thumb and forefinger in a pincer-like movement is not "putting a coin into a vending machine." A parrot that says "Polly wanna cracker" is not really speaking our language (unless, maybe, we give it crackers when it asks). These particular activities are "meaningful" only in their proper contexts. Behavioral analysis, then, entails the analysis of behavior in its context whether in the natural environment or in a laboratory.

Contextual Definition of Behavior: Contingency as a Logical Relation

The central model we will use to examine the causes of behavior is the consequential contingency paradigm. It serves as the basis for defining the details of context for what we would consider meaningful behavior.

Consequential contingency is a special "if/then" relation between behavior and its consequences in a given environmental context. It describes situations in which certain events will occur only if particular behavior occurs in a specific setting. The consequential contingency relation is at the heart of the behavioral assessment procedures described and discussed in this book. In this section, we will first define the contingency as a formal/logical relation (just as in a math or formal logic course) and briefly examine a few of the different kinds of contingency relations that might be important for the behavioral sciences. We will then focus at length on contingency relations as we encounter them in our dealings with real behavior, whether in the laboratory, at work, in school, or in our homes.

Contingencies, in one form or another, are probably familiar to most people. Although one might not recognize the name, one probably would recognize examples of the various kinds of arrangements commonly called "contingencies." When an umbrella is taken to work, even though it's not yet raining, one has a contingency plan for possible afternoon showers: if it rains, then use the umbrella. If one's stock goes up dramatically, then it may be sold for a profit. If the opportunity to attend a concert by one's favorite musical group presents itself, then tickets will be purchased to attend. Prescriptive contingency plans are, stated most simply, planned "if/then" arrangements: if this happens, then I will do this; if that happens, then I will do that. They prescribe alternative actions given sets of predetermined conditions.

Formal/Logical Definition of Contingency

Let us now consider the formal contingency relation, or what we mean, logically, when we say a contingency relation exists between behavior and contextual variables. We will begin with the assumption that a relation can exist minimally between two things (or events), but it may include several or many things or events. For the sake of convenience, and in accord with the behavioral paradigm we will be discussing, let's consider a formal relation among three sets of objects or events.

Thus, there are three main elements to this relation: for purposes of the logical exposition, let's call these variables X, Y, and Z. For us to say a consequential contingency relation is involved, these three variables can be related only in the ways shown in the following table ("0" means the element is absent, while "1" means it is present).

X	Y	Z
0	0	0
1	0	0
0	1	0
1	1	0
1	1	1

This table (called a logical "truth table") shows that Z can occur only if Y occurs when X is present. Row 1 shows that if the X is not present (X=0), and Y does not occur (Y=0), then we will not observe Z to occur (Z=0). If X is present (X=1) but Y is not (as in Row 2), Z is not observed; it does not occur. If Y occurs, but X does not (Row 3), then Z is also not observed; it does not occur. In some instances (depicted in Row 4), X is present (X=1), and Y occurs (Y=1), but Z remains absent (Z=0); it is not observed. In the case where Z is observed (Z=1), both X and Y must occur; Z is present if only if Y has occurred in the presence of X. If a relation among three variables meets these requirements, then we say a contingency exists between variables X, Y, and Z and that the occurrence of Z is contingent upon the occurrence of Y in the presence of X. We can also define variable Z as a consequence or outcome of the joint occurrence of X and Y (X•Y). The consequential contingency relation can thus be depicted formally as: Given $x \in X$, $y \in Y$, $z \in Z$, $(x_1 \cap y_1) \cap (z_1 \cup z_0)$; z_1 only if $(x_1 \cap y_1)$.

Extending the Formal/Logical Definition of Contingency to Behavioral Relations

We can now apply our formal definition of contingency to relations among behavior and other variables. Let's say that X represents specific elements of the environmental setting that can be present or absent, the occasions for behavior (Ocn), and Y is a particular kind of behavior or pattern (Bhv). Consider the following examples.

In our first example, Ocn is a parent reading quietly in a room where a small child is playing on the floor nearby. The child cries out (Bhv), and the parent stops reading and immediately goes to help the child (Z, the consequence of the child's crying out, [Csq]). The child's behavior can be said to result in the parent's help, or stated another way, the parent's help is contingent on the child's crying out when the parent is close by.

In another example, you are trying to leave a large, complex building. You look around and see a sign that says, "This way out," with an arrow pointing the way out (Ocn). You then walk in that direction (Bhv), continue to follow like signs, and more efficiently arrive at the building's exit (Csq). Quickly reaching the exit is contingent upon following the directions provided.

Bill, a psychiatric patient living in a group home, is sitting alone in his bedroom. Ocn: Another resident enters his room uninvited and begins looming menacingly over him. Bhv: Bill stands up and begins ranting about bugs on the walls of his room crawling into his clothes and under his skin. Csq: The intruder leaves in a hurry.

The three examples above describe simple contingency relations between particular occasions (Ocn), specific behaviors (Bhv), and their respective consequences (Csq).

$$Ocn \bullet Bhv \to Csq$$

More complexity is introduced when multiple contingencies are considered. Here behavior not immediately considered "rational" when a single contingency is considered may be shown to be quite rational when the interaction of multiple contingencies and their histories are considered.

$$Ocn \bullet Bhv \to Csq$$
$$Ocn \bullet Bhv \to Csq$$

The following sections will show how we can use this definition of contingency and the simultaneous occurrence of multiple contingencies to offer a more comprehensive approach to clinical intervention.

Note

1 (1967/2004)

4

What Does It Mean to Be Constructional?

Many approaches may be taken to changing consequential contingencies. The approach taken in here is a constructional one. People usually seek help when they are distressed or suffering from what outcomes accompany the presence or absence of certain behavioral repertoires. The constructional approach is an orientation that offers solutions to such problems based on the establishment of new alternative repertoires, rather than on the elimination or deceleration of problematic ones. Instead of considering problems in terms of pathologies to be eliminated, it attempts to increase clients' adaptive options and extend or improve existing repertoires for producing those outcomes that are important to the client. This is a direct approach to producing "desirable" outcomes, rather than an indirect approach, with desirable outcomes as hoped-for by-products of the elimination or acceptance of pathology.

Therapeutic programs taking an actual constructional approach comprise five critical elements, including:

1. terminal repertoires;
2. current relevant repertoires and resources;
3. change procedures;
4. maintaining consequences; and
5. means of monitoring progress.

Stated otherwise, these program elements may be described in terms of five simple questions posed to the clients: Where do you want to go from here? Where are you now? How can you get there? What would keep you going? How will you know where you are along the way? Accordingly, the approach begins with administration of the Constructional Questionnaire. This is an interview conducted with the client to gather basic information for an initial functional assessment of what the client would view as a desirable resolution to the presenting problem. Specific questions address each of the elements of the programming approach. The interview also serves to acquaint clients with the particular therapeutic

DOI: 10.4324/9781003141365-4

approach ahead of them. Answers to these questions are crucial, whether or not the client is verbal. If necessary, the questions can be answered by the clients' caregivers, therapists, parents, or other informants familiar with the clients' daily lives.

Terminal Repertoires, or Successful Program Outcomes

The first program element addressed during the interview is the terminal goal, or the target repertoires sought. Here, the client (or another inform-ant) is asked, "Assuming we were successful, what would the outcome be for you?" This question might surprise some clients, especially those who have previously sought help for their problems elsewhere. They might instead expect to be asked about what their problem is, how bad it is, and what behavior they are looking to eliminate. In contrast to their expectations, the constructional therapist seeks clearly observable targets or outcomes of a successfully completed program. The therapist asks, "What would others observe when the successful outcome is obtained?"

The client is asked for examples of what life would be like once the outcomes are obtained and how this prospective outcome differs from the current state of affairs. This is important for two reasons. First, the outcome is stated in terms of a repertoire or repertoires to establish, and not pathologies to be eliminated. Second, it gives clear criteria for the successful completion of the program. When the initial terminal reper-toires become the current repertoires of the client, the program is com-pleted and successful. In other words, the clients got what they came for!

For example, clients who come in with complaints about feeling depressed and anxious might reply to the question, "Assuming we were successful, what would the outcome be for you?" with, "I wouldn't be depressed and anxious" or "I would be happy." But neither of those answers state clear repertoires to be shaped or other explicit behavioral changes to be sought. In such a situation the question, "What would others observe when the successful outcome is obtained?" can be of great help.

One should also ask about examples: "Can you give an example of what you would be doing?" Often this evokes answers such as, "I will be spending more time with friends, working only six hours a day, and I would be exercising three times a week." This answer gives clearer out-comes that are observable and measurable. Another example could be a client seeking help with his or her dog. "The dog won't be jumping at people who come into the door, and it won't be pulling on the leash the whole time when we go for a walk." Again, this answer only addresses what behaviors the pet owner would like to eliminate. In this instance, more questions would be asked to get at what the dog *will* be doing rather than what the dog *won't* be doing. It would be more helpful to ask such questions as, "What will the perfect dog look like? When someone walks in the door, what will the dog be doing? When you take the dog for a walk, what will the dog be doing? What will others see when they are observing your perfect dog?" These sorts of questions are more likely to yield answers stated in terms of repertoires to be established: "He will be sitting on his mat, waiting there to be petted by guests. And while on a walk, he will be walking at my pace and right by my side." These stated outcomes guide the client to train the dog to sit on the mat when guests come and to walk by the owner's side on a loose leash. Once the therapist has an idea of where the client wants to go, the next step involves learning about where the client is currently.

Current Relevant Repertoires and Resources

Accordingly, the second element of the program is to identify the client's current relevant repertoires and resources. This includes their potential for change, their assets, and any strengths they could direct at attaining the terminal repertoires. Questions here cover multiple attributes: related skills ("What skills or strengths do you have that are related to what you'd like to program?"), stimulus control ("Are there conditions when the present problem is not so difficult as at other times?"), and relevant problem-solving repertoires ("In the past, what related problems did you tackle successfully? What related change programs did you succeed in and how?"). It is also important to ask about other skills or assets clients have that might seem unrelated to the current change attempt.

Clients may be unaware of how some repertoires they already have can help in the current effort. For example, one client wanted to improve her diet and increase her exercise. When asked about her skills and strengths, she mentioned that she had been an athlete in college and loved journaling. She also shared that she was a planner and showed how she had everything in her day planned a week ahead. Such information is invaluable for the behavior analyst. The eventually arranged change program capitalized on all of these repertoires and strengths. Her experience with athletics in college was enlisted to create an exercise regimen that was comfortable and familiar to her; her love for journaling was transferred to her keeping records of her workouts, meals, and snacks; her planning skills were later utilized to plan what she would eat daily and what meals she would prepare in advance.

The stimulus-control question, "Are there conditions when the present problem is not a problem?" can also prove useful. A child might engage in repetitive behaviors in one classroom but not in others, or during one part of the day rather than at other times. Such information can provide a place to begin looking for relations that might inform the analysis and intervention.

Responses from a constructional interview with a woman seeking help for self-described depression and social anxiety show how a rather complete picture of goals and current functioning can be obtained. This is an abridged version of a much longer and detailed patient interview. A typical interview may take three hours and be several pages long. The following transcript has been edited to highlight the salient points.[1] A guide to the use of the Constructional Questionnaire is provided in Appendix A.

Identifying information:

Sally is a 27 y/o w/female, divorced, no children, who has a history of a serious medical disease that is now under control and is not currently life threatening. A serious operation was required four years prior to the interview—it was very successful.

1. Stated outcome?

I wouldn't be as depressed or frightened. I would have relationships with people who are emotionally together; more balance especially with men; especially with more assertive men. I would get to know women [who are] more on the ball. I would increase the number of relationships I have. I wouldn't have to tell the other person what to do.

2. Observed outcome?

I would have three new relationships—close friends. I would be working in an office [and be] in charge of at least two people. I would have at least one close male friend (lover). You would see us taking a trip somewhere, staying overnight, half the time would be spent in bed, athletics, sport events, see us participating in active things—dancing, bicycling, volleyball, etc. You would see me affectionate—touching, kissing, smiling, holding hands. You would see him acting the same toward me; you would see him doing things for me—little things, a card, flowers, calling, soup if I am sick.

3. Current state?

I do nothing, go to work, can't look coworkers in the eye. No boyfriends; there are a couple of women I talk to, but I don't spend time with them. Have trouble talking to a man; get upset—never can think of anything to say. I was married. After one year retreated into a shell. I had to tell him (husband) what to do. I couldn't get what I wanted unless I did. Last year of marriage almost no interaction. I now have great feelings of avoidance, act busy, won't look at men.

4. Times when problem is less of a problem?

Clubs at school, if I am doing something—something I am focused on, I can talk with other people. It's at work with men and women and on purely social occasions that I feel the worst.

5. Current skills?

Intellectual abilities: can be a good conversationalist, can alter what people do by attending to what they say; I'm nice looking, good at sports, read a lot, good student, very introspective.

6. Benefits from the problem?

Makes people want to take care of me—very protective, give me things, help me out. Example, need a ride can't get there by myself, family or someone will give me a ride. Example, father got lawyer for me for divorce. Sometimes I feel superior because I can get people to do things for me.

7. Excused from things?

Less expected of me, fewer decisions, excused from taking care of myself.

8. Those helpful?

Mother, father, sister, four female friends.

Once there is a good picture of the outcomes and the current relevant repertoires, the next programming element is the change procedures themselves.

Change Procedures as Program Steps

The third element is the change procedures; these are the program steps that will evolve the entry repertoires into the target repertoires. Some cases necessitate shaping, whereas for other cases, transfer of stimulus control over existing repertoires can be used. The governing contingencies determine which course the program takes. These are *not* treatment packages that are targeted at problems or symptoms. They are not procedures matched with topographies. These days it seems common for people to state, "I have a client who has stereotypy, a client who is a picky eater," and so on. "What procedure should I use?" Such questions are commonly met with, "Use a DRO; use escape extinction; teach them meditation." These kinds of approaches are not constructional, and they are often too general to be particularly useful.

A constructional program takes into account the targeted outcomes and the entry repertoire (along with other more detailed considerations described in the following chapters). The entry repertoire is the starting point in the shaping procedure, and notably, no program-extrinsic consequences (reinforcers) are used. There are two sources of reinforcement used in a constructional program. The first derives from those reinforcers already maintaining the current disturbing pattern, and the other is progress towards the terminal repertoire—those reinforcers that will become available with the new repertoires being shaped.

There are some situations where new repertoires need to be established, and others where control over existing repertoires can be readily transferred to new occasions. An example of a situation where shaping is called for might be a child who engages in self-injury maintained by attention. The target outcome would be teaching less costly ways of getting people's attention—specifically walking up to people and tapping them on the arm. Currently, the child walks up to people but then engages in the disturbing pattern—say, some form of self-injury. A possible plan would be to utilize the current relevant repertoire, walking up to people, separately teaching tapping on objects and then people, putting both repertoires under the guidance of a separate stimulus, and then combining the two stimuli such that walking up to people and tapping occur together, resulting in the attention. As much as is possible, the reinforcers used are the same as the reinforcers maintaining the disturbing pattern, perhaps staff or parental involvement.

Other cases might involve transferring some repertoires that clients already have under different conditions. Goldiamond[2] described the example of a woman who reported having no social skills, and because of that, she did not invite people over to her house. The same woman had once worked as the director of a television talk show. Her intervention included discussions about treating her living room like a television studio, and her houseguests like talk show guests.

Another example is that of a man who wanted to have a woman he was dating come to his house for dinner. The client was worried because his kitchen was very messy, and he did not know how to organize it. Answers to the questionnaire revealed he was an auto mechanic and that his tools at work were perfectly organized. He mentioned that he placed the tools he used the most much closer to him, and the ones he used less farther back, and so on, in a tier system. For this client, the plan was simply to organize his kitchen the same way he organized his garage. The therapist recommended that the client "treat your kitchen, like you treat your garage."

Though none of the solutions involve targeting some vague cognitive construct or thoughts and feelings directly, thoughts and feelings are included as indicators of important contingencies, and when those contingencies change, the result will be a change in reported thoughts and feelings. A recommended Case Presentation Guide is provided in Appendix B.

A final example here concerns a problem on the organizational level. A hospital reported that its intake staff were unfriendly and short with clients. The hospital wanted staff to be friendlier with the clients—to ask clients about their day, how they were doing, and so on. Previous interventions included posting sticky notes as reminders to be more pleasant and recommending a response cost system where an observer would keep data on who was or was not friendly, with penalties for those staff who were not being pleasant. Additionally, they suggested sending staff to workshops so they could learn how to be friendly with clients, using performance checklists to hold them accountable. A few observations in the cafeteria to observe the staff at lunch revealed that they were all friendly and decent with one another and with others—they *had* the desired repertoire. They question was then raised: Why did being unfriendly on the job make sense; how was it adaptive?

An investigation into the primary criteria against which staff were evaluated revealed that they had to meet a certain quota for how many clients they processed per hour. There was the problem! Stopping to be friendly and chatting a bit slows down the number processed per hour. It was not a repertoire problem—they were behaving perfectly rationally, given the contingencies governing their behavior. So instead of reminders, a response cost system, sensitivity or perspective-taking training, or having leadership holding them accountable, it was suggested that the institution increase the time allowed for workers to intake each client, as well as train the staff in how to politely terminate conversations with more talkative individuals. No *direct* intervention was recommended.

Typically, once outcomes and likely procedures are determined, a program worksheet is introduced at the end of each session. The program worksheet describes the subgoals the client will work on during the upcoming week, the current repertoire upon which each subgoal is based, and program notes or guides that suggest how the client might go about achieving the subgoals (see Figure 4.1). After a short time, the self-control worksheet is typically introduced (see Figure 4.2). This worksheet is filled out by the client or patient prior to attending a session. The self-control worksheet has six entries: subgoals agreed upon (from the previous week); extent to which each subgoal is accomplished; relations noted and comments; proposed subgoals (for the next week); rationale, justification; and, suggestions for future agenda, and feedback to be provided. In-session discussion centers on how the client decided on each entry and how the logs were used to inform the entries. Feedback

Name:	Date:
Current Relevant Repertoire:	Subgoals:
Program Notes:	

Figure 4.1 Example of a between-session worksheet

Name:		Date:
Subgoals (previous session):	Extent Accomplished:	Relations Noted, Comments:
Proposed Subgoals:	Rationale; Relation to Terminal Outcomes:	Feedback Requested, Areas of Discussion:

Figure 4.2 Example of a between-session self-control worksheet

is provided on the client's own contingency analysis. At the end of a session a new program worksheet (Figure 4.1) is produced for the upcoming week that reflects this process.

Once the constructional therapist has a clear idea of the outcomes to be sought, the client's current repertoires relevant to reaching those outcomes, and the procedures that might be necessary for change, the next element to be accounted for is maintaining consequences.

Maintaining Consequences

It is important to ascertain what consequences are maintaining the current pattern so that any program the analyst and client develop will stand a better chance of being effective. The Constructional Questionnaire again provides several questions meant to uncover these reinforcers—positive and/or negative. One of these questions asks, "Has your problem ever produced any special advantages or considerations for you?" This question specifically addresses positive reinforcers. Another, aimed instead at negative reinforcers, asks, "As a result of your problem, have you been excused for things you have done, or excused from things that you might otherwise be required to do?" Yet another question seeks potential social reinforcers, asking, "Who else is interested in the changes you're after?" To learn about the costs of the current patterns, we ask, "How is your problem a drag, or how does it jeopardize you?"

The client previously described who wanted to improve her diet and increase exercise gave an interesting and informative answer when she was asked about being excused from things. She said that because she was overweight, people no longer asked her for help when they were moving. When asked about any advantages, she said people usually give her the better seat at gatherings. When asked about who else is interested in the change she's after, she said her boyfriend is and that his encouragement and attention meant a lot to her. Such information can be very helpful when developing a program.

It is important to ask these analytical questions. Again, regardless of the client's verbal repertoire, caregivers and parents can be asked. These questions are useful in painting a picture of how the current patterns make sense. We know that the organism is always right, but there are cases where people start doubting this because of how disturbing some behaviors seem. In those cases, just as with all cases, it is important to always remember that the behavior is rational and makes sense regardless of how bizarre it may seem. In the constructional approach, no behavior is considered maladaptive. Behavior is considered always to be adaptive, although it can also often be very disturbing or costly.

To clarify this point, let us consider the bizarreness of the behavior of a young man who regularly fights the strongest, meanest people he can fight. He fights them until he knocks them out, or they knock him out, or someone stops the fight. This continues for several years. The behavior seems costly, perhaps criminal, and reckless. Until we consider that the person's name is Ali, Mayweather, or McGregor. Now we see that although fighting is a costly operant, it is a sensible repertoire providing otherwise unobtainable reinforcers.

Other person • Fight → Injury, big payday
Other person • Refuse fight → No injury, work for hourly wage

For those of you who don't know, in their last fight against each other, McGregor made $85 million and Mayweather made $275 million—in one night.[3] Patient/Client behavior makes equal sense if we look carefully at not only the costs of the disturbing behavior but at its benefits, and at the costs and benefits of the available alternatives as well.

A Case Presentation Guide is provided in the Appendices and is often used to plan the intervention. The abbreviated Case Presentation Guide that follows illustrates how the information gained from the Constructional Questionnaire and Daily Events Logs (described later) provides a constructional diagnosis and a plan that is shared with the client or patient. We will use the information we gathered from Sally.

A1. Identifying information:

Sally (not her real name) is a 27 y/o w/female, divorced, no children, who has a history of a serious medical disease that is now under control and is not currently life-threatening. A serious operation was required four years prior to the interview—it was very successful.

A2. Background for the program:

As a result of her past illness Sally has come to rely on others, particularly her family, for almost all her personal needs. When she could not get what she wanted from her husband, she withdrew, resulting in him trying to please her, ending in a deteriorating relationship and divorce. During her life-threatening illness she was indeed helpless. Her family rallied around her providing everything required. Her helplessness resulted in her family shopping for her, running her errands, and attending to every need. Her father arranged for her divorce. As she recovered from the physical illness over a long period of time, she found herself alone, now without a husband, a job, or a social life, which further made contact with the family more potent as a reinforcer. That is, family support was contingent on her helplessness. She maintained her successful withdrawn pattern even after recovery, gaining her family's continued support. To become more socially involved and independent may mean losing the family involvement upon which she has come to rely. Becoming more involved and self-sufficient at work may lead family members to question why she could not be more self-sufficient at home and put their continued involvement in her life at risk.

Helpless at home and work → Family involvement, others help her
Self-sufficient at work or home → No or greatly reduced family
involvement

A3. Symptom as a costly operant:

Independence at work likely would require independence at home, which would lead to less family involvement and Sally having to do more for herself. Whereas this was necessary during her illness, she is beginning to miss out on important consequences available to others. Her return to work brought her into contact with career possibilities and the possibility of a more active social life. Her patterns, so effective at maintaining her family's involvement, are now preventing her from a more meaningful work and social life. This inability to access these opportunities has become increasingly aversive and jeopardizes her advancement and social life, leading to reports of hopelessness and depression.

Helpless at home and work → Benefits: Family involvement, others help her with tasks and decisions. Costs: No social life, unlikely work advancement.

Self-sufficient at work → Benefits: Increased likelihood of a social life, chance of advancement, more control over schedule. Costs: Family question why she can't be more self-sufficient at home, possible confrontations, greatly reduced family involvement.

B. Tentative program directions:

1. new friends where the relationships are reciprocal;
2. career advancement indicators established;
3. a romantic relationship;
4. continued close, though less frequent, relations with family such that contact is maintained by mutual enjoyment of one another's company; and
5. making own decisions and doing own tasks.

Though the outcomes are focused on work and non-familial relationships, it is clear that changing the current familial interactions will be important to changing work patterns. By slowly changing the patterns at home, it should be possible for reinforcers otherwise precluded to have their effect at work. The goal will be to provide similar familial consequences for different patterns, thus resulting in making the changes required for increasing work and social consequences more likely.

Self-sufficiency at home while maintaining family involvement → Benefits: Family involvement continues, make own decisions, do own tasks, can expand work and social repertoire; Costs: Effort to change, more time alone, faced with more difficult decisions, more work around the house.

C. Current relevant repertoires:

1. Sally is an articulate and well-educated woman. She will have no problem gaining the analytical repertoires required for contingency analysis and self-control programming.
2. Sally has had to follow complex medical regimens during her treatment and recovery. She graduated from college and has very good conversational skills. Her family has been willing

to spend a great deal of time taking care of her; enlisting their assistance should not be an issue. Her helplessness and overall "warm personality" have resulted in others providing for her when she found it difficult to provide for herself. These patterns were quite successful and can perhaps be a starting point for the program.

D. Change procedures, programing guides:

1. Sally will keep daily records with an entry every hour. These records will be reviewed in each session and used to analyze the consequential relations and the emotions that describe them. They will also be used to ascertain the achievement of weekly subgoals. Graphs depicting what was wanted vs. what was actually achieved may be generated, as well as graphs of subgoals achieved during the week.

2. Since Sally had a good social life in college, was married, and is a good conversationalist it does not appear that specific social-skills training, etc. will be required. She has a love for sports and was at one time athletic, and she enjoys skiing. Transferring historically successful repertoires to her current activities may be required. It is likely that the program will focus upon changing the relationship with the family as she takes over responsibilities at home in such a way that contact is maintained. Incremental steps where her activity is substituted for theirs is where the program will start. Concurrently, steps will be taken to establish and transfer past social repertoires to the work environment. Weekly subgoals will be agreed upon that lead to the eventual outcomes as agreed upon. The upcoming week's subgoals will cumulatively be based on the success of the previous week's subgoals. Analysis of the logs will provide the basis for evaluation and planning of subgoals. The self-control worksheet will be introduced as soon as possible, whereby Sally will come to the session with her own plan for the upcoming week based upon her own analysis.

E. Maintenance guides:

1. The logs, work product, documentation from outings (ticket stubs, etc.), and other items will serve to provide evidence of success along with the charts and graphs noted earlier.

2. Follow-up meetings and telephone calls will be scheduled after formal sessions end. Sally will acquire the analytic repertoire required to reinstate the logs and plan goals if a setback should occur or other problems arise.

Monitoring Progress

Therapists, regardless of orientation, are well aware that clients have lives outside their therapeutic sessions. Accordingly, contemporaneous records of events during those times between sessions can be extremely important for the success of the helping process. Constructional therapists instruct clients to keep prescribed kinds of records every day in their home ecologies, and then to bring these records into their weekly sessions for examination and discussion. These daily logs serve several functions, including:

1. providing basic assessment information;
2. acting as the primary basis for discussions during therapeutic sessions;
3. providing details essential to establishing the discriminative repertoires necessary for clients being able to analyze their own behavior and surrounding contingencies;
4. providing clients with clear evidence of their progress, and an easily discriminable source of program-intrinsic reinforcement;
5. supporting the ongoing fine-tuning of elements of the program; and
6. facilitating continual control over the program's direction by the clients themselves.

Nearly all the logs clients are asked to keep briefly describe time of day, others present, locations of various events, what the clients did under those circumstances, and what followed immediately after their own behavior. In other words, clients' log entries describe occasion • behavior → consequence cycles in their everyday lives.

As part of initial assessments, this kind of information can be invaluable for what it may reveal about recurrent and influential contingencies in clients' daily lives. Moreover, through joint examination and discussion of the entries, the therapist can directly observe the clients' verbal behavior with respect to the nature and personal meanings of events covered by the logs. Client entries will reveal whether they can distinguish the occasions for their actions from the consequences, their behavior from their feelings, and so on. This sets the stage for any potential discrimination training that may be necessary at the start of the therapeutic program. Modeling and shaping of appropriate log-keeping may be needed initially to produce logs that are useful and informative. The critical reinforcer for keeping logs should be their utility in the program and to show clients they are getting closer to their goals. Clients are repeatedly encouraged to compare current logs with previous ones to assess whether or how much they have progressed.

Subsequent weekly sessions, as already noted, then focus almost exclusively on the content of the logs. The logs provide direction and the basic data for each interview, supplemented by what clients have to say about them during the sessions. The monitoring that logs provide enables the therapist and client to have an ongoing fine-grain analysis and evaluation of the program. If a given subgoal is not met, the reasons surrounding it will likely be evident in the logs, and that information is critically important. Emotions and thoughts are entered and serve as useful indicators of important contingencies. The program steps are under constant evaluation.

The logs are not restricted to a single form. Optimally, the therapist uses particular logs tailored to fit the client's current repertoires and particular situations being tracked. Initially, the logs may require simple general entries, such as times and places, clients' actions, and what followed. However, as a program progresses, the logs may become more specific and more complex.

Different types of logs may be used to gather specific kinds of information that may be helpful to the therapeutic process. These include Daily Events Logs, Specific Event Logs, and Interaction Logs (Transaction and Conversation Logs) (see Figures 4.3, 4.4, and 4.5). There may be times

No.	Time & Duration	Audience, Place, Conditions	Activity Intended, What I Wanted	Activity, What I Got	Comments, Emotions

Figure 4.3 Example of the Daily Events Log

No.	Time, Duration	Audience, Place, Conditions	Concurrent Activity	Behavioral Description	What Followed	Comments, Emotions

Figure 4.4 Example of the Specified Events Log

No.	Time, Duration	Audience, Place, Conditions	Antecedent, or Intent	What I Did	What Others Did	My Behavior	Comments, Emotions

Figure 4.5 Example of the Interactions Log

where one type of log is kept simultaneously with another, or a log is invented to meet a specific program requirement.

The Daily Events Log is the most general type, and it may be the only log employed. It usually follows the initial session in order to provide more clarity and definition surrounding the problem presented. It is also used when detailed data on frequency of a behavior is needed. During the initial interview (the Constructional Questionnaire), clients usually talk about their problems in general terms. The information gathered by the Daily Events Log can clarify and supplement the information obtained in their initial interviews.

With Daily Events Logs, clients keep data on the times, places, other people present, what the client wanted or the activity planned for that hour, what the client actually got or the actual activity that occurred, and comments. The main purpose for this type of log is to provide information for the in-session contingency analysis, to monitor the frequency of behaviors prescribed in weekly subgoals, and to indicate cumulative progress.

The main purpose for the Specific Event Log is to obtain information about the frequency of a target behavior, or another behavior or particular interest, and the events bracketing it. The clients keep data on the times, places, other people present, the behavior, what followed the behavior, and comments. That is, they keep data on possible occasions, behaviors, and possible consequences. Interaction Logs (see Figure 4.5) may be used when the problems reported involve interpersonal relations. In these situations, information on actions of people who are significant to the client is essential. This information enables the therapist and client to analyze social transactions. These types of logs are usually very useful for problems such as marital conflicts, social inadequacies, interpersonal interactions on the job, and stuttering.

The means of monitoring client progress through their programs are critical elements in the constructional programming process. The accuracy and completeness with which clients keep logs often are the strongest predictors of achieving successful outcomes.

In summary, the main overarching question guiding the approach is, "What repertoire needs to be established, the absence of which is the problem?" This is the question we always ask, and it allows us to focus on what needs to be provided, not what needs to be eliminated. The problem behavior is never the focus in a constructional approach. A full case study is provided in Appendix C.

Notes

1 For a more detailed example see Goldiamond and Schwartz (1975), The Smith Case.
2 1974
3 This example, with different names, comes from Layng & Andronis, 1984.

5

NCA as a Constructional Approach

Nonlinear contingency analysis is a constructional approach[1] that seeks to help individuals "establish patterns the absence of which is the problem." It does not seek to directly decelerate or eliminate behaviors, thoughts, or emotions.[2] That is, it is not a pathological approach, which seeks to eliminate behavior patterns. As we described, a constructional approach seeks to make sense of disturbing behavior and understand its function within the context of a person's life. It recognizes not only the costs of the behavior but its benefits as well. To do this requires that not only the disturbing behavior be considered but its available alternative behaviors as well. Finding ways to produce the same, and often, additional benefits, but at far less cost, is typically the goal of an NCA constructional intervention.

The history of the disturbing behavior is critical to understanding the behavior. How the pattern was shaped and how it is now maintained are of importance to making sense of the behavior in its current ecology. The Constructional Questionnaire was designed to help provide these answers. The Case Presentation Guide leads us to explicitly describe the likely history. Such a history does not attempt to assign blame or to suggest that triggering or other reactive events are the cause of the behavior. As Goldiamond noted, a forest fire is not caused by an arsonist; it is caused by the presence of oxygen, combustible material, and a locus of heat at a certain temperature. We may blame the arsonist for the fire, but locking someone up will do nothing to the blaze. The fire will only end when one of the three elements required for fire (the causes) are addressed. Accordingly, early experiences or trauma may be to blame, but the cause is found in how the consequential contingencies unfolded, into which the behavior entered. After a particular traumatic event or series of events, for example, what transpired to shape and maintain the behavior we see today? Eliminating the disturbing behavior, thoughts, and feelings is never the goal. Instead, establishing patterns that provide important outcomes, and enjoyable thoughts and feelings, is the goal.

DOI: 10.4324/9781003141365-5

It is the nonlinear context that frequently accounts for the patterns that occasion their classification as disturbing, either by the individual, or others. The assessment's nonlinear analysis helps an individual to understand the disturbing behavior (DB), which at times may be referred to as the referent behavior (RB), as the adaptive outcome of the consequential contingencies comprising an individual's environment, given that individual's available alternative behaviors (AAB) and other linked contingencies that may account for the potency of the consequences maintaining the disturbing patterns. In so doing, it may become possible to establish new patterns, or target behaviors, (TB) that provide the same (and often additional) benefits of DB but at a much lower cost. Briefly,

> A nonlinear approach involves analysis of (a) the contingency of which the target behavior is a member (the direct or linear relations); (b) alternative sets, or matrices, of consequential contingencies, of which the target behavior and currently available alternative patterns are members; and (c) the contingencies or relations that can potentiate the matrices (the nonlinear relations). This analysis is applied to gain an understanding of the patterns of observed learner behavior, which occur as a result of the interaction of these matrices.[3]

Interventions are developed jointly with the patient to constructionally address the presenting complaint or the precise contingency matrix into which it enters. A topical intervention might be implemented whose target is DB (disturbing behavior) or the immediate matrix of DB and AAB (available alternative behaviors) and their costs and benefits, or, alternatively, a systemic intervention may be developed that does not directly target the disturbing pattern or its contingency matrix but instead targets other contingencies that potentiate the consequences maintaining those relations in the matrix. In essence, as described in the following text, the entire contingency context is considered.

Accordingly, this requires an assessment that reveals the consequential contingencies that rationalize the DB in the context of AAB and their respective consequences. As noted in preceding chapters, the Case Presentation Guide provides the framework for the assessment. The direction to "weave in various items from questionnaire and other sources to present a coherent picture of a person functioning highly competently, given his circumstances and implicit or explicit goals" is a powerful statement. The patient is not to be regarded as possessing "a bundle of deficits," as Goldiamond was fond of saying, but as a person whose behavior had adapted to its environment.

At times the consequences of maintaining DB are not immediately clear to the patient nor to the therapist. On these occasions it is helpful to ask the patient what would happen if they were to do something other than the disturbing behavior. The patterns considered are those currently available to the client, that is, something already learned. Sometimes we find that the alternative is worse, more costly—or benefits are uncovered that previously were overlooked. The patient's competency is expressed as a resolution of the alternative contingencies in favor of the patient, even if substantial cost is involved. Stated differently, what first may appear as dysfunctional or maladaptive is instead the adaptive response to the available alternative contingencies.

One does not set out with any preconceived notions other than that the behavior is a sensible operant maintained by the consequences not only of the disturbing pattern, but the consequences of its alternatives as well, and that those consequences are often characterized by positive reinforcement, particularly in terms of the alternative contingencies (and contingency matrices) available.

The reader will recall the case of the young woman presented in Chapter 3 who reported she felt she was inadequate for her job, could not make friends, and found socializing at work aversive to the extent that she had difficulty looking people in the eye. Only by asking what would happen if she did not engage in the disturbing pattern, and whether there were any benefits to her problem, would we have uncovered the positive reinforcement maintaining the disturbing behavior. Instead of considering her work patterns as maintained by avoidance contingencies (overt or covert), defective rule governance, or a maladaptive pattern, they were considered adaptive—and a perfectly sensible way of maintaining the involvement of her family. As time passed, however, the cost of maintaining the involvement grew and occasioned seeking help. As she learned how to do things for herself while maintaining family involvement, the work problems were easily replaced with the outcomes she valued, and the anxiety and self-deprecating thoughts ceased.

In NCA it is very important to have a clear description of what success actually looks like in the form of clearly stated, observable quality-of-life outcomes. Though the initial interview may take some time to complete, it often decreases the time spent in sessions trying to ascertain many of the relevant variables. The goals, once described, are broken into subgoals based on each person's current relevant repertoire. Each week's subgoals are based on the past week's performance and the analysis of the contingencies responsible for that performance.

The Daily Events Log is often the key to success. Weekly subgoals are typically determined after a contingency analytic therapist and the patient analyze daily logs kept by the patient between all meetings. Each subgoal is chosen based upon its relation to the final goals. Using the logs, patients can identify whether they are getting what they want out of their daily interactions and activities. They can determine whether the reinforcers important to them are likely to occur because of what they are doing. They can test different approaches and adjust their behavior in order to achieve what is important to them. Patients make an entry every hour on average. At the outset, an assessment is made as to the recording and analytical repertoires possessed by the individual. Logs may be modified accordingly. An example of typical a log is provided in Figure 4.3.

Of significance is the distinction between what one wants versus what actually transpired ("What I Got"). "What I Wanted" speaks to the potentiating variables operative at that time, that is, what the likely consequences were at that point and why they were important. These may be either positive reinforcers ("Him to ask me out") or negative reinforcers ("Mom to stop nagging me about homework"). Emotions are extremely important to the process and are used as windows into the operating contingencies. Accordingly, the "Comments, Emotions" field in the logs is used to suggest the consequential contingencies operating. For example, after the entry on Mom nagging, an emotional response might be "irritated, but want closeness." "Want closeness" might be identified as indicating that there may be a positive reinforcer operating, thus occasioning a clarifying question that would not otherwise occur.

Through a series of questions and a dialogue with the patient, instances are examined cumulatively and analyzed until next steps emerge. For example, we may discover that the only real interaction with Mom comes in the form of nagging, with few other instances of close interaction recorded. This suggests that the consequences of nagging and what occasions nagging may be critical to understanding the contingencies of which the overall pattern is a function. That is, when combined, what isn't in the log may be as important as what is in it. We may find that although the nagging is aversive to a certain extent, it is also reinforcing, bringing close social contact with the mother that is not otherwise available. In essence, the nagging is actually acting as a positive reinforcer for those behaviors that occasion its occurrence. We would try to determine what happens if those behaviors that occasion nagging were absent. We may discover the duration of interaction occasioned by other behaviors currently in the repertoire is far less. In fact, we often discover that other behaviors have occurred but did not reliably produce as intense an interaction as those such as nagging. The behavior occasioning nagging, therefore, is the sensible outcome of these alternative consequential contingencies, even if it leads to substantial costs as well.

This raises the question, "How can a valued and meaningful interaction with Mom be developed without the behaviors that occasion nagging?" Stopping nagging, eliminating the behaviors that occasion nagging, or working on the feelings or thoughts associated with the nagging would not be a goal of the intervention. The logs would be examined to look for a place to start—where a brief, meaningful interaction could occur. The interaction would be a subgoal for the next week, and the results would be evaluated during the next session.

In the next week's logs we might see:

Activity Intended, What I Wanted: A nice interaction with mom.

Activity, What I Got: Asked mom about how she picks out handbags since hers always look so great. She explained it was a balance between utility, activity, and matching one's clothes.

Comments, Emotions: Felt really good to have these minutes just talking; I almost cried.

And in a later entry: "I noticed she nagged me less, too. Maybe this IS how we have learned to interact with each other." (The patient is performing her own functional analysis.)

The Constructional Questionnaire and logs provide highly valued patient end-goals, where the initial and subsequent subgoals are based upon an iterative analysis of the logs. This analysis involves evaluating the nonlinear relations that account for the behavior, thoughts, and emotions presented. In a nonlinear analysis, as noted earlier, one considers not only the occasions and consequences for the disturbing pattern, but those of its alternatives as well. Often the first question to be answered is, "What would happen if the person didn't behave as described?," that is, "What are the consequences of doing something else?" A matrix is produced that describes what might be called the "costs and benefits" of each pattern. What typically emerges is that the disturbing behavior is a "rational" outcome of the matrix, that is, the joint effect of the costs and benefits for all patterns favor the disturbing pattern. While the costs are often the focus and the source of the described distress, there are often real benefits, especially as measured against the alternatives. This is what underlies the instruction at the start of the Case Presentation Guide described earlier to "present a coherent picture of a person functioning highly competently, given their circumstances and implicit or explicit goals."

Notes

1 Goldiamond, 1974, 1975b
2 Goldiamond, 1974, 1975b; Layng, 2009; Layng & Andronis, 1984
3 Twyman, Layng, Stikeleather, & Hobbins, 2004, p. 62

6

Within the NCA Session

Conversation during a session is considered a reflection of current and past nonlinear contingencies. The goal is to always uncover or address these contingencies. Even instances of resistance are considered a sensible response to being asked to give up certain benefits provided by the disturbing pattern. Denial is taken as a strength; the client/patient does not want to forgo consequences they have previously experienced as important. "I will walk again," can be restated: "I will obtain the reinforcers provided by walking."

As described in the previous chapter, much of the within-session discussion surrounds the logs. Logs are not used to simply record behavior but as a basis for teaching the patient how to perform their own contingency analysis. Initial sessions involve identifying and analyzing important events. This transitions to the patient as the one to identify and analyze events. All of this occurs in the effort to move toward the goals, or terminal outcomes defined by the patient. The emphasis is never on stopping or reducing a behavior, thought, or feeling. Thoughts and feelings are treated as part of the contingencies under discussion and are used to analyze and change them. As contingencies change, so will the thoughts and emotions.

The use of the self-control worksheet (as depicted earlier in Figure 4.2) helps the patient take control of their situation and prepares them to deal with new problems that might arise long after sessions have ended. The patient begins by listing the subgoals targeted for the latest week, followed by the extent these were accomplished. Next, any relations noted and comments are entered. An evening out this week with one's wife might be a subgoal. "It was good to be alone without the kids, just talking; I felt close to her," might be a comment. A possible relation noted might be: "When I listen to her talk about her day, she is more interested in what I say." From this, the patient proposes subgoals for the upcoming week. The next entry results in reflection and analysis; this is where the rationale and the subgoals' relation to the terminal outcomes are described. A subgoal might be to spend at least 20 minutes each day

DOI: 10.4324/9781003141365-6

listening and talking to his wife about her day. Given how much she liked talking about her day, doing this every day is good next step to getting to having the type of relation the patient wants. Feedback occasions such entries as "How can I do this?" and "Is it too much too fast?" The logs would be examined for listening opportunities that may have been presented and that occur naturally, rather than scheduled.

Once patients learn to use their thoughts and feelings to analyze contingencies, they have the behavioral flexibility to solve a range of unforeseen circumstances. This is not limited to one class of issues or another. Israel Goldiamond[1] described a patient diagnosed as schizophrenic who learned to do this.

> I shall cite the report of an out-patient upon his return from vacation. He had had a history of hospitalization for schizophrenia and his brother was recently hospitalized for the same problem. During his vacation his wife walked out on him, leaving him alone in the motel. "I found myself sitting in bed the whole morning, and staring at my rigid finger," he said. "So I asked myself: 'Now what would Dr. Goldiamond say was the reason I was doing this?' He'd ask what consequences would ensue. And I'd say: 'Hospitalization.' And he'd say: 'That's right! Just keep it up and they'll take you away.' And then he'd say: 'But what would you be getting there that you're not getting now?' And I'd say: 'I'll be taken care of!' And he'd say: 'You're on target. But is there some way you can get this consequence without going to the hospital and having another hospitalization on your record?' And then I'd think a while and say: 'Hey! My sister. She's a motherly type, and she lives a hundred miles away.'" He reported that he dragged himself together, packed, and hitch-hiked to his sister who took him in with open arms. The education occurred in the process of the analysis of several months of written records.

Challenging Verbal Behavior

Often, verbal behavior that appears nonsensical or obscure can change within a session when the alternative contingencies are considered. That is, what happened to this person when they attempted to speak directly about their situation? At a staff meeting at a regional in-patient mental health facility, a psychiatric resident described how it was impossible to make sense of what a newly admitted patient was saying. The resident asked whether the patient could be brought to the meeting and interviewed on the spot so everyone could see the process in action. The interviewer agreed as long as the patient was willing to attend. The patient was a woman in her late seventies who had become distressed, continuously calling social services over the past few months. The calls had recently become more frequent, and she was showing signs of delusional speech. A worker visited and recommended hospitalization.

She was asked, "If you could make the changes that would solve your problem, what would they be?" She said, "Help my grandson." The interviewer asked what type of help he needed. She said that he shrank; he was tiny. When asked how tiny, she used her thumb and forefinger to indicate that he was about three inches tall. She went on to describe how he had not only shrunk, but at times he was on top of cabinets, etc., out of reach. Hearing this and knowing she had made a continuous effort to call social services, the interviewer asked, "When did you realize he had shrunk?" "About a week ago," she said.

This response suggested that she was likely calling about issues with her grandson, and no one was taking action. By engaging in the current form of verbal behavior, she got the attention to her situation she was seeking. But why was she saying he shrunk? The interviewer reasoned that if someone has shrunk, communication would not be easy. Also, one condition where people look small is when they are far away. When far away, communication is impossible. The interviewer then said, "When people look small often they are far away. Has your grandson grown farther away?" She looked up, nodded, and said, "Yes." "And when far away, even if you shout, they don't respond," the interviewer commented. She said, "He doesn't listen; he doesn't care." Had he always been that way? No. She went on to describe how he was a sweet boy, and that is why she invited him to live with her after he returned from the Army. "He changed?" she was asked. She went on to describe how he was not the warm, caring boy anymore, keeping to himself, being short with her, and finally stealing money from her. She tried talking to him, but nothing helped. She tried calling social services agencies, but no one helped, and she was becoming frightened. What began as a description of a shrunk grandson had been replaced with what was a very "rational" discussion. The interviewer had discerned the metaphor she was using and reinforced the theme of the "delusion." Further, the interviewer removed any punishment for directly talking about her situation. Her verbal behavior changed within the course of the interview from references to a shrinking grandson to her inability to reach him. She was assured she would get help; a social worker was assigned to her case who would work to remove the grandson and to protect her income. She remained delusion-free for the duration of her stay.

By considering the multiple, alternative contingencies involved, her delusions made perfect sense. Her delusion resulted in her removal from her house and in people sitting down to speak with her. Prior to hospitalization, her attempts at directly speaking about her concerns were ignored. The combination of her grandson becoming behaviorally unrecognizable, more socially distant, and refusing to listen to her combined to produce her use of the shrinking metaphor dressed up as a delusion.[2] Speaking to the theme, and reinforcing her speaking to it, resulted in the replacement of delusional, metaphorical conversation with direct conversation about her situation.

When we say we may reinforce the theme in a verbal episode, we are not suggesting simply paying attention to normal discourse and ignoring disturbing discourse. Instead we are advocating speaking to the contingencies reflected in the verbal behavior. By so doing, we are aligning our interests with that of the patient. We can then jointly pursue what is important to them.

Patients are often acutely aware of what therapeutic staff are doing. In an inpatient facility, where one of the authors worked, some staff decided to look at the effectiveness of reinforcing "normal" conversation by continuing to converse and ignoring "abnormal" conversation by remaining silent until the topic changed. They showed their data, which showed a marked decline in abnormal conversation when the procedure was implemented. The patient was interviewed and asked whether she enjoyed talking to the staff. She said yes, but that she knew what they were doing. "As long as I say things they like, they keep talking to me; when I don't, they stop. I just keep what I am really thinking to myself."

In some cases, the effect of the verbal behavior on the therapist is as or more informative than the content of the conversation. As Layng and Andronis[3] describe,

> One "obsessional" patient wove a detailed and interesting story concerning her search for a dentist to solve the problems she had with her teeth. The story lasted for over three hours. Seeing how involved he himself had become in her story, the programer [therapist] began to investigate how other people in the patient's life reacted to her heroic quest for a dentist. As it turned out, the woman was recently divorced after 25 years of marriage, and was now alone for the first time on a very important holiday. She developed an ill-defined periodontal pain, and called her ex-husband for assistance. He immediately came to her home and took her to a dentist, who found nothing wrong with her teeth or gums. . . . Nonetheless, the problem developed to such an extent that relatives she hadn't seen in ten years now came to stay with her, and tried to help her with what they all thought was a medical problem. The program's outcome had become clear. Repertoires needed to be established that would maintain the close contact with others that her obsessive delusional pattern now made available (note, the mand here was assumed, but the actual content of the delusion was viewed as being governed mainly intraverbally).

Often a theme may arise within the therapeutic context that the therapist can use to further the analysis and help the patient contact the relevant contingencies. From Layng and Andronis[4]:

A 40 year old man was admitted to a locked psychiatric unit for behaving "irrationally" (e.g., trying to pull the clothesline poles out of the ground in his backyard), and speaking "irrationally" (e.g., shouting that the poles were blasphemous statues of the cross and that Jesus had told him to tear them down). During a constructional interview (after Goldiamond, 1974), the man began by saying how little influence he had on his family, that he had, in fact, no effect upon them, and that he had no hope until he began hearing the voice of Jesus. He spoke for an hour about what the voice had told him and that he felt compelled to follow it. Nothing could be done for him; he had no control over his life. When asked about what his family might think of his hospitalization, he said, "I guess I've disappointed them. . . . They've been upset for a long time." When asked what had upset his family, he looked up and said, "I did. I'm to blame. It's all my fault." The interviewer seized this opportunity and replied, "If indeed it is your fault, and you are to blame as you say, then you do have control, you do have an impact on your family, you can influence your own life. Maybe your family is ready to listen to you now." He looked surprised and asked, "Do you think so?" In the discussion that followed, he described his behavior as being ineffective at providing critical family consequences. From this, it was inferred that his "irrational" patterns were attempts to produce the involvement by his family he so valued. Steps moving successfully toward this outcome could be used as reinforcers to maintain his working on a program to establish such family involvement, and would provide a test of our original inference. . . .

A program was designed to engage his wife in meetings with the programer and a social worker. Conversations during these meetings indicated that, indeed, all the man's attempts at involving his wife in his often demanding business problems had failed. Only when he became very morose did she comfort him and show concern for his situation. A programmatic sequence of contingencies, thereby, had been arranged, inadvertently reinforcing increasingly "pathological" patterns. During treatment, a similar program, but one targeting different behavior patterns, was implemented, including measures to reduce the response requirements imposed upon him by his business. Both the man and his wife were required to keep records, and both were trained to analyze these records in terms of consequential contingency relations. Concurrently, they were trained to develop procedures that could make available the consequences which, through their records, were identified as being critical to both of them.

At times, questions about the past can point to important contingencies. A young woman who claimed she had no goals and could not think about anything worth working toward was asked if she could remember a time when she was happy. She said yes, when she stayed for a while on her uncle's farm. She was asked what made it so pleasant. She said that she loved helping him. They would get up very early in the morning, milk the cows, feed the chickens, and even clean stables. She said she felt very accomplished and pleased with her work. She was asked whether she would like such a situation now. She hesitated and then said, "You know, I would." A consistent routine with observable accomplishments that are pleasantly acknowledged by others became the starting point for her program.

Other times, dreams or childhood memories will be reported. Contingency indicators can often be derived from these childhood memories. Recently, a young woman reported a nearly debilitating phobia of lizards. It was so bad she could not view a commercial airliner from the front without it reminding her of a lizard and creating a feeling of panic. She was asked when this first occurred. She said she was about 8 years old and remembered having a panic reaction when seeing a lizard. She was asked what happened. She said her family immediately rallied around to her and came to her rescue. From then on it only grew worse, requiring further family involvement. She came from a family where high expectations were placed on her in all areas. It was apparent a main source of control was the phobia. That is, it was by-and-large maintained by positive reinforcement. It grew to be more debilitating, but in spite of this the woman was quite professionally successful. She still had to do careful planning in order not to put herself into situations where she would encounter lizards, pictures of lizards, or representations of lizards. Again, success at doing this was interpreted as a sign that she could be effective at controlling her world. She had recently developed a hobby, at which she was quite talented, and a related social environment that made coming into contact with lizards more likely. The phobia was making it increasingly difficult to fully pursue the hobby and related social activities.

With control over her world being an apparent potent reinforcer, she was provided with a suggestion that she use the same skills she used professionally and the training skills she had acquired in her hobby to develop a program for herself. The program had two components: one, the application of a topical program involving providing control over overcoming the phobia; and two, a social component such that her success would provide greater social consequences for her success in her program. Since lizards had become a conditioned aversive stimulus, from which distancing from the stimulus was a reinforcer, a program was designed that provided that distance, not by removing oneself, but by removing the lizard. An image of a distant lizard was self-presented;

when she first "alerted" to the stimulus (began to notice a negative reaction forming), the image size increase was halted; and once she felt calm, it was self-removed. Now the distancing was contingent on calmness, not panic. This was repeated, systematically increasing the size and type of the image until she could comfortably view an image of a lizard. She extended the program to other reptiles and lizards, and finally to live animals. The other component was social. She posted her progress and what she was doing to achieve it in social media frequented by fellow hobbyists. The social support flooded in, as did some very good program suggestions. Now solving the problem generated the social involvement and control, the lack of which occasioned the behavior in the first place, a systemic intervention. She wrote in one of her public posts:

> Lizard stuff update
> I watched a first person perspective video for the first time on my phone on the train today of a lizard walking onto a person's hand, facing the camera and being carried forward towards the camera.
> I then rewatched the same video twice in my bedroom before going to sleep. This is a location where if I had previously even so much as imagined a lizard in my head, I'd have had to throw all the sheets out and check everything until I was sure that there was no actual reptile army trying to get to me.
> It simply blows my mind that focusing purely on the behaviors I can do something about in a systematic way also changes the emotion, the hallucinations and the physiological responses, all of which I believed would live with me for the rest of my life.
> I wonder if I'm ready to go see some live snakes now. There is a reptile shop near where I live. Maybe I can go into the shop to see the cute snakes where there also happen to be some lizards.

She was able to travel to a location for a workshop where she encountered a lizard on her patio and took a picture. When sending the photo she said, "I believe the little guy was more afraid of me than I was of him."

As is often the case in an NCA intervention, the private accompaniments of disturbing behavior change as the contingencies change. While no attempt is made to intervene directly in reported thoughts or emotions, those reports are not only tracked but, as noted previously, used to analyze the contingencies of which they are a function. Changes in these reports are good indicators of the success of the procedures, but it is the actual attainment of their stated goals that is used to evaluate the program.[5]

NCA has the potential of providing the next systematic step in behavioral intervention. It builds on traditional linear approaches, which have had some success, and provides analytical tools and interventions over-looked when nonlinear relations are not considered. Appendix E provides a comparison of Topical Direct, Topical Functional, Topical Nonlinear, and Systemic Nonlinear Interventions. By considering the relations involved in a nonlinear analysis, variables that otherwise may not be considered can enter into analysis and treatment. Further, such analysis may offer explicit and concrete alternatives to moving consequential contingencies and other causal postulates into a patient's head while accounting for important thoughts and feelings. It also reduces the temptation to postulate hypothetical language or covert-based accounts of what maintains DB in the apparent absence of maintaining consequences.

Notes

1 1976a
2 See Layng & Andronis, 1984 for a more detailed discussion of delusions and hallucinations as metaphor.
3 1984
4 1984
5 Layng & Andronis, 1984; Merley & Layng, 1976; Goldiamond, 1974, 1975b; Goldiamond & Dyrud, 1968; Goldiamond & Schwartz, 1975 provide even more examples of within-session behavior.

7

NCA and Patterns Arising From Organic or Medical Issues

NCA has been extended to those conditions that may have identified organic origins. Here, though the origin, or at least a contributing variable, may be organic, the behavior is still considered a rational outcome of the contingencies into which it enters.[1] For a successful intervention, it is critical to focus not simply on the behavior but on the contingencies into which it enters. Drossel and Trahan[2] describe the importance of a contingency analysis for those exhibiting diagnosed cognitive decline:

> This constructional stance is also maintained when behavioral problems occur, typically once the person has become increasingly disoriented, has begun to mis-interpret contextual cues, and fails to render accurate self-descriptions (see also Bem, 1972). To illustrate, topographical assessments developed within the medical model, such as the Neuropsychiatric Inventory (Cummings et al., 1994) or the Cohen-Mansfield Agitation Inventory (Cohen-Mansfield, Marx, & Rosenthal, 1989) can identify "wandering" as a behavioral target, with descriptions of form, frequency, and perceived severity. However, these assessments do not inform about the function of wandering, i.e., what the behavior accomplishes. Consequences may be very idiosyncratic: Joe may have a long history of golfing, and for him so-called "wandering" away from home represents the mere continuance and maintenance of his daily walking regimen. Miko's progressive degenerative condition decreased her English skills, and her "wandering" from home reliably takes her to a restaurant where people speak her first language. Andra has a chronic pain condition, and "wandering" is a reliable sign of increased pain that she is unable to verbalize. Behavioral interventions prescribed for these three scenarios will differ based on the function: Joe's intervention involves access to supervised exercise or a walking companion, Miko's support plan gives her access to meaningful social interactions, and Andra receives pain management. In none of these cases are psychotropic medication trials indicated. Indeed, in the latter case they

DOI: 10.4324/9781003141365-7

would be especially contraindicated, as psychotropic medication would further reduce Andra's ability to communicate her exacerbated pain condition.

Another case illustrates how such a nonlinear contingency analysis may be extended to understanding and intervening in verbal behavior, which itself seems to be a product of cognitive decline. The first author was contacted by a woman of his acquaintance about her mother. The mother was not well and suffering from a terminal illness that required her daughter's care. The mother had received multiple medications but was taking relatively few when the author was contacted. She had begun to engage in behavior the daughter and physicians considered hallucinatory. The treatment recommended was patience and continual "reality checks." For example, the mother would become agitated and exclaim there was water coming from the walls (DB). The daughter would wheel her mother to the wall and have her touch it, showing her it was dry. This had little effect. The daughter was distraught, and the mother appeared agitated and uncomfortable. Other patterns consisted of asking for dead relatives and concern for imaginary people.

One approach is to assume that the condition was entirely a function of the disease or its treatment and simply make the mother as comfortable as possible. As Drossel and Trahan[3] note:

When a person with a progressive neurodegenerative disease engages in these types of interactions, inaccurate verbal descriptions—or confabulations—typically result (Trahan, Donaldson, McNabney, & Kahng, 2014). The person fills in memory gaps, gives plausible reasons, or simply escapes from a social demand by providing an explanation that strikes the conversational partner as contrived. These confabulations alarm family members, who label them from a pathological perspective ("psychoses," "delusions")—possibly cued by their interactions with providers trained in the biomedical model—rather than viewing the individual's efforts to maintain social interactions as a continued functional strength.

Another approach is to assume that the contingencies that normally evoke typical verbal behavior are present, but for some reason responding verbally to those contingencies is difficult (likely related to the illness). Being unable to respond effectively may lead to increasing agitation and an escalation of symptoms as the mother escalates her attempts at obtaining what she is after (all of these are predictable outcomes of extinction). Speaking with the daughter, it was suggested she view her mother's behavior as a sensible attempt to meet current contingency requirements made incredibly difficult by the illness. That is, the verbal behavior was likely more of a mand, a request made to the daughter, than a tact, a description of the environment.[4] The apparent tact was possibly more easily voiced than the direct request. Usually, mands are evoked by some form of aversive event needing attending to, or some form of deprivation.[5] The mother could keep quiet (AAB) and suffer through whatever she currently faced, or she could attempt to communicate and at least have a possibility of producing the assistance she was after. The AAB would never provide the critical consequence,[6] but the hallucinatory behavior, DB, might on occasion do so. The daughter was provided a copy of Layng and Andronis[7] and told her job was to find the reinforcer being requested. In essence, her job was to find the words her mother could not. She was instructed to consider her mother's verbal behavior to be a metaphor and told to find the theme. Once identified, she was to speak to the theme and take action accordingly. Here is an excerpt from the daughter's logs:

Nov. 28: Goes to bed for nap at 1 p.m. 3:00 still awake but not reading. She is asking for Wesley, my father's brother. (FIRST TRY on metaphor. Sue don't say "Wesley is dead." I think, okay, lonely?)

Mother, are you lonely?

Yes, she replies.

Would you like to get up when I finish tutoring, and we can get ready for dinner?

Yes.

(Wesley gone.)

Nov. 29: 5 or 6 quiet conversations to what seems like a relative early in the morning. I am still in bed and can hear her on the monitor. She seems peaceful so I don't worry about it.

During nap she shouted for "Matilda" (her grandmother) and was frightened. I stopped tutoring and went downstairs. (Second try on metaphor. Sue don't say "Matilda is dead.") She said she had a bad dream. I rubbed her head for a bit, and she went to sleep. Rest of day was good.

I don't have dates, but there were other times the last month of her life that I used what I learned from you and it worked:

Aunt Elsie and Uncle Harold again:

Would you have them come downstairs so Uncle Harold can fix the fireplace?

Mama, would you like your favorite sweater on?

Yes!

(No more Elsie and Harold. She was just cold.)

Getting ready for the President. After breakfast one morning she was insistent that I bring in the folding chairs to the living room and pick things up a little because the President was coming to see us. She was persistent and kept watching out the window. I couldn't figure it out at first. Then I had it: she wanted something to happen social and perhaps get some recognition. (She had, in her real life, gotten an award for teaching adult literacy, and the President and his wife handed the award to her at a literacy dinner in a nearby city.)

Ma, want to try to beat me in Scrabble?

Yes!

(President gone. She beat me at Scrabble).

Several more water hallucinations, which I could stop on a dime:

Uh, Oh Suzie, there's water coming out of the wall again.

Mama, would you like your diaper changed?

Yes!

(Water gone.)

Dec. 1: Very normal today. She has had no long, tiring hallucinations for several days. Very strong humor is back.

To find the sense in such patterns we assume that there is something that is making a reinforcer (positive or negative) potent, that is, worth working for. A cold room potentiates putting on a sweater as a reinforcer; a leaking diaper potentiates a diaper change as a reinforcer. Next, we look at the occasion for the behavior, when and where does it occur, and finally we look to see if there is an escalation, increased demands, or agitation, suggesting the reinforcer is not attained. Finally, we look closely at the verbal behavior itself. We consider that the potentiating variables are making a class of requests or descriptions that in the past has provided something or removed something more likely to occur. The historically typical verbal behavior is for some reason blocked. Other patterns may occur that are linked to the potentiating variables and the occasion. This linkage provides the theme of the verbal behavior. Layng[8] described the process this way.

> Evocative or potentiating conditions often result in an individual seeking occasions or cues upon which behavior has been reinforced in the past, what B. F. Skinner[9] called precurrent behavior. To illustrate, if a person has a piece of paper and an important phone number to remember, but no pencil or pen, that person is likely to seek out and ask another individual for a pencil. The reinforcer here is receiving the pencil, the behavior is asking for it, and the occasion is the other person. The precurrent episode is evoked because the pencil can now be used in another episode: piece of paper—write with pencil— have the number. If the request for a pencil or pen is not successful, requests for something that will make a mark on paper may occur. A piece of burned matchhead may eventually be used. The matchhead may share little in physical resemblance to a pen, but it can serve the function of a pencil—readable marks on a paper. Procuring

the match head satisfies the writing requirement evoked by the necessity of having that important phone number. Further, one can predict that asking for a pencil or pen on these occasions is much more likely than asking for the time. It is also predictable, given that obtaining a pencil or a pen is not possible, that other behaviors related to writing will occur until the number is written down. These evocative or potentiating variables are what helps us understand when, where, and what behaviors might occur. That is, we can predict that given a set of evocative conditions, behaviors will occur on occasions that have previously produced changes in those conditions; and further, where a pattern is unavailable other patterns historically related to the function of the unavailable pattern will occur. Deprived of water, we would predict water related behaviors—asking for water, opening a water faucet, buying a bottle of water, drinking from a river, etc.

In the case of the verbal episode of seeing water coming from the walls, we ask what would make references to emerging water more likely. And why in the presence of the daughter? We can then explore if wetness, or water coming from something in some way, could be occurring. It is a search for the potentiating variable; we are in essence looking at the disturbing pattern as a kind of synonym for what is typically said under those conditions.

Nonlinear analysis may provide a basis for making sense of a pattern that might otherwise be considered entirely organic in origin, and for which no behavioral treatment is considered possible. By considering the pattern a sensible outcome of the interaction of the effects of the illness, the contingency matrices, and their potentiating variables, not only can the pattern be understood but relief provided for both the patient and the caregiver.[10]

Notes

1 Goldiamond, 1979
2 2015
3 2015, p. 127
4 Skinner, 1957
5 Skinner, 1957
6 Given several different consequences that may occur, the one that governs the contingency is the critical consequence. A potentially positive outcome of a particular medical treatment may govern my treatment selection even though the "side effects" are potentially quite aversive.
7 Skinner, 1957
8 2006, p. 161
9 1953
10 See Drossel & Trahan, 2015, for extensions to yet other areas of cognitive decline.

8

Distinguishing Between NCA and Other Approaches

Though many approaches may be constructional in nature, few if any typically make use of a nonlinear contingency analysis. Goldiamond[1] provided a somewhat detailed and technical description of linear and nonlinear contingency analysis that bears examining. He begins:

> The terms "linear" and "nonlinear" have a variety of usages, both within mathematics and among the various disciplines that employ them. They are used here in the context of the causality of a specified pattern of behavior; or, stated otherwise, in the context of the variables of which the referent behavior (RB)—that is, the specified behavior pattern at issue—is a function. Stated heuristically, the term "linear" is applied to those cases where the RB is considered to be a function of variables (which may include history) that a particular explanatory system assigns to the RB as its exclusive domain. Examples are the reinforcement history of a particular RB, its conditioning history, its maintaining variables, and so forth. The values of these variables in a given functional relation to the RB determine the value of the RB at any time.

Here Goldiamond is describing the typical behavioral contingency analysis often called an Antecedent, Behavior, Consequence or ABC analysis. Accordingly, the investigator considers what precedes the behavior of interest and what follows. A range of variables may be considered that impact on any of the As, Bs, or Cs.

> The term "nonlinear" is applied to those cases where, although the RB may be functionally related to the variables noted, the values in its exclusive domain enter into, but do not determine at any time, the values of the RB. To obtain its values, one must also consider similar, but exclusive, domains of alternative behaviors (ABs)—that is, behaviors other than the RB that are then functional. Stated otherwise, *no matter how extensive one's knowledge of the behavior*

DOI: 10.4324/9781003141365-8

at issue and of its linear determinants, one cannot make adequate predictions about the behavior in such cases.

This point is critical to nonlinear analysis. No matter how thorough one's ABC analysis might be, or how closely one examines the verbal relations involved, one cannot understand or identify the variables affecting the referent behavior of interest (RB) without considering the available alternative behaviors and their consequences.

> The crux of the distinction between linear and nonlinear behavior analysis is not whether one can diagram the RB and its determinants by a straight or curved line of the stimulus-response (S → R) type, or the operant occasion—behavior → consequence (S • R → S) type, or by a model requiring multiple lines of a decision theory type. Rather, the distinction lies in the causality, the determinants, and the domains, of which the RB is, respectively, the effect, the resultant, and the range. Stated otherwise, the issue is whether or not the RB can be understood (or predicted, etc.) solely by, or as a resultant of, variables assigned exclusively to it at any time by an explanatory system, regardless of whether one (unilinear) or more lines (branching, converging linear) or feedback loops (feedback linear) are used in the diagram. If it can be so understood or determined, the analysis or determination of the RB will be considered linear. Given an RB depicted linearly (in accord with the requirements of a particular explanatory system), if, *no matter how historically adequate that explanatory system has been at explaining RB, it cannot be explained on its own, but requires simultaneous attention to the determinants of one or more ABs, then the analysis or determination of the RB will be considered nonlinear* (italics in the original).

The issue is one of causality. The behavior of interest is determined by the prevailing contingency arrangements. In the laboratory and other highly controlled settings, behavior may be in fact a function of and analyzed in accord with linear ABC variables. However, outside the laboratory, behavior may be understood only in the context of multiple contingencies and not by any one contingency alone.

> A theoretical implication is that when a unilinear operant analysis, say, of the RB does not provide adequate explanation of the RB, the answer is not necessarily to reject operant analysis in such cases in favor of, say, a cognitive analysis.

This point is an important one. When confronted with behavior that appears to have no immediate reinforcing consequence, the tendency may be to "turn inward." That is, it is tempting to postulate that variables residing in some private domain, inaccessible to the therapist, must be determining the observed pattern, or that the patient may be following some form of maladaptive rule that makes them insensitive to certain consequential contingencies. These variables may be considered as part of either cognitive or behavioral explanations and are not restricted to either. The variables can be, alternatively, thoughts, emotions, defective verbal relations, or subconscious motivations. Accordingly, therapeutic efforts are then conventionally targeted at those variables either pathologically (eliminating or reducing unwanted thoughts or emotions), constructionally (establishing desired thoughts and emotions), or through acceptance and goal setting where the disturbing behavior is considered a type of public or private avoidance behavior that is, at least in part, a product of defective verbal relations. But as Gambrill[2] notes,

> We are often aware of our thoughts and thus they are readily available to view as the cause of behaviors and events that befall us in our lives. The same can be said of our feelings. These too are readily available. (See also later discussion of cognitive biases.) This availability, combined with the tendency to think that we have discovered the cause (and thus the remedy) regarding behaviors or consequences of interest, lull us into thinking we have discovered how to change things for the better. There is an illusion of understanding. If this is not true, they are false prophets (a kind of false positive) which get in the way of further inquiry.

And therein lies the problem. When causality is moved inside, either the individual or a hypothetical verbal relation, the search for past and current environmental variables may be overlooked. Accordingly, a consideration of the nonlinear variables may provide an alternative to more mentalistic or defective verbal relations accounts.

Topical and Systemic Interventions in NCA

Often, it is enough to consider the (nonlinear) matrix of which the disturbing behavior is a part. The intervention for the nagging described in Chapter 4 is an example of intervening directly in the matrix in which DB participates. We call this a Nonlinear Topical Intervention.[3] Topical interventions may be based on either linear or nonlinear analysis. In topical interventions, treatment is often directed at eliminating the presenting complaint (punishment, extinction, time out, differential reinforcement of other behavior [DRO], differential reinforcement of alternative behavior [DRA], etc. procedures) or at substituting another less costly pattern for the disturbing pattern (teaching an alternative behavior that has the same maintaining consequence as DB). Accordingly, as in some applications of DRA procedures, the procedure may or may not include attention to the function of the disturbing behavior.

Topical interventions may include procedures directly addressing the presenting complaint: *Topical Direct*; those that address the function of the complaint without reference to the available alternative behaviors: *Topical Functional*; and those that not only address the consequences of the disturbing behavior, but the consequences of the available alternative behaviors as well: *Topical Nonlinear*. The latter produces a matrix of alternative behaviors and consequences in which the presenting complaint participates. In this formulation, DB is a function not only of its consequences but also of the consequences of the AABs. Accordingly, DB cannot be fully understood in the "linear" context of its consequences alone. As we have maintained, a more complete understanding requires the "nonlinear" consideration of the AABs and their consequences as well, creating a "matrix" of occasions, behaviors, and consequences that together determine the occurrence of DB. In this way, such Nonlinear Topical Interventions differ from typical DRO or DRA programs. However, as noted earlier, at times another type of intervention is required: *Systemic* intervention.[4]

In a systemic intervention, a matrix of contingencies is identified that typically does not contain the presenting complaint (DB), yet when addressed, affects the disturbing pattern. A person who leaves his desk at work to eat a candy bar when "stress" and "anxiety" build seeks help with weight reduction. It may be determined that leaving the desk and eating the candy provides a needed break from the demands of coworkers and accumulating unfinished work and gives the patient time to gather his thoughts. The patient may report self-deprecating thoughts along with the feelings of stress and anxiety. One might approach this by focusing on the feelings of stress and anxiety and the thoughts that may be occurring at those times. Procedures directed at coping with these feelings and thoughts might be prescribed through reframing, acceptance, or diffusion, among others. Another (topical) approach might be explicitly to explore escape alternatives healthier than getting candy that also provide the same relief.

A nonlinear contingency analysis would take a different approach. To begin, the feelings of stress and anxiety would be used to search for the consequential relations they describe.[5] A contingency analysis of stress implies increasing work requirements with falling reinforcement rates, and anxiety suggests behavioral requirements the patient may be unprepared to meet.[6] The therapist and patient first would scan the daily logs for indicators that those are indeed happening. The daily logs might reveal how the patient controls work requirements and how the patient evaluates and prioritizes them. Instead of dealing with the candy eating, a program of assertiveness training, along with another focusing on organizational skills, might be recommended as part of the subgoals. No action is taken directed at candy eating or feelings of anxiety or stress. Once the new assertive and organizational patterns are established, providing greater control over the work environment, the candy eating should no longer be required and would be expected to drop out without direct intervention, as would the self-deprecating thoughts and feelings of stress and anxiety that previously were part of a contingency that is no longer potent. Figures 8.1–8.6 depict how some topical and systemic intervention strategies might be applied in this case.

The therapist and patient continually monitor the logs for evidence that the frequency of candy eating changed. A reduced frequency of candy eating and lack of reported anxiety would suggest that the systemic procedures worked. The anxiety, stress, self-deprecating thoughts, and the

Disturbing Behavior	Costs
Get candy when work piles up	Increased calories and fat

Target Behavior	Costs	Benefits
Decrease candy eating by sending money to Ku Klux Klan for every candy bar eaten	Money, recording, mailing	Fewer calories and less fat

Figure 8.1 Example of a possible Topical Direct Intervention, where the intervention is targeting the disturbing behavior without regard to function

Disturbing Behavior	Costs	Benefits
Get candy when work piles up	Increased calories and fat	Temporarily escape work requirements

Target Behavior	Costs	Benefits
Walk to get healthy preprepared snacks	Takes preparation	Temporarily escape work requirements; fewer calories and less fat

Figure 8.2 Example of a possible Topical Functional Intervention, where the intervention is targeting the possible function of the disturbing behavior

Disturbing and Available Alternative Behavior	Costs	Benefits
AAB: Stay at desk	Work piles up, coworkers on back, no time to think or plan	Fewer calories and less fat
DB: Get candy when work piles up	Increased calories and fat; work not done when away from desk	Break from work and coworker requests, time to think what to do next
AAB: Get up, walk out of office	Co-workers wonder why standing in hall, socially awkward	Break from work and coworker requests, time to think what to do next

Figure 8.3 Example of a Nonlinear Topical Functional Analysis, where the consequences of the available alternative behaviors are used to understand and make sense of the disturbing behavior

Target Behavior	Costs	Benefits
Walk to get healthy pre-prepared snacks; While snacking, make notes about what to do next	Takes preparation	Break from work and coworker requests, time to think about what to do next and seen working away from desk; better able to meet requests; fewer calories and less fat

Figure 8.4 Example of a Nonlinear Topical Intervention, where the target contingency attempts to provide same function uncovered by a consideration of the consequences for the available alternative behaviors as well as the disturbing behavior

costs and benefits of candy eating are a function of another matrix altogether that, when addressed, also affects the presenting complaint. The patient is taught that recurrent distressful thoughts and feelings are to be treated as part of the broader contingency ecology in which the patient lives. Imposing change procedures targeting DB may have only transitory effects unless there are changes to the other contingency matrices responsible for DB in the first place.

Emotions and Thoughts

The occurrence of the disturbing pattern, including any reported thoughts or emotions, may often be found to be a function of nonlinear relations

DB & AAB Matrix	Costs	Benefits
AAB: Stay at desk	Work piles up	Fewer calories
DB: Get candy	Increased calories	Break from work
AAB: Walk out	Socially awkward	Time to think

Systemic Matrix	Costs	Benefits
Disorganized, acquiescent	Increased work, others take advantage	Keeps job, work eventually completed, pleases others
Quit job	No $$, etc.	No work hassles

Potentiating Contingencies

Figure 8.5 Example of a Nonlinear Systemic Analysis, where contingencies of another matrix potentiate the consequential relations of the matrix in which the disturbing behavior resides

DB & AAB Matrix	Costs	Benefits
AAB: Stay at desk	Typical workday effort	Work completed
DB: Get candy		No longer required
AAB: Walk out		No longer required

Systemic Target Behaviors	Costs	Benefits
Organizational skills	Time to learn and practice	Good planning, organized work day
Deal effectively with others	Time to learn and practice, possible early setbacks	More easily handle requests, co-workers more respectful of time

Depotentiates Contingencies

Figure 8.6 Example of a Nonlinear Systemic Intervention, where changing the systemic contingencies results in a change in the disturbing behavior with no direct intervention in the disturbing behavior or the matrix in which it resides

traced directly to the individual's environment. Thus, emotions and thoughts play a crucial role in identifying these relations, not as causes or forms of maladaptive rule-following, but as descriptors of the nonlinear contingencies of which they are a part.[7] Stated otherwise, the reported emotions may be used as indicators of specific relations involved and can be quite useful in identifying and programing alternative contingencies. Such programming may result in a different set of reported emotions that occur in accord with changes in the nonlinear relations. Hence, patients are taught to be very sensitive to their emotions—not to try to change them, but rather to understand that they are the sensible and natural outcome of the consequences of everyday life as they experience it.

The emotions experienced are not maladaptive or pathological, or the product of self-defeating personal rules. By learning how emotions describe and are a function of certain contingencies, patients can use them to change their patterns by changing their contingencies, and as part of that change other emotions describing these new contingencies are likely to supplant the others. This is not limited to basic emotions but extends to such complex feelings as those of shame, guilt, or embarrassment, and even freedom and happiness.[8]

This approach emphasizes the acceptance of emotions and thoughts, but with a twist. It is acceptance of experienced emotions and thoughts as part of, and indicators of, the nonlinear contingencies of which they are a part. Accordingly, the task is to harness emotions and thoughts as indicators of contingencies and teach patients to use them to make changes in those contingencies.[9] As Goldiamond[10] said at the end of his address "Emotions and Emotional Behavior" to the (then) American Association for Behavior Therapy:

> The emotional descriptors are descriptors—they're not stimuli, they're not responses, I don't believe they're respondents—they are descriptors of a contingency relationship. They're a bit more complex, just as words can be even more descriptive. Now, what is their use? What use do they have? As Skinner has noted, it's been very important in psychotherapy and this kind of change. And I submit it is not only important for psychotherapy, I submit that it is crucial for any therapy which utilizes a radical behaviorist analysis. This is so for the following reasons.
>
> Number One: I will state that emotions are private descriptors of publicly observable consequential contingencies.
>
> Number Two: The person often lacks the repertoire to describe publicly those contingencies. Can't put them in words. After all, not all of you—not all people have had the advantages of reading the books that we have, or utilizing that language. The person, especially

if in contact with the popular psychological literature, may describe other events and relations, often past indignities.

Three: However, most people can experience, and can report, the private emotional events. There are some who do so poorly, or they could use—they use emotional subterfuges such as guilt, or phobias, or conflict, or something of the sort.

Four: A sensitive analyst working can use such report to attempt to specify the operating contingencies, and to teach people how to program the change in these contingencies. Thereby, the patients may not only behave in a manner better suitable for the consequences they consider to be important, they will also feel better, because the contingencies have been changed.

Notes

1 1984
2 2015, p. 124
3 Goldiamond, 1978, 1984
4 Goldiamond, 1978, 1984
5 see Goldiamond, 1976c; Layng, 2017
6 cf., Dyrud, 1971
7 see Goldiamond, 1975, 1979b; Layng, 2006, 2009, 2017
8 Cardinali de Fernandes & Alexandre Dittrich, 2018; Goldiamond, 1979b; Layng, 2017
9 Goldiamond, 1974, 1975b, 1978; Layng, 2006, 2009; Layng & Andronis, 1984; Merley & Layng, 1976
10 1979b

Measuring NCA Outcomes
Avoiding Response Bias

We begin with what appears to be a simple experiment. An observer is seated facing two panels. When the panels are illuminated a triangle is projected on one of the panels. The observer is instructed to press the panel upon which they think the triangle was projected and confirm the presence of the triangle by saying "Yes, I see it," or "No, I don't see it." The occurrence of "Yes, I see it" is thereby a function of the occurrence of the triangle. In this arrangement there are two indicator responses. One is the panel touch, and the other is a verbal response saying, "Yes, I see it" or "No, I don't see it." Both the touch and the spoken response are occasioned by the presence or absence of the triangle.

The triangle is presented at various levels of illumination. Sometimes the triangle is quite visible, while at other times it fades into the background and is difficult to see. When the data are analyzed, and the accuracy of their responses calculated, it is found that panel touches are indicating the correct presence of the triangle more frequently than is saying "Yes, I see it." That is, the accuracy of the motor response is greater than the accuracy of the verbal response. How can that be? It is the same triangle projected on the same panel. Perhaps the observers' responding is controlled at a level below awareness. They see the triangle, but aren't aware of it, so they press the panel, but do not say "Yes, I see it." That is what defines so-called subliminal perception. But perhaps there is another explanation.

What if we examine the history of consequences for the two behaviors, panel pressing and speaking? In the case of speaking, when an observer says, "Yes, I see it" and what they are claiming to observe is there, it is a hit—they are being truthful. If they say, "No, I don't see it" and it's not there, it is a correct rejection; again they are being truthful. If they say, "No, I don't see it" and the event is present, it is a miss—they may be inattentive or confused. But, if they say, "Yes, I see it" and it is not there, this is a false alarm—they are hallucinating or perhaps lying. Given all four possible outcomes, the one that is likely to have a history of being punished is saying, "Yes, I see it" when something is not there. Panel presses, however, likely have no such history.

DOI: 10.4324/9781003141365-9

This was an actual experiment conducted by Israel Goldiamond.[1] The differences in accuracy disappeared when procedures were changed to mitigate the effects of past consequences for false alarms. It was one of the first experiments that showed that it is not simply the presence or absence of a stimulus that guides the behavior, but the consequence of responding among alternative responses as well. Where behavior is not controlled by the simple occurrence or nonoccurrence of the stimulus, but by the effects the indicator response has in its own right, it is called response bias. Accordingly, two aspects of discrimination must be considered when evaluating an individual's response to events: 1) the discriminability of the stimulus; and 2) response bias that may be produced from a range of variables not related to the simple presence or absence of a stimulus.

In the clinic, response bias as well as discriminability must be considered when making observations about patients, and when patients make observations about themselves. Using procedures derived from Signal Detection Theory (SDT), which allow for the separate measurement of discriminability and response bias, Robbins, Layng, and Karp[2] investigated the ability of trained observers to detect (diagnose) psychiatric inpatients from individuals with no such diagnosis based on the house-tree-person (H-T-P) projective test. Fifty H-T-P drawings were collected from psychiatric inpatients, and 50 H-T-P drawings were selected from college students and others from the general population. Observers previously trained on the use of the projective test were asked to simply say "yes" or "no" after studying an H-T-P drawing to indicate whether or not the drawing was made by a psychiatric inpatient. The responses fell into one of four categories: a "yes" when the drawing was made by a psychiatric inpatient was a "hit;" a "no" response when the drawing was made by a psychiatric inpatient was a "miss;" a "no" response when the drawing was not made by a psychiatric inpatient was a "correct rejection;" a "yes" response when the drawing was not made by a psychiatric inpatient was a "false alarm." In essence, there were two categories of correct responses (hit, correct rejection) and two categories of incorrect responses (miss, false alarm). The investigators asked the observers to rate their answers as to their certainty. Once the observer indicated "yes" or "no," they were asked to indicate whether they were very certain, certain, or not certain their response was correct.

The investigators provided the 100 drawings in random order one at a time. After a baseline was established, the observers were provided feedback on the degree to whether their "yes" or "no" responses were incorrect. When incorrect responses were made, the investigators presented a loud, shrill sound after blocks of either five or ten drawings. The duration of the aversive sound was determined by the number and type of disagreements that occurred during the blocks. The more disagreements, the greater duration of sound. Feedback was not presented after each drawing to prevent memorizing the results of their responses. After some blocks, the aversive tone was presented for "miss" errors; after other blocks the aversive tone was presented for the "false alarm" errors. Three of the four observers showed great sensitivity to the tones and changed their responses to minimize its occurrence. To summarize, the observers experienced three conditions: baseline, tone contingent on misses, and tone contingent on false alarms.

As predicted by SDT, all four observers' ability to discriminate patients from non-patients (*discriminability*) remained unchanged across all conditions. Their ability was not good, with accuracy just above chance. With each of the feedback conditions, however, three of the four observers saw a marked change in *response bias*. That is, they went from saying "yes" to nearly 90% of the drawings in the aversive tone for misses to saying "yes" to only 30% of the drawings during the aversive tone for false alarms. Observers maintained the tone did not have any effect on their decision making and that their rules for making their decision remained unchanged.

This experiment was a demonstration of the effect of nonlinear contingencies on a simple response, yes or no. Describing only the consequences for a "yes" response in the presence of the discriminative stimulus (S^D) will not account for the observed behavior. One must also include the consequences for the alternative responses. Under all conditions the consequences for hits and correct rejections remained unchanged. Figure 9.1 shows the results for one of the observers and the changes that occurred as a result of the changes in the experimental conditions.

This experiment demonstrated that the subjective evaluation of one's response to the environment has two components: discriminability of the stimulus, and response bias. This is particularly important when assessing a patient's discussion of private events. Private events are by their very nature ambiguous. It is impossible to know whether the feelings or thoughts the client is describing are the feelings or thoughts they actually had, even when they are "certain" they are. It is similarly impossible for the patient to know. Our attempts to clarify patient descriptions of those events or bring the patient into better "contact" with them may turn out to be exercises in aligning patient response bias with that of the therapist. As Israel Goldiamond once said, a patient obtains "insight" when they come to describe their behavior as their therapist would.

Understanding the effect of nonlinear relations has important implications for the clinic, Robbins et al. remarked:

> Accordingly, this experiment may have implications for the clinic where ambiguity may be more the rule than the exception. It suggests that a least one class of verbal behavior may be altered by nonlinear

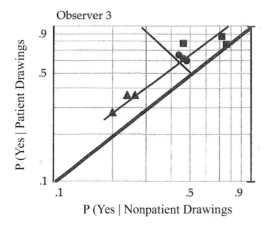

Figure 9.1 The graph depicts the probability of saying yes to a psychiatric
in-patient drawing as function of the probability of saying yes to
a non-patient drawing for Observer 3. The filled circles depict
baseline performance; the filled triangles depict noise contingent
on "false alarms" performance; filled squares depict noise contingent on "misses" performance. The solid, thick diagonal line
represents chance discriminability. The parallel, thinner diagonal
line, the Relative Operating Characteristic (ROC) curve, depicts
unchanged discriminability as response bias changes as a function
of changes in consequences for false alarms and misses.

consequential relations. Verbal behavior which may appear to be
"out-of-sync" with observed "reality" may instead be the sensible
outcome of unobserved (by the clinician and the client) nonlinear
consequential contingencies. Second, it suggests that a client may be
perfectly able to discriminate one event from another, even where
there appears to be a discrepancy in how the client sees the world versus how the therapist sees it (see Layng & Andronis, 1984). Where
nonlinear consequential relations are overlooked, there may be a
tendency to explain what appears to be pathological or maladaptive behavior through the postulating of defective self-instructions,
abnormal schema, the effects of rule-governed behavior, governance
by private events, or some other inferred process.

(Goldiamond, 1974, 1984; Layng & Andronis, 1984)

Recognizing that response bias plays a major role when describing
ambiguous events extends to our consideration of our choice of independent variables when conducting clinical research. Barry Farber and Matt
Blanchard[3] have provided evidence that patients are often knowingly less
than truthful with their therapists. In a survey of 547 patients they found

that 72.6% reported lying to their therapists. Often, the patients claimed more progress than they were making. Some commented that they liked their therapists and didn't want them to feel bad. If we combine this recognized deception with descriptions influenced by variables responsible for response bias, we are presented with a real dilemma. How can we accurately evaluate patient progress and how their thoughts and feelings enter into that evaluation, and to what extent can we use patient description of their private experience and behavior in our clinical work? Let's tackle those questions one at a time.

Today we see an increasing reliance on surveys and questionnaires in studies evaluating clinical interventions. Patients provide answers to a questionnaire prior to therapy, and then again at the end of therapy. Any pre-test vs. post-test differences are then assessed to determine the effectiveness of the therapy. These questionnaire responses are often compared to others who either participated in no, or a different, therapy in order to determine which approach was most effective. Many therapists use questionnaires to determine their own effectiveness. Unfortunately, few studies explicitly consider the effects of response bias. They appear to assume that patients evaluate strictly on the presence of absence of stimuli, often described as private events. A study conducted nearly 60 years ago raised serious problems with this approach.

Azrin, Holz, and Goldiamond[4] replicated the results of a major survey on the subjective effects experienced by pilots in aerial dogfights during the Korean War. The remarkable results of the study were the consistent subjective experiences described by almost all the pilots surveyed. The replication, however, did not survey fighter pilots but college students who had never been in combat, many of whom had never even flown. Prior to the survey, students were given the following instructions:

> Imagine that you are a combat flyer who has flown many missions over enemy territory. Your commanding officer gives you this questionnaire and tells you to fill it in. Fill in the answers, keeping in mind what your commanding officer expects you to have felt.

The students produced questionnaire results that correlated just as highly with the pilots as the pilots' responses correlated with one another. Here they were providing detailed descriptions of the subjective effects of combat without ever experiencing it. In essence it was not the presence of private stimuli or responses that guided the students' behavior, but consequences of their responses—that is, their response bias. As the investigators noted:

> The response pattern obtained from the students by means of the questionnaire is almost completely predictable on the basis of response

bias. Therefore, it is quite likely that the same type of response bias operated on the combat flyers. Any conclusion concerning the actual symptoms must await study by a method that provides a more direct and objective measurement.

The point raised is of critical importance in the clinic. To what extent are the questionnaire responses of patients a product of response bias and not of therapeutic intervention? Perhaps one could argue that the nature and construction of modern questionnaires make them more reliable indicators of actual changes in private experience. To test this, Russell Layng[5] devised a study to see whether he could replicate the findings of Azrin et al., using a sample of individuals willing to take online surveys for payment. The payment is simply for taking the survey, not for the answers provided. Layng provided a copy of the Acceptance and Action Questionnaire known as the AAQ-II to group of 31 online responders. He first asked the responders to fill out the survey. He then provided the AAQ-II again, this time after the following instructions:

> Now, imagine you have just successfully completed an 8-week course in Acceptance and Commitment Therapy. The course is intended to improve your psychological well-being. Take the survey, keeping in mind how your therapist would expect you to feel.

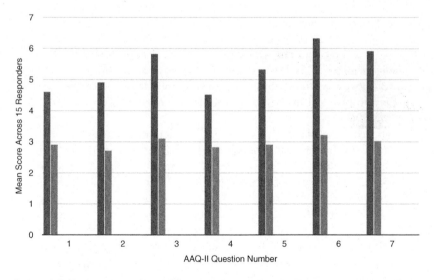

Figure 9.2 Responders filling out initial questionnaire are depicted in dark gray. Questionnaire responses after instructions are depicted in lighter gray. A higher score indicates greater experiential avoidance. A lower score indicates greater psychological flexibility.

The changes were large and dramatic. The results are depicted in Figure 9.2 for a sample of 15 responders who showed high experiential avoidance as measured by the initial survey. The higher the score, the greater the reported experiential avoidance; the lower the score, the greater the reported psychological flexibility. It is evident that simply specifying what one thinks a therapist would expect one to feel is enough to produce statistically significant results. The question is raised: To what extent are the outcomes of studies using questionnaires the result not of therapeutic intervention, but of response bias?

To further investigate this question, Layng replicated a published study using the AAQ-II. A study had been conducted using middle school teachers faced with many classroom challenges. The teachers went through an 8-week course of ACT. The AAQ-II was used pre- and post-training. The teachers showed a statistically significant difference in their questionnaire responses, with a decrease in experiential avoidance and an increase psychological flexibility. Layng again found 30 respondents willing to participate in a survey, and he provided the AAQ-II with the following instructions:

> Imagine you are a middle school teacher. You are failing to meet your goals with your students. Keep this in mind while making your choices.

The respondents were then provided the AAQ-II again along with the following instructions:

> Now, imagine you have just successfully completed an 8-week course in acceptance and commitment therapy. The course is intended to improve your psychological well-being. Take the survey, keeping in mind how your therapist would expect you to feel.

The effectiveness of the "intervention," depicted in Figure 9.3 for a sample of 15 responders who showed high experiential avoidance as measured by the initial survey, was nearly identical to that obtained in the actual study. It is quite conceivable that the same variables resulting in the response bias that produced the results in the Layng demonstration may also account for the results in the published study. Layng's study indicates that modern questionnaires may be no more reliable as indicators of private experience than the surveys of 60 years ago.

Another way response bias can affect outcome studies is suggested by a study conducted by Goldiamond and Hawkins[6] in which observers were asked to identify nonsense words studied when they were briefly flashed on a display. The more the words were studied, the more often the words were correctly identified. This replicated many similar experiments that

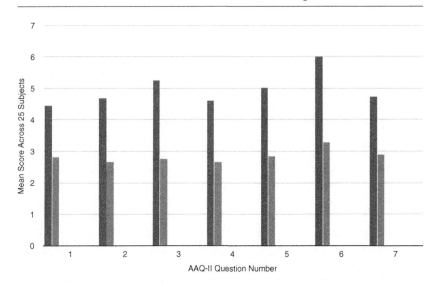

Figure 9.3 Responders filling out initial questionnaire after reading a middle school teaching scenario are depicted in dark gray. Questionnaire responses after instructions are depicted in lighter gray. A higher score indicates greater experiential avoidance. A lower score indicates greater psychological flexibility.

sought to evaluate the effects of training on perception. One difference, however, in the Goldiamond and Hawkins study was that no words were flashed on the display, only smudges. How was this possible? Experimenters used a scoresheet to track observer responses and determine their accuracy. If a trial specifies a particular word is to be presented, there will be a corresponding entry on the score sheet. If ZEQ is scheduled on Trial 3, then ZEQ will appear on the scoresheet next to Trial 3. If the observer says, "ZEQ" the response matches the scoresheet and is counted as being correct. What Goldiamond and Hawkins did was to show that they could obtain an increased frequency of scoresheet matches without presenting the scheduled stimulus. It turned out that the more the words were studied, the more likely observers were to say the nonsense words compared to less-studied words, thus resulting in more scoresheet matches for the studied words. There was no change in perception—there couldn't be, since no words were presented. There was a change in response bias toward saying the studied words.

Now consider a patient in therapy. Certain words and characterizations will be repeated and emphasized during sessions. The likelihood of these words being used by the patient may increase with no other real change occurring. A questionnaire is provided that contains words or characterizations that match the words or characterizations used in session (the scoresheet). Changes in responses from pre-test to post-test can be a function of increased scoresheet matches based on changing word usage, not other treatment effects. Control groups who have not experienced the word use and characterizations will not be affected by a similar response bias. Randomized control studies may, therefore, be only reflecting the differences in response bias from, as we have seen, a variety of potential sources. As Azrin et al. first noted 60 years ago:

> The present findings may well be considered for their implications for the use of interview and questionnaire methods in general. Unless an objective and direct means of measurement is available, the questionnaire responses may be independent of the behavior being studied.

Clinical studies, even randomized control studies, that rely on questionnaires may be considered only as weak evidence for therapeutic effectiveness.

Accordingly, NCA does not rely on questionnaires when evaluating its outcomes. This does not mean reports of subjective events are not considered; indeed, they are noted and often recorded. However, the primary means of evaluation centers on patient accomplishments. As we see in Chapter 10, a patient's goals are stated as:

"I will be enjoying a full social life: going out with friends attending entertainment events such as museums, movies, etc.; able to make new friends; develop ways of entertaining myself through crafts, sewing, and various projects.

"I will be financially able to maintain myself, outside the halfway house, and be working, if possible.

"I will be living in my own apartment or with friends out of the halfway house.

"My children will be returned to me. If not possible, increased visiting will be established."

She of course no longer wanted the hallucinations that she reported plagued her; she wanted to enjoy life and to feel good. Our goal was to help her achieve her goals, but we needed to see them in the context of a better quality of life. We feel much more confident that those private experiences will be more likely if they accompany changes in consequential contingencies. If a patient obtains their explicit outcomes and expresses a corresponding change in affect, we consider our intervention to have been successful. In the case of our patient described in Chapter 8, she achieved the following outcomes:

1. new friends and hobbies;
2. relationships, but not married;
3. out of halfway house living with sister and brother-in-law off and on;

4. part-time work;
5. GED; and
6. kids never lived with her but maintained close relationship, frequent visits.

Though not identical to her stated outcomes, they were quite close. She also reported an absence of hallucinations and feeling content and much happier. She reported no longer feeling depressed about her situation or fearing losing contact with her children. We feel justified in considering the intervention successful. We see identifiable accomplishments, and we have subjective reports that one would predict from those accomplishments.

Response Bias Within the Session

Earlier we raised questions about the role of response bias in ongoing therapy. Where any ambiguity exists in describing intrapersonal or interpersonal events, response bias may enter into a patient's descriptions. We have found that patient verbal behavior is very sensitive to environmental consequential contingencies, and these will exert their influence over patient descriptions. Patients may exaggerate problems to ensure they are taken seriously; they may under-report problems so as not to make their therapists unhappy; they may align their descriptions to more closely match those of the therapists; they may have a history of punishment for false alarms, which results in their saying they cannot achieve certain outcomes, etc. The issue, however, is not the truthfulness of any particular statement, but the functional relation of that statement to its environment. A factual lie may be a truthful metaphor. A patient may describe being abandoned in a mall by their mother, when that event never happened. The question is raised: Why that lie among all that could be said? Perhaps contingencies that describe being alone and helpless in an unfamiliar environment need to be addressed, or perhaps abandonment is a recurring theme expressed by the therapist. In the first case, we will often see indications of the conditions responsible for those feelings in the Daily Events Log. In the second, we need to recognize how our verbal behavior biases patient verbal behavior. In all cases patients are being genuine. Their observations are considered an adaptive outcome of a history of nonlinear contingencies and an indicator of those contingencies.

NCA broadens and extends the concept of context to embrace the full ecological contingency context and its history, of which behavior is a function. It provides a basis for understanding private experiences without assigning them causal status, without moving consequential contingencies inside the head or necessitating the construction of questionnaires in order to have some form of observable and recordable indicator responses.

Notes

1 1964
2 1995
3 <u>2015</u>, also see Farber, Blanchard, & Love, 2019
4 1961
5 2016
6 1958

10

Topical and Systemic NCA Interventions

A Case Study

There are two forms of nonlinear analysis. One assesses alternative behaviors and their consequences. The other considers alternative contingencies whose effects on the disturbing behavior (DB) may not be readily apparent and may occur at different times or places than DB[1] but potentiate the contingencies into which DB may enter. Stated differently, the first form primarily focuses on an intra-matrix resolution, while the second form primarily focuses on an inter-matrix resolution. We will refer to the first as *topical nonlinear relations* and to the second as *systemic nonlinear relations*.

For the first, topical nonlinear, making sense of the disturbing behavior pattern may be as simple as asking, "What would happen if the person did not behave this way?" At a recent conference one of the authors was presented with a case of a boy who would make progress at a special school only to sabotage his progress and "regress." All methods had failed, including tokens, time-outs, and, most recently, attempts at a form of acceptance and commitment therapy. The first author asked, "What would happen if he made continual significant progress?" The answer: "He would return to the school from which he was referred." It was pointed out that one could view this as a response to mounting fear of return to the original school, with escape from that fear reinforcing the boy's acting out, or one could view this as a result of the new school's having created such a welcoming environment that the child is willing to suffer unpleasant tantrums and setbacks in order to stay in a place he loves. They said, "But he claims he wants to leave and does not want to stay as he is screaming and tantruming." And the result? "He shows he is not ready to progress," they said. One of the authors suggested that after a period of some progress they tell him they have decided to let him stay as long as he wishes to stay, and that going back to his old school or another will be his decision. It was recommended they tell him that as long as he continues to make the great progress he is making he can remain at the school. The staff agreed to try it and said they had not thought of approaching it this way. It also made them think a little

DOI: 10.4324/9781003141365-10

differently about the boy and his needs. After a couple of months with no tantrums, the team was asked to please let the first author know if and when the next tantrum occurred. No notice was received. We do not know whether this recommendation was entirely successful, but the point here is to demonstrate that when the entire matrix of behaviors is considered, in this case the consequences of tantrums and of doing well, a different intervention is suggested.

Topical Interventions

We can specify three types of topical interventions: Topical Direct, Topical Functional, and Topical Nonlinear.

1. The focus of **Topical Direct Intervention** is on the disturbing pattern (DP). The intervention may include eliminative procedures, reinforcement procedures (e.g., DRO), teaching incompatible behaviors, and other procedures whose aim is to change the frequency of the disturbing pattern without regard to function.
2. The focus of **Topical Functional Intervention** is on trying to substitute new target behaviors (TB) that produce the same consequence as the disturbing pattern, but at less cost. These interventions may also attempt to alter the function of certain (perhaps private) stimuli. Other patterns may be encouraged that provide additional benefits (reinforcers).
3. The focus of **Topical Nonlinear Intervention** is on the matrix into which both the DB and the available alternative behaviors (AABs) enter. This includes substituting alternative behaviors; reducing costs for available alternative behaviors; or establishing new behaviors that provide increased benefits, reduced costs, or both as compared to AABs. The target behaviors (TB) are, therefore, patterns that resolve the matrix by providing the same or other benefits of the DB at lower cost in relation to specified AABs.

Figures 8.1, 8.2, 8.3, and 8.4 depicted a series of simplified intervention matrices that describe the three types of topical intervention.

Systemic Interventions

The focus of **Systemic Nonlinear Interventions** is on the interaction between matrices such that the existence of one (or more) potentiates another matrix of which the disturbing pattern is a member. The goal in systemic treatment is not to address directly either the DB or the matrix of which it is a part, but another matrix that makes the consequences of the DB important to the person.

Figures 8.5 and 8.6 depict simplified matrices that describe the systemic intervention discussed so far using the example of candy eating.[2]

Illustrative Case Examples of NCA

To better illustrate and distinguish between topical and systemic interventions, we will use a case example. The patient participated in an inpatient research treatment group where the first author was the group and programming supervisor, and occasional group co-leader.[3] This case illustrates a constructional approach to treating a woman who reported a history of frequent auditory and occasional visual hallucinations that resulted in repeated hospitalizations in psychiatric facilities. The analysis is nonlinear, and the interventions are both topical and systemic. The patient's identity has been disguised.

The case is that of a 36-year-old woman whose log entry was first introduced at the beginning of this book. She had been admitted to a locked psychiatric unit after making suicidal statements and complaining of hearing voices. She had been admitted to psychiatry from a medical floor of the same hospital. She had spent several years in and out of various psychiatric facilities. The most recent was a three-year stay in a state psychiatric hospital ending one year prior to her admission to a local halfway house. She spent the year between her previous and current admissions there. The patient reported a four-year history of auditory and some visual hallucinations, beginning with her admission to the state hospital. The reported hallucinations included hearing voices telling her to jump out of open windows, to throw herself off bridges, to run away, and to engage in sexual acts she stated she found morally reprehensible. She reported the most troublesome hallucinations centered on religious themes and are discussed in greater detail in the following paragraphs.

The patient was married, although separated from her husband for the last four-and-a-half years. She had two children, one of whom lived in a foster home and the other in an orphanage. A variety of treatment strategies, including pharmacological, had been tried with little success during the last four years before the program reported here was attempted. Further, her medical condition, which occasioned her admission to the medical unit, ultimately precluded the use of most psychotropic medication.

A Constructional vs. Pathological Approach

The reported hallucinations were the symptoms most responsible for her admission and subsequently required stay in a halfway house. One approach might be to implement procedures that might reduce the reported hallucinations. That is, the reduction of hallucinations could be made explicitly the main goal of therapy. Such approaches comprise what Goldiamond termed as "pathological" in orientation. That is, intervention focuses on the disturbing pattern, with attempts to reduce or eliminate it. Another approach might be to encourage the patient to accept the hallucinations as part of her life, and to try to get on with her life by establishing some meaningful goals that she might achieve in spite of the hallucinations. This approach has constructional elements since it does not focus on eliminating the pathology. It does, however, accept the reported hallucinations as maladaptive or pathological, and it strives to help the patient live with that pathology, making as best of it as she can. NCA goes further. It does not consider the pattern pathological; instead, it frames the pattern as a successful and sensible operant—that is, it is behavior maintained by its environmental consequences, even though it may have organic origins or components (as described earlier).[4] This raises the question as to how that can be, given the suffering that so often appears to accompany symptoms such as those demonstrated by the woman discussed here. The costs of the pattern seem obvious. In this patient's case, she is kept away from her children, must live in a halfway house, relations with those outside the psychiatric community are limited, and of course, she lives with the stated anguish in experiencing the hallucinations. What therapists (and our patients) may often overlook, however, are the benefits of such patterns. And further, therapists may often overlook the costs and benefits of the patient's available alternative patterns. We shall discuss that in more detail in the next section.

Constructional Diagnosis: The Benefits of the Disturbing Pattern

The analysis began with identifying those consequences that may have shaped and maintained the disturbing pattern, along with the events that occasioned the hallucinatory episodes. Data from the initial constructional interview, Daily Event Logs kept by the patient,[5],[6] and previous hospital records, along with information forwarded by social workers from the halfway house all contributed to the analysis.

The resulting history revealed that the patient's husband had left her for a male lover a few months prior to her three-year stay in the state hospital. He left the care of the household, the children, and the entire financial responsibility for maintaining the family with the patient. Her husband was the only man the patient had ever dated, and she had relied on him for everything since she was 20 years old. She reluctantly reported enjoying sexual relations and male companionship; however, since her religion did not sanction it, she had not filed for divorce. As a result, she had not dated or had any close relationships with men during the preceding four years. She reported missing her children deeply and that she wrote to them every week and telephoned occasionally.

The patient was considered (constructionally) to be functioning in a highly competent manner, using the only means she had at her disposal to deal with an intolerable situation. As a result of relying on her husband for 12 years and having no employment history or preparation of any kind, the response requirements of caring for two children, maintaining a household, and providing financially for the family were enormous. Escape from these requirements, eventual avoidance of them, and providing the best outcome she could for her children maintained the entire class of disturbing behavior. Being "sick" may also have provided a way for the removal of aversive consequences usually applied to those who cannot adequately support their families. In other words, being sick rationalized her not being able to take care of her family.[7] Individual disturbing patterns that made up the "sick" repertoire were viewed as necessary components of the larger pattern, maintained by their immediate effects in the institutions where she resided. That is, her symptoms allowed her to navigate the milieu of the halfway house.

She had managed to get herself discharged from a state hospital to a halfway house, which allowed for an expanded social life (a benefit) while still meeting the conditions necessary to maintain the benefits described earlier. Her brief stay on the psychiatric unit, where she first met one of the authors, seemed to demonstrate the effectiveness of her behavior in its particular ecology. The patient was admitted to a medical floor for tests and treatment. After a week, she began complaining of hallucinations, which resulted in her immediate transfer to the psychiatric unit. On the second day of her stay, she remarked, "I knew this unit would be more fun; it was so boring down there." After a stay of about three weeks, the patient was discharged from the hospital immediately after all the medical tests were completed, her hallucinatory behavior at an "acceptable level" for the halfway house. Because of her medical condition, psychotropic medication could not be prescribed.

The Costs of the Disturbing Pattern

Even though her symptoms were successful operants in her present ecology, they did not allow for a life outside the halfway house subculture, and they deprived her of the company of her children. The patient indicated she cared very much about her children and was afraid that as they grew older they would become embarrassed at having a mental patient for a mother. The result she feared would be a complete loss of contact with them.

General Constructional Outcomes

The analysis of the relevant contingency history, along with her current circumstances, indicated that new patterns would need to be established that would: 1) maintain the reduced response requirements described earlier, or provide the repertoires necessary to meet increased requirements, i.e., allow her to provide for her children; 2) allow for the development of meaningful relationships; and 3) expand her social life away from the halfway house subculture.

Terminal Repertoire

Following the constructional assessment, the patient negotiated an agreement following the guidelines specified by Goldiamond.[8] The negotiated terminal outcomes are listed here:

1. I will be enjoying a full social life: going out with friends attending entertainment events such as museums, movies, etc.; able to make new friends; develop ways of entertaining myself through crafts, sewing, and various projects.
2. I will be financially able to maintain myself, outside the halfway house, and be working, if possible.
3. I will be living in my own apartment or with friends out of the halfway house.
4. My children will be returned to me. If not possible, increased visiting will be established.

Final agreement on target outcomes was reached a week after discharge from the hospital. It is noteworthy that reports of her hallucinating would likely prevent Outcomes 1 through 4, but a reduction in such reports would not likely be enough to provide them. Accordingly, reducing or eliminating hallucinations or their reports was not stated among her goals.

Current Relevant Repertoire

Patient strengths relevant to the program were evaluated to determine the starting point. The patient had a high school education and had received good grades, suggesting that recording and analytical requirements could be introduced early in the program. In addition, she had kept a diary for a few years in the past, indicating a history of record keeping. The patient was already working with a social worker on her financial situation and still had a room in the halfway house to which she could return. The patient was well groomed, had a good sense of humor, and made many friends at the halfway house. She enjoyed short walks and window shopping. The patient also maintained consistent contact with her children.

Program Strategy

The terminal outcomes were to be achieved through the development of procedures jointly constructed by the patient and therapist. This would require her to keep Daily Event Logs that would serve as the basis of individual sessions between the patient and therapist, where continuous assessment of her growing current repertoire and analysis of controlling contingencies would be undertaken. From this analysis, subgoals relevant to the achievement of the terminal repertoire would be agreed upon and programed for each coming week, along with the specification of notes or guides to aid in achieving the subgoals. The patient agreed to become a member of the Personal Effectiveness Group while she was still an in-patient, with the option of continuing her participation as an out-patient. The Personal Effectiveness Group comprised an assembly of in-patients and out-patients working on their own individual constructional pro-grams.[9] The group format allowed for behavioral rehearsal and problem solving related to achieving each patient's particular terminal outcomes.

From observations made while the patient was on the psychiatric unit, it was noted that she could carry on normal conversations, was helpful to others, and had a good sense of humor, putting whomever she was talk-ing to at ease (as noted earlier). We would try to transfer these behaviors to situations outside of the psychiatric facilities.

Her window shopping would be the starting point to shape longer walks to specific destinations, such as zoos, stores, libraries, etc. Because she had done such things previously, this was looked at as a reinstatement of a past repertoire rather than shaping a new one.[10] With its high prob-ability of success, this would be one of the first repertoires worked on.

As noted previously, reducing hallucinations was not a goal. Instead, the program targeted achieving important outcomes that could succeed only if the hallucinatory behavior was addressed successfully. Hallucina-tions would be treated in two ways. Some would be considered as private events to which only the patient had access. The reports of these events in her logs would be used as indicators of consequential contingencies of which they were a part.[11] Engaging in hallucinatory behavior could be monitored,[12] and thus examined as to the function the hallucinations served in the patient's life. The focus would not be on the topography of the hallucinatory behavior, but what effect such behavior was having on the patient's social environment.

As the program progressed, the possibility of her substituting less costly behavioral patterns that could have the same effect (functionally defined) as the hallucinatory behavior would be a prime objective. As described in the following text, both topical and systemic interventions[13] would be employed. Also, as part of a constructional approach, the therapists wanted to emphasize success or movement toward terminal outcomes as represented in the program worksheets, not the reduction of pathology. Session discussions would thus center on times when the patient was successful in meeting subgoals leading to the terminal outcomes, rather than on the hallucinatory behavior. Where hallucinatory behavior was reported, discussions focused on establishing alternative patterns that would produce the same environmental effects, which in turn became subgoals for the upcoming week. That is, the patient and therapist would work jointly to discover the variables controlling her hallucinatory behavior, leading to procedures for establishing alternative behaviors, for altering the potency of certain consequences, or for establishing new sets of contingencies. Emotions were recorded in Daily Event Logs (see following text) and used by the patient, with assistance of the therapist, to discover the consequential contingencies of which the emotions were a function.

Maintaining Consequences

We assumed that no extraneous consequences would be necessary. Establishing a closer relationship with the children seemed to be a potent enough consequence around which the program could be centered. In general, we assumed that progress toward the terminal goals would maintain working through the program. Also, the Personal Effectiveness Group might offer immediate social reinforcement for such progress. Where alternatives to the hallucinatory patterns needed to be established, the same beneficial consequences maintaining those patterns would be used as guides. We predicted that as the patient's ability to travel to new places and establish new relationships improved, new sources of reinforcement would develop. Log keeping would be maintained by therapist interest as well as by her subgoals being based on material in the logs, making log keeping a reinforcer necessary for program success. Program steps were kept small enough to ensure success.[14]

Performance Data

Evaluation of the patient's performance was carried out jointly by the patient and therapist. The current repertoire, as ascertained through the patient's logs and clinical discussion, provided the basis for the following week's subgoals. Validity of the patient's logs was established, when possible, by discussions during the Personal Effectiveness Group meetings and with other patients and staff from the same halfway house. Other means of establishing that subgoals were completed included bringing certain items to the sessions such as magazines or newspapers that could only be obtained by leaving the halfway house.

The Program

The approach was exclusively constructional, the analysis was nonlinear, and all three types of topical as well as systemic interventions were involved. Following the initial constructional interview and setting of treatment goals,[15] the program began by introducing the patient to the Personal Effectiveness Group.[16] The "hospital" part of the program consisted of regaining her room in the halfway house and beginning to establish social and self-entertainment skills. Also, an attempt began to improve her financial situation. The patient's first in-patient program worksheet is shown in Figure 10.1. The first program worksheet after her discharge from the hospital is shown in Figure 10.2. It was at this time that the patient started logging her behavior. She made entries an average of once every two hours as shown in Figure 10.3, which is a half day's log. The patient saw the therapist twice a week at the start of the program and later once a week. Cumulative hours of reported hallucinations during the baseline period are depicted in Figure 10.4.

From the first two weeks of Daily Events Logs, it was evident to the therapist and patient that when the patient was painting pictures or working on other projects, she did not report any hallucinations. Conversely, sitting idly around the halfway house appeared to occasion reports of hallucinations. Since reporting hallucinations was a symptom that required that she remain in the halfway house, situations that occasioned such reports needed attention. The logs seemed to indicate that the behavior was under discriminative control of the environment and not haphazard. Accordingly, subgoals were programed immediately to increase those activities that did not occasion reports of hallucinatory behavior. Subgoals targeting

Current Relevant Repertoire	Subgoals for Week
1. Has room at halfway house.	1. Keep room at halfway house!
2. Talked to lawyer with social worker about finances.	2. Lawyer will call social worker or you (Find out what is going on, keep on top of it!)
3. Likes to walk and window shop.	3. Talk to (psychiatry) resident about getting campus with staff privileges.
4. Friends (from halfway house) have been visiting.	4. Following from 3, try and go out on walks with friends.
Program Notes:	
1. Talk with social worker again.	
2. Resident is here (on unit) every day.	

Figure 10.1 Early program worksheet while an in-patient

Current Relevant Repertoire	Subgoals for Week
1. At halfway house concerned about diet and related problems (medical)	1. Talk to social worker and dietician!
2. Interested in volunteer work at nearby hospital!	2. Go with friends to find out about volunteer work!
3. Back with friends at halfway house, expressed feeling that they were always around; no time alone!	3. At least one afternoon before Thursday ask friends to give you some time to yourself in the afternoon. Also keep helping friends and keep up interactions with them that help through rough spots.
4. Kept diary in past.	4. Begin logging behavior on forms supplied.

Program Notes:

1. Find out if dietician is coming. If not, and they cannot provide needed diet, examine alternative living situations.
2. Tell friends you are tired and need some rest, and they should come back and wake you in a couple of hours!
3. Follow directions supplied by consultant.

Figure 10.2 First program worksheet upon return to the halfway house

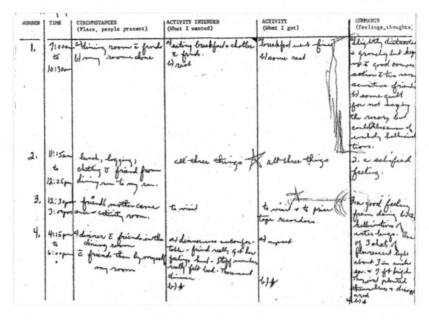

Figure 10.3 Example of patient log with hourly entries

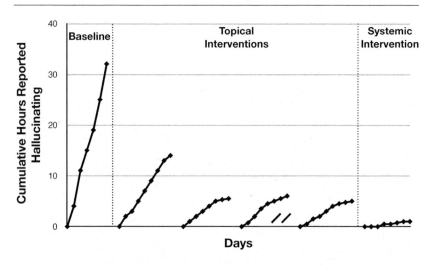

Figure 10.4 Cumulative hours of reported hallucinations for the period employing Topical and Systemic Interventions. Reset lines indicate one week of data. The break lines indicate six weeks removed for presentation purposes where no change was recorded week to week.

Current Relevant Repertoire	Subgoals for Week
1. Felt good after walking and during meditation.	1. Try and go for longer walks, then spend time by yourself meditating
2. Told yes after asked if more painting was possible.	2. Try and do some painting this week!
3. Noticed things seem to cram together!	3. Try and have one hour for yourself each day, and watch logs for increased activity!
4. Noticed hallucinations come and go.	4. Log all hallucinations.
5. Feeling relaxed after tapes.	5. Continue with listening to tapes!

Program Notes:

1. Try 1-to-2 mile walk; watch what people are doing. How are they enjoying themselves? Savor walk when alone!
2. Need to recognize when crammed feeling begins. Try and log what you feel the requirements of the situation are.

Figure 10.5 First program worksheet depicting topical interventions

increasing project engagement, thereby reducing periods of prolonged inactivity, were agreed upon by the patient and therapist. Figure 10.5 depicts subgoals that may be considered a Topical Direct Intervention.

The patient also reported difficulty sleeping. She stated that she would lie in bed worrying and at times hallucinating. Procedures were implemented to bring sleeping under stimulus control of the bed. She was instructed that, if possible, she was not to try to stop worrying but, instead, to get out of bed when she was doing anything other than sleeping. She was told she could worry as much as she liked, but not in bed. She was to do any worrying, hallucinating, or other discomforting activities elsewhere. This pattern was postulated as an example of adjunctive behavior, often observed in the laboratory during periods of infrequently reinforced responding.[17] The goal was to provide a low-cost alternative that could also occur adjunctively. A relaxation tape was given to the patient, and she practiced relaxing, concentrating on her breathing, and so on, while lying in bed, a reasonable approximation to, and possible prerequisite for, sleeping. If she began hearing voices, fine; simply get out of bed and hear them elsewhere. These subgoals may be considered to be a Topical Functional Intervention since they attempted to change the function of certain stimuli, namely the bed, and to provide patterns that could substitute for the worrying. Often when someone is instructed to "not think of pink elephants" it becomes difficult not to think of them, but if the instruction is "now think of blue elephants" the shift from thinking of pink elephants is relatively effortless. Hearing and thinking about the relaxation tapes was a low-effort response alternative to hearing voices.

At times, the patient reported that she would have "highs" and then seem to end up in "lows." These episodes were represented in her logs as periods of high activity followed by periods of low activity. She reported that things just seemed to "cram" together. This cyclic pattern resembled what in the laboratory might be termed *ratio strain*.[18] Following from this, periods of meditation and relaxation were programed into the day to occur after completing an enjoyable, higher frequency activity. Care had to be taken to assure that the relaxation period was a specific activity that avoided occasioning hallucinations, but one that required low rates of behaving.

It should be noted that procedures were arrived at jointly by the patient and the therapist. The patient was encouraged to examine her daily logs on her own so she could discover the functional relations between her behavior and her environment (a prerequisite for self-control). For example, she discovered that she often reported hallucinations occurring after prolonged periods of interaction with her friends at the halfway house. The crammed feeling, similar to what was discussed earlier, would occur, followed by some form of hallucinatory behavior (such as telling her friends what she is hearing or seeing, or holding her head). Seeing the patient in distress, her friends would immediately leave the room. It appeared that her friends' leaving the room maintained this pattern. But why was this necessary? In the past she had abruptly asked fellow residents to leave and was treated rather harshly. In other words, the available alternatives to hallucinatory behavior produced much more cost for the same benefit than did hallucinating. Stated otherwise, given the current behavioral matrix, the behavior made consequential sense and was considered quite adaptive. The patient discovered that the crammed feeling indicated she was facing increasing response requirements. She began using the crammed feeling as an indicator to change the situation before hallucinatory behavior occurred, in this case, by acting very tired and asking her friends if they could leave so she could rest for a while, enabling her to spend more time with them later—she devised other variations on this theme. The patient rehearsed these variations in the Personal Effectiveness Group before implementing this procedure. By doing so, she was careful not to occasion a harsh response from fellow residents. These subgoals may be considered as a Topical Nonlinear Intervention as they were derived from her available alternatives.

Figure 10.4 shows the change in reported hallucinations as a result of the Topical procedures. Though there was a noticeable reduction in durations of reported hallucination as the various subgoals were achieved, her reports of hallucinating remained at fairly constant frequencies. The patient acknowledged that her ability to sleep had improved and that her reports of the frequency and duration of hallucinations decreased substantially from baseline. It was apparent, however, that other, systemic, interventions might be required.

Systemic Intervention

It will be recalled that the goal in systemic treatment is not to address directly either the DB or the matrix of which it is a part, but another matrix that makes the consequences of the DB important to the person. Such an intervention was required for the remaining reported hallucinations and disturbing behaviors. Though there was a substantial reduction in total duration, some episodes of hallucinatory behavior persisted even though the patient was making good progress in her program. She reported that her remaining hallucinations, both visual and auditory, were the most personally disturbing. The entry in the patient's log that introduced Chapter 1 is a good example:

> I am hearing our Lord and demons. On the bus, a man took out his wallet and began flashing his money. I started to nudge my girlfriend to say, "It sure would be nice to have all that money!" Before I could nudge her or say it, I heard a voice in my heart say, "Meet me when we get off the bus and you can have it." My voice in my mind was saying, "This is crazy, Lord, please stop this from happening." But again the voice in my heart took my voice and said, "OK," while I almost yelled out, "Lord, OK nothing! It's not OK!" Then the man put the money back in his wallet.

The content of this and similar episodes always involved men and were often sexual in nature. An examination of the logs revealed that sexual referents, as well as references to God and the devil, were common to all these hallucinations. A contingency analysis of several of these episodes, including the patient's history and available alternatives, made sense of this behavior.

As previously mentioned, the patient was brought up deeply religious and had sexual relations with only one man, her husband. She said she enjoyed these relations very much and missed them. In fact, her husband had been the only man she had ever even dated. Her upbringing and religious training forbade relationships with men outside of marriage. Even if she were interested in a man, her repertoire in dealing with men in social situations was lacking. The logs indicated that when she happened upon a man she found attractive, or a situation that could lead to anything but the most superficial interactions with men, the patient would begin to hallucinate. The content was described usually as sexual, with the "devil" urging her on, and "God" or "Mary" telling her these sexual urges were bad. At other times, conversations with friends about their relationships would occasion reports of hallucinating. At yet other times, she reported seeing men gesturing toward her and engaging in other suggestive behaviors that, upon further consideration, had not actually occurred.

The hallucinations as described by the patient were regarded as impure and distorted tacts,[19] that is, descriptions of the environment influenced by deprivation, punishment, or other variables. The descriptions did not appear to be simply intraverbal operants,[20] since the reported hallucinations did not change thematically, but did change topographically.[21] Because the patient was deprived of the kind of relationship that had been reinforcing in the past, the likelihood of a response containing elements of a mand (verbal behavior which specifies a characteristic reinforcer) was greatly increased. The descriptions (e.g., of a man taking out his wallet) were treated as tacts, greatly influenced by deprivation of certain types of relationships and further distorted by historic punishment contingencies.

What these episodes suggested were conflicting contingencies. On the one hand, the patient could try to develop a relationship with a man, but at the cost of losing the support of her church. She could refuse relationships, maintaining her church support, but she perhaps would lose any chance of developing relationships with men. When her lack of social repertoires was added to the picture, such situations became even more difficult and aversive. The patient was accurately describing her situation in the best way she knew. We thought these hallucinations might also have functioned as a self-control procedure that could be used to avoid those situations and gain support and comfort from her friends. A program that removed the punishment contingency and attempted to provide repertoires that would lead to good relationships with men (as specified by the mands implied in the hallucination reports) might be successful in replacing the remaining hallucinations with a more direct way of talking about her needs and possibly provide a way to fulfill them. The function of the hallucinations in escaping these situations and recruiting the comfort of friends would not be addressed directly. Instead, other contingencies related to her relationship with the Church would be the target so as to change the potency of the consequences maintaining the disturbing pattern.

It turned out the program used to help the patient gain control of these situations was independently arrived at by the patient a year before we had any contact with her. She had gone to see a priest and asked whether there was any way she could begin to have new relationships with men since her husband had left her. The priest, being rather traditional, said no. The Church could not condone anything but "friendships," and she should consider herself still married. We concluded she had the right program but the wrong priest. By first removing the aversive consequences for socializing with men, a social-skills program could be designed to help establish those relationships.

Accordingly, a liberal priest was located, and the patient's situation (within the limits of patient-therapist confidentiality) explained. He agreed to a meeting with her. One of the therapists arranged for the priest to attend the next session. The priest assured the patient that the Church did not want her to cut off relationships with men, that he would help her get her marriage annulled, and that he would continue to serve as her moral advisor. He said that she should begin to see men, if that was what she wanted to do. After these assurances, the entire class of hallucinatory behavior related to sexual themes dropped out, leaving only incidental reports of hallucinatory behavior of any sort. The results are depicted in Figure 10.4.

A program worksheet that illustrates a social skills program, which was implemented immediately thereafter, is depicted in Figure 10.6. The patient was instructed not to avoid a man she found attractive, but to continue whatever she was doing when she encountered him. She said she thought that men she was attracted to could tell she was attracted to them and might take advantage of her. She was instructed then to record the responses of men she was attracted to and of those she was not. As expected, given her reserved manner, we saw no difference in their reactions to her. The Personal Effectiveness Group was used at this time to work on social skills. Increased interaction with her children was also encouraged at this time. Low-cost outings such as visits to pet stores and the park were programed as part of this effort. This intervention was entirely Systemic Nonlinear. It targeted her relationship with the church. By changing that relationship, there was no reason any longer to avoid men. In essence, the "subconscious motivation" for the hallucinatory pattern was removed. One might say the escape provided a "secondary gain" potentiated by the "primary process" involving her relationship to the church and her history of interacting with men.

Current Relevant Repertoire	Subgoals for Week
1. Attracted to new man at the half-way house	1. If you run into him at the halfway house, just act as you would toward anyone else. Say hello if he says hello to you!
2. Feels good when walking	2. Try to take another walk before the next meeting
3. Spanish lesson Sat.	3. Go if you can make it
4. Felt proud when making ornaments!	4. Try to make at least one more each Day
5. Talking to friends about positive things	5. Continue

Program Notes:
1. Just go your own way, don't avoid him
3. Tell friend you want to talk about what's going good and that you'd rather not talk about depression, etc. Try to set it up so that to talk to you, she has to talk constructionally.

Figure 10.6 Program worksheet immediately following visit with the priest

Summary

Figure 10.4 presents a cumulative record of hours spent hallucinating as reported in the logs. The condition designated as baseline comprises the last six days of log analysis and rehearsals in the Personal Effectiveness Group of asking friends to leave. The relaxation tapes and sleeping procedures were also introduced during this period. The second condition demonstrated the effects of using the crammed feeling as an indicator for slowing her rates of activity and asking friends to leave temporarily. The instructions to work on concrete, accomplishable projects were also introduced during this period. The final phase reveals the effects of meeting with the priest and the social skills program. The drop in reported hallucinations was so immediate that the meeting with the priest must be given credit for at least the initial change in rate. More important, observable activities that the hallucinatory behavior had prevented were now beginning to occur.

Figure 10.7 shows the percent of subgoals completed as specified in the program worksheet. The figure reveals a high degree of engagement was maintained throughout the program. Within the program, each step increased the behavioral requirement while remaining small enough as to ensure success and prevent "ratio strain."

Figure 10.8 shows a program worksheet near the end of formal sessions. The sessions had been interrupted by medical problems (discussed later in more detail) and a short stay in the hospital. This worksheet was

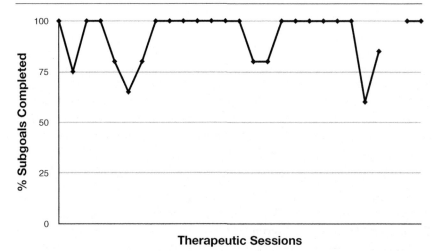

Figure 10.7 Percentage of subgoals completed each week; break indicates no sessions for 1.5 months

Current Relevant Repertoire	Subgoals for Week
1. Has opportunity to move in with sister	1. Consider ways of living with sister and her boyfriend without getting entangled in moral issues!
2. Concerned about possibility of son living with his father	2. Call social worker, or priest at orphanage!
3. Working 1/2 day per month	3. Continue, increase time as physical condition allows!
4. Wants to continue flute lessons and meeting people!	4. Call the learning exchange for a list of community classes!
5. Walking when feeling jittery; asking people to leave, and leaving when you have to; plays music and tapes at night!	5. Continue using your procedures.
6. Finances need settling, and has straightened them out in past.	6. Call M.D., have him fill out forms.

Program Notes:

1. Idea of going a week before Christmas for a trial stay is a good one.
2. Taking more responsibility for children, relates to terminal outcome #4.
3. Relates to terminal outcome #2!
4. Terminal outcome #3!
5. Terminal outcome #1!

Figure 10.8 Program worksheet near completion of formal program

the first after the illness and shows considerable progress relative to the earliest worksheets.

The patient achieved her goal of increased interactions with the children, as well as arrangements to move into her sister's apartment. She terminated formal sessions but continued contact with the therapist by telephone and informal meetings. Unfortunately, a series of medical problems resulting from side effects of the various medications given to the patient over the years prevented the full accomplishment of the precise terminal outcomes specified in the program. She suffered kidney, liver, and intestinal problems that required surgery several times over a period of a year and a half. However, when the patient was not in the hospital, she spent time with her children and relatives. She managed to do volunteer work and established a romantic relationship. After ten years, following the termination of formal sessions, the patient, who was in constant contact with a social worker who assisted with the case, reported none of the hallucinations that had plagued her during the four years prior to treatment. Though there were frequent medical hospitalizations for kidney problems, the following outcomes were achieved:

1.   out of halfway house living with sister and brother-in-law off and on;
2.   kids never lived with her, but maintained close relationship, frequent visits;
3.   part-time work;
4.   GED;
5.   new friends; and
6.   relationships, but not married.

One of the more interesting results was the consistent log-keeping by the patient over a period of several months. The logs had been an essential part of the program, used to formulate subgoals for the following week's session. Since program progress was explicitly contingent upon conscientious log-keeping, it appears that it was an effective reinforcer. Supporting evidence comes from the fact that when the program was interrupted, the patient asked whether she could reinstate log-keeping so she could monitor her own progress. She reported in follow-up telephone conversations that she had initiated log-keeping on her own when she ran into troublesome situations to help her figure out what was going on. It appears that a self-control repertoire based on a contingency analysis transferred to the patient's current repertoire.

Layng and Andronis[22] have provided an analysis and a guide for treating similar systems of delusional speech and hallucinatory behavior in both in-patient and out-patient settings. It has also not escaped our notice that the procedures described here overlap with those comprising what is called Recovery-Oriented Cognitive Therapy. In this approach, establishing and working toward patient-stated goals has shown promising effects in the treatment of those diagnosed with schizophrenia.[23] Differentiating the approaches is that in NCA, goals and the procedures for their attainment are derived from a thoroughgoing contingency analysis.

No constructional intervention is precluded. NCA procedures often arise from the examination of patient records and logs as well as from the basic and applied literature. Evidence of ongoing behavior change is used to continually ascertain the effectiveness of NCA procedures. Setbacks are treated as occasions for investigation, and new procedures are often introduced. There is no cookbook or therapeutic recipe other than a commitment to understanding behavior as a sensible outcome of the prevailing nonlinear consequential contingencies and intervening accordingly.

It is our hope this (re)introduction will occasion renewed interest and research in the constructional approach, Nonlinear Analysis, and Topical and Systemic Intervention, pioneered by Israel Goldiamond.

Notes

1 Goldiamond, 1984; Layng & Andronis, 1984
2 Further accounts, examples, and important aspects of the approach can be found in Drossel and Trahan (2015), Gambrill (2015), Goldiamond (1970, 1974, 1975a, 1975b, 1976, 1979, 1984), Layng (2006, 2009, 2017), Layng and Andronis (1984), and Merely and Layng (1976).
3 Merley & Layng, 1976
4 Also see Drossel & Trahan, 2015; Goldiamond, 1979b
5 see Goldiamond, 1974
6 Daily logs were not initiated until the patient was discharged from the hospital and returned as an out-patient.
7 see Goldiamond, 1964
8 1974
9 see Merley & Layng, 1976
10 after Isaacs, Thomas, & Goldiamond, 1960
11 after Layng, 2017
12 cf. Layng, 2006
13 Goldiamond, 1979b, 1984; Layng, 2009
14 see Goldiamond, 1974, 1975b; Goldiamond & Schwartz, 1975; Layng, 2006
15 after Goldiamond, 1974
16 see Merley & Layng, 1976
17 Falk, 1977; Wetherington, 1982
18 see Ferster & Skinner, 1957
19 after Skinner, 1957
20 Skinner, 1957
21 see Layng & Andronis, 1984
22 1984
23 Grant, Bredemeier, & Beck, 2017

A User's Guide to Goldiamond's Constructional Questionnaire

The Constructional Questionnaire (Goldiamond, 1974) is used to obtain information specifically for behavioral programs in clinical, educational, industrial/organizational, as well as other applied settings. This instrument helps assess: 1) clients' current behavior and personal attributes that contribute in significant ways to their behavior problems; 2) historical and current ecological variables that actually support or maintain their problematic patterns of behavior; 3) any personal, behavioral, material, social, or environmental resources the clients have that could help them complete the program successfully; and 4) explicit behavioral objectives that they could reasonably attain by participating in the program.

This document is meant as a guide for programmers, to help them use the questionnaire effectively. Interview questions themselves are given here in **bold-face type**—the interviewer may simply say aloud those parts written in plain text. The interviewer may change the specific wording of questions (when respondents do not quite understand the given form of a question, or need further prompting), but both the explicit and implicit intent of the questions should be preserved. Accordingly, in this guide, many questions are followed by brief notes commenting on any implicit objectives behind questions, suggesting follow-up or alternative questions, and various common examples that may serve as useful prompts. These notes and commentaries are indented and shown in a compressed typeface.

Introduction

I am going to ask you some questions to help us both understand exactly what we should work toward in this program. The questions have three purposes:

- First, we'll need some information to help us get to know you—about the way you live, what things you enjoy and those you dislike, what have you done in the past, and what do you want in the future.

DOI: 10.4324/9781003141365-11

- Second, from the questions people ask, you can learn things about them, so this should help you learn about our approach in this program.
- Third, to see what kind of progress we are making, we need records, and "befores" and "afters." The information we get from you during this interview will be a kind of "before" on how you see things now, and what your goals are now when you are just beginning our program. So please relax and speak up. You are the important person here—so tell us about yourself.

Question 1: Outcomes

I am first going to ask you a group of questions to help us decide exactly what our goals should be. You are here because you want certain changes to occur—you want to be healthier, to feel better, to live longer, to look better, or something else.

Question 1a. (Presented outcomes) Assuming we were successful, and you got everything out of this program that you came for, what would the outcome be for you? In other words, what exactly do you want from this program?

This question gives clients a chance to tell in their own words exactly why they have sought help. Common responses here will include: "I have to lose weight;" "I want to lose X pounds;" "My doctor says I have to stop worrying so much because of my _____;" "I want to stop yelling so much at my kids;" "I can't afford to quit working, but I also can't keep doing the same job I've had in the past;" "I am filled with anxiety, and I want it to stop," or "I just want not to feel so depressed all the time." Because answers to this question are typically given in negative terms (losing, getting rid of, not hurting, not being so tired, avoiding, feeling less of, etc.), they are often inadequate for defining constructional program directions. Nevertheless, these kinds of answers can provide clues about how invested respondents are likely to be in the program. Also, this is a good question for collecting important medical information, like past diagnoses of diabetes, hypertension, or atherosclerosis; family patterns of cardiac or vascular disease; and so on. In this respect, answers to this question can help identify whether there are any immediate and distinct physical benefits the respondents expect to gain from the program (like relief from arthritic pain in the knees, being able to breathe more easily, etc.) or whether they have been referred to the program simply because of future risks to their health. Unfortunately, fear of impending death is a (surprisingly) weak and (only) temporary motivator for changing behavior, and the longer people live after hearing about personal health risks, the less they are motivated by fear. Finally, this question gives respondents the opportunity to immediately state their own agendas, to express their own concerns, and simply to begin talking to the interviewer on their own terms. There should be no effort to rephrase or redirect any answers given to this question, except where the interviewer requires some clarification or wants additional factual information.

Question 1b. (Observable outcomes) Now, this may sound silly, but suppose one of these flying saucers we keep hearing about is real. It lands and 2,000 little Martians pour out. One of them is assigned to watch you (they got your name from a computerized junk mail list). It is now some time after L-Day—Liberation Day from your problems—and your little Martian follows you around invisibly. He records his observations of you and enters them on his computer when he gets home each night. Based on his observations, his bosses are either going to blow up the earth or give us a chance to try their great new interplanetary fast-food chain. What does your Martian see you doing? Remember: you have already finished this program successfully, and you look and feel the way you want to. What does the Martian see?

This question may indeed sound crazy, but it is very effective in getting respondents to think (often for the first time) about some truly positive outcomes they can expect if they participate successfully in the program. It is just "goofy" enough to make respondents feel comfortable—it allows them to give offhanded answers, without feeling pressured to come up with the kinds of completely rational and intellectual goals they think the interviewer wants from them. Saying a Martian is the observer of the program's outcomes allows the interviewer to focus respondents' efforts on describing: concrete, observable aspects of their future lives; explicit and objective lists of recreational, occupational, and routine daily activities they would engage in if not for their health problems; any existing interpersonal relationships that are important to the respondents, or a lack thereof; available social networks that might support behavior change; and so on. The form of this question also helps clarify (without making the interviewer seem out-of-touch or judgmental) any apparently idiosyncratic habits or practices that might simply be obscure to people unfamiliar with the respondent's native culture or a particular subculture. By being required to talk in concrete terms and in the "here-and-now," rather than talking in subjective terms or "befores-and-afters" (like, "I want to be happier," "to look better," "to go out more," "to have more friends," "to be able to wear nicer clothes," etc.), respondents will provide answers that can be used immediately to formulate useful treatment goals and objective measures of their progress through the program. The interviewer can use such prompts as: "How often does the Martian see you go bowling once you don't tire so easily?;" "Exactly what style of clothing will you be wearing?;" "Are you working at the same job (or do have your present friends, husband, wife, etc.) when the Martian sees you?;" or "What would the Martian see you do that would tell him you are happy (energetic, healthy, better able to handle stress, in a good mood, popular, etc.)?" This question can also help pinpoint hidden personal problems that, even though unrelated to program goals, might nevertheless interfere with a respondent's adequate commitment to and participation in program activities. A final note: This question has been used effectively with a wide range of psychiatric clients, including some who were extremely paranoid at the time of their interviews; others who complained of chronic or acute anxiety, phobias, obsessions, compulsions, or pain (with no apparent physical causes); and many who simply sought relief from troublesome habits or more seriously disturbing patterns of behavior. Psychiatric clients do not generally expect a therapist to begin talking about Martians, so the effect of this question is usually quite disarming, especially with people who otherwise might be extremely guarded or uneasy in a clinical setting. If you have any serious reservations about using this question with a particular client, skip the Martians and ask an alternative form, like: "Pretend you can see yourself after you have successfully completed this program. What do you see?" While this form of the question may seem less bizarre or provocative to you than the original version, it also will almost certainly be less effective in getting the client to talk freely or in the concrete terms of the Martian observer.

Question 1c. (Present state) How is this different from the way things are now?

This gives clients a chance to tell you what is currently wrong in their lives, but it forces them to tell you what is wrong by comparison to the way they would like things to be. The answers they give you here will usually tell you what you probably already knew quite well: about some of the ways in which their medical/behavior problems are costly or disturbing to them. This information is usually suggested, if not spelled out quite clearly, by the clients' presenting complaints. If clients give you vague or (too) general answers, like, "Oh, just about everything in my life now is different from what the Martian would see," ask them to give you some concrete examples of those differences, and prompt them if you must by recalling some of the things they said the Martian could see.

Question 1d. (Example) Can you give me an example?

Question 2: Areas to be changed and unchanged by the program

The next group of questions concerns things in your life that are going well, and other things that are not.

Question 2a. (Areas unchanged, things going well) There are probably things about your life right now that are going well for you—things you don't want changed by our program (including some favorite foods you absolutely refuse to stop eating, or distinctive habits that have made you "famous" with your family and friends, which you don't want to give up). Can you describe some of these things that are going well for you, or that you like too much to change?

Answers to this question can provide you with two helpful kinds of information: 1) details about certain aspects of clients' lifestyles that are likely to compete with their reaching their targeted program outcomes (and hence may present potential problems with their adherence to intervention protocols); and 2) examples of some things or activities that you might be able to use within the program to help motivate the clients to continue with or adhere to the requirements of intervention. Nevertheless, clients often will answer this question with short, uninspired, and somewhat superficial statements, like, "Nothing in my life is going very well, so I wouldn't mind changing everything!" You can prompt them to say whether they would in fact change their spouses, their jobs, their homes, and so on, if they had the chance to do so; this usually gets them to be considerably more specific, but also, for many of these clients, this may be the first reminder in a long time for them to "count their blessings," so to speak.

Question 2b. (Things not going well that will not be improved by program) Are there things going on in your life right now that you don't like, but that are not going to be affected by our program?

This is a deceivingly simple and harmless question, but don't you be fooled by it. What you get here will often be the most important bits of information in your entire interview. This is sometimes called the "hidden agenda" question, because it usually gets clients talking freely about the problems that are most important to them in highly personal ways, and that they might not otherwise admit having. The form of the question implies to clients that you really do not want to pry too much into those few special, private problems that are bothering them, but that they may, if they want to, tell you about them anyway so that you both know what problems lurk in the background; it gives clients a chance to talk about these problems in their own terms, at their own rates of confiding in you, and to whatever extent they feel is comfortable and "safe." You will often get surprisingly graphic accounts of certain kinds of problems (e.g., highly personal problems in marital, sexual, parental, or other social relations; secret admissions of low self-esteem or low self-confidence; secret fears and so on) that the clients are either too embarrassed to bring up themselves, or that they feel are too painful to discuss with mere acquaintances, yet which often will constitute the most important areas of their lives needing programmatic intervention.

Question 2c. (Byproducts of the program) What other things in your life might change, besides those we'd work on directly in this program?

This question often obtains answers similar to those given to the previous "hidden agenda" question, but it takes a more positive tack. It also begins shaping the clients' thinking about some of the real-life benefits they are likely to experience from successful intervention, and it often represents some of their first opportunities to "think through" the desirable outcomes of adherence to their intervention programs, rather than focusing exclusively on all the hard work and difficult changes in lifestyles required to reach their goals.

Question 3: History of changes
Question 3a. (Present attempt) What made you want to start a program like this now? How come?

This question prompts the clients to disclose whether they are currently seeking help because of recent worsening of their problems, important changes in their private lives (e.g., loss of home or job, spouse running off with secret lover, etc.), windows of opportunity (e.g., newly instated insurance coverage by policy provided on recently acquired job, slack time in professional or occupational activities, etc.), coercion by other people who are important to them, and so on. Some of this information can be helpful in defining Axis IV of their DSM-IV diagnoses, namely, severity of psychosocial stressors. It also helps you to find out whether the clients are seeking help for reasons that will actually help support their recovery or simply meet somebody else's requirements, wholly unrelated to the clients' own needs.

Question 3b. (First attempt) When did it first occur to you to try to change? What was going on in your life at that time? What did you do about it? How did it come out?

Answers to this (and the following) question can help provide you with complete histories, whether medical, behavioral/psychiatric, or occupational. You can prompt clients to give very specific information about their past medical treatment and attempts to change aspects of their lifestyles, their reasons for doing so at those times, what professionals they consulted or resources they used, how hard they tried, what other people were helpful, how successful they were, and so on. In trying to give you chronologies of their health status and past attempts at treatment, clients also often recall biographical details about concurrent events and circumstances to help jog their own memories; you can surely record these additional bits of data for later reference—sometimes, you can bring up these ancillary facts at later times, either with the clients themselves or with their families, to help verify the quality of information you obtained during this initial assessment interview. Besides, every little bit of historical information helps give you more complete pictures of the clients as people, whether that information is accurate or not! Even the lies people tell, their distortions of the past, the facts they avoid telling you, or their merely faulty recollections, all say something about the people you are interviewing.

Question 3c. (Intervening attempts) What did you do then? What was going on? How did it come out? (Series continues until present.)

Question 4: Assets

The next series of questions is about areas where you are strong, and certain skills or resources you have that we can build on in our program. Everybody has some things at which they are pretty good, so nobody has to start out completely from scratch.

Question 4a. (Skills related to program goals) What skills or strengths do you have that are related to what you'd like to achieve in this program?

You can prompt clients about some specific skills they are likely to need in their own programs and assess to what extent they may already have these skills. For example, basic knowledge about good nutritional habits, and an interest in and aptitude for certain sports, are useful repertoires for people who must change their dietary and activity habits; record-keeping experience on the job, or histories of keeping personal diaries or journals, are extremely useful for clients whom you want to keep logs detailing their daily activities or specific habits; college students may (or may not) already know how to draw and read graphs; diabetics may already know how to give themselves insulin injections; and so on. Given the goals that the clients state in response to the first questions in this interview, along with your general understanding of what the intervention in their particular problems is likely to entail, you can guide and prompt the clients through the assessment of their current relevant repertoires—"current" in the sense that they can already do these things, "relevant" meaning directly related to their most likely prospective treatment program, and "repertoires" meaning sometimes complex and large-scale "cognitive" as well as physical abilities and skills.

Question 4b. (Other skills unrelated to program goals) What others do you have? Any special resources (like special equipment at home, membership in organizations that might be helpful, new financial resources for which you now qualify, etc.)?

Here you can get information about clients' general competencies and their social and financial resources. You can assess: 1) whether the clients can in fact read, or how well they do so (reading is a pretty basic, but also often inconspicuously missing, skill that is crucial to almost any program of behavior change for adults); 2) whether they have any hobbies, favorite crafts, or special interests (e.g., building model airplanes, sewing ragdolls, making scented candles, cooking traditional Russian peasant dishes, or reading mystery novels, all of which might be useful, for example, in "stress-reduction" and relaxation programs); 3) whether they already belong to any organizations that are likely to support changes the clients attempt to make in their own lifestyles (e.g., community, religious, or professional organizations; Alcoholics Anonymous; birdwatching clubs and the like; marital or various other therapeutic groups; and so on); and 4) what financial resources are available to the clients and their families (e.g., special insurance coverage for outpatient treatment, extended workers' disability benefits and compensation, independent family fortunes, rich uncles who would offer the clients free use of their villas on the French Riviera, and so on). You can use this question to assess what in general the clients have going for them, both inside and outside their own skins.

Question 4c. (Stimulus control) Are there any times or places when the present problem is not a problem, or when it is at least a little less troublesome?

Stimulus control refers to the observation that a given pattern of behavior is most likely to occur under certain specific conditions (often because it is most likely to "pay off" or because its alternatives do not pay off under those very conditions). Rather than focusing on worst cases, bad times, and accomplished failures, give clients a chance to tell you about those times and circumstances when things are not so bad, or about times when they are actually able to deal a little more effectively with their problems. Try to draw attention here to any effective coping and adaptive skills the clients might already have but might not be aware of having. Because you are asking, "Are there any times when. . .," you are actually conceding to clients that you know their problems are there most of the time, but with some effort, they might be able to think of a few very extraordinary circumstances when they get some small measure of relief (as a general rule, clients can readily think of numerous occasions when their problems are not so severe, but they are afraid to admit it because they think this might call the legitimacy of their symptoms into question).

As a general rule, avoid asking clients directly about when their problem behaviors themselves occur, or when their problems are particularly bad—you might have to wait a long time for any satisfactory answers to such questions, especially in cases where the problems allow clients to avoid or escape from certain unpleasant tasks or duties they might otherwise be stuck doing. It is like saying to the client, "I think you're probably just faking your symptoms to get sympathy, or to get out of having to fulfill your household or family responsibilities. Can you tell me exactly when you have these particular problems, so I can prove that you're only faking?" What clients in their right minds would admit to such things by answering your questions put this way? Moreover, clients usually have automatic litanies they recite whenever asked to describe their symptoms (even "just one more time, for our special records"), and so the information clients provide often gets less accurate and less helpful each time they are required to repeat it. They also do not generally need any more practice at complaining; most are pretty good at this by the time you see them. They usually could, however, use all the practice they can get at thinking and talking constructively about their problems, about how to solve them, and so on.

Do something that is probably completely different from what the clients (and often other staff as well) expect: ask the clients about times and circumstances when things are not so bad, or when they do a little bit better or maybe even particularly well. In response, clients often give fresh, well-thought-out answers, and can sometimes learn as much about their problems as you can from their answers,

Question 4d. (Other problems solved) What other problems have you tackled successfully? How?

This question (and the next one) asks clients indirectly about general skills and resources they might have going for them; it is similar to question 4b, but it helps you to get the client talking in concrete terms about specific problem-solving skills, which they may already have but which they might not simply recall out of context. This is a roundabout but very effective way to get clients to provide real examples of areas where they are well-endowed with special personal attributes or with other available resources. This is another way of getting clients to "count their blessings," by having them recall specific historical lines of evidence.

Question 4e. (Past control) Did you once have mastery of the present problem area? If so, when and under what circumstances? Any idea of how?

Question 5: Consequences

I am going to ask you some questions about some effects produced by your problem, or effects you'd like to produce by solving that problem.

Question 5a. (Symptom reinforcers: positive) You've probably heard the proverb, "It is an ill wind that blows no good." With regard to some advantages or good things that have "blown your way," has your problem ever produced any special advantages or considerations for you (like, in school, on the job, or at home)? Please give specific examples.

You can do a couple of things with this question. First, by virtue of its form, you can use this question as part of your assessment of the clients' mental status (e.g., Do they understand the proverb correctly, or do they interpret it in particularly disordered or distorted ways?).

More important, you can begin to identify what outcomes of the client's problem behavior might actually maintain the pattern, despite its medical or social costs to the client—in other words, in what ways might the client's symptoms actually be "adaptive" or be considered somewhat beneficial, in spite of their obvious "dysfunctional" aspects? Sometimes, clients are extremely wary of answering any questions about "what they get" out of their symptoms, again because of possible implications that the symptoms are faked. After assuring them that you believe their symptoms are indeed real and beyond question, you tell the clients that, even so, there are normally some good things that come out of people's illnesses. The clients often then respond accordingly (e.g., "Well, for the first time in 20 years, my husband says he loves me, and misses me, and can't wait for me to get home from the hospital," or "My boss finally gave me the big office, so I could be closer to the washroom," or "When I stay home from school with a headache, Mommy lets me eat lots of ice cream to help me feel better").

Question 5b. (Symptom reinforcers: negative) As a result of your problem, have you ever been excused for things—or *from* things—that you might not be otherwise?

This one is tough, for the same reasons as are cited in the notes for questions 4a and 5a. You can provide whatever prompts you think would work here to let the clients know quite clearly that you aren't suggesting they're just malingerers. Again, the issue here is to assess whether and to what extent the clients' disturbing patterns of behavior actually pay off for them, in this case by buying their ways out of certain undesirable or unpleasant tasks, duties, requirements, or circumstances, or by getting them "off the hook" when they do things they would not otherwise be forgiven for doing. Most clients will sheepishly say, for example, that "My family is so helpful and concerned that they won't let me do anything around the house yet, none of the housework or yardwork—I'm getting stir crazy from having nothing to do, but they just won't let me!" (Remember: Br'er Rabbit said, "Oh, please don't throw me into the briar patch!" If instead he had begged to be thrown in, would Br'ers Fox and Bear have obliged him?)[1]

Question 5c. (Symptom costs) How is your present problem a drag, or how does it jeopardize you? (Simply omit this question if the client gave a satisfactory answer in 3a: "Why start now?")

Question 5d. (Possible current reinforcers) What kinds of things do you really like to do? Is there anything that really sends you?

These are things the clients enjoy doing, or things they are willing to work hard in order to do. You can systematically arrange opportunities for the clients to do some of these as incentives for meeting treatment goals or as activities which, in and of themselves, have therapeutic aspects. Most of the time, clients will talk very freely about these things, but depressed clients often make you pull out their teeth and fingernails before giving you suitable answers—just make it clear to them that you understand they probably haven't had much fun lately, but back in the good old days, before they got depressed, what kinds of things did they enjoy?

Question 5e. (High probability behaviors) What do you find yourself doing instead? (or getting instead?)

This question can get you several important kinds of information, about whether the clients: 1) actually miss the things they described in 5d, or whether they are now doing what they really like to do; 2) are actually capable of doing the things they say they enjoy, or whether their present situations allow them to do these things; 3) are presently doing what they have to do, at the expense of their preferred activities; and 4) are doing simply what comes most easily to them, even though it means in the long run they can't do the things they say they enjoy; and so on. The main purpose of this question, in general, is to find out whether the clients are doing any of the things they enjoy, and if not, then why not?

Question 5f. (Social reinforcers) Who else is interested in the changes you're after?

This will provide a list of "significant others," including immediate family members, more distant relatives, friends, coworkers, acquaintances, and so on, who could be recruited as participants in the clients' programs. Ostensibly, the clients will work toward their goals if that would please these people. But clients' answers to this question can often tell you not only who else might be interested in the clients' well-being, but also who is likely to be "obstructionist" with regard to the intervention program. Sometimes, clients' problems thrust other people into the limelight, or provide them with special family or other social roles that they could not occupy if the clients were well—these significant others would stand to lose something important to them once the clients recover, and if these people are genuinely important to the clients, or can exert strong influence over their actions, then the intervention program would do well to take these other people's needs into account as well as the clients'.

Question 5g. (Social reinforcers) What people have been helpful to you in the past? How did they go about it? How did you obtain this help from them?

The purpose of this question is not only to identify significant others from the clients' past, but also to assess the extent to which the clients can effectively ask others for help, and whether they even need to turn to other people for help or support when faced with problems. You can prompt responses here to remind clients that they have not been alone in the past at times of need, and are not now alone if they need help or emotional support. (You will find out just how much social support given clients have actually had in the past, whether they sought it out, whether it was offered "freely," or whether it existed for them in the first place.)

Question 6: *Completion*
Is there anything we left out or didn't get enough information about? Was there something we overlooked—or made too much of? Are there any impressions you'd like to correct?

If guarded clients come to feel more comfortable with you by this point in the interview, they might now wish to supplement their previous answers with more detail. Also, some facts or details that the clients simply could not recall earlier may come back to them now, after they have talked at length about distantly related matters. On the other hand, clients with borderline or antisocial (sociopathic) personalities often take this opportunity to substantially change previous answers, or to give information that obscures or changes the underlying meanings of their earlier responses, especially if they now suspect they may have divulged something that will later work against their hidden agendas. The answers to these "completion" questions are sometimes more implicitly informative about the clients personalities than are their direct answers to previous "content" questions. For these reasons, it is generally a good idea to let the clients' original answers to content questions stand, and to clearly identify any information they later added or changed in answer to the completion question. Accordingly, you should note any impressions you get at this time about such attributes as compulsiveness, paranoia, emotional hypersensitivity, obsessive worrying over or preoccupation with certain recurrent themes, self-aggrandizement, and so on. You can later summarize these impressions, and note them on Axis II of a clients' DSM-IV diagnoses, for example.

Question 7: Turnabout

Turnabout is fair play. We have asked you a lot of questions. Are there any questions you'd like to ask us? Any comments? Kicks? Anything you'd like to know about our goals or approach?

This question is self-explanatory and has no great hidden meanings. It gives you a very natural point at which to introduce the client to the program's general treatment philosophy, rules and procedures, and available institutional resources. Be prepared occasionally to receive some constructive (or nasty personal) criticism about your interviewing style, or to bear the brunt of a client's anger at having problems or simply being ill. Just count these kinds of incidents as opportunities for your own personal growth and adjustment.

Note

1 The Br'er Rabbit tales have their origins in traditional West, Central, and Southern African trickster stories, representing extreme forms of behavior that people may be forced into for survival in extreme circumstances. They became part of an oral story-telling tradition among African-Americans, particularly in the Southern United States.

Modified Goldiamond Case Presentation Guide[1]

A. Introduction

1. Identifying information:
   Brief description of patient and a few qualifying statements that are relevant to what follows

2. Background for the program:
   Use A3 as the resolution toward which this presentation is directed. Weave in various items from the Constructional Questionnaire and other sources to present a coherent picture of a person functioning highly competently, given their circumstances and implicit or explicit goals. Consider the available alternative behaviors. Describe how the costs and benefits of these behaviors in relation to the costs and benefits of the disturbing behavior make the disturbing behavior a sensible and competent resolution of their situation. Present the history of the person as an example of such competence, giving evidence wherever available. Use a contingency matrix to illustrate your analysis.

3. Symptom as costly operant:
   Infer how, as a result of A2, the patterns shaped and reinforced up to now are now too costly or otherwise jeopardizing the patient. Infer what reinforcers are presently maintaining patterns, sources, and type of jeopardy and its source. This should be brief and simply stated as a logical outgrowth of A2, which presented in more detail what led up to this. Use a contingency matrix to illustrate your analysis.

B. Tentative program directions

1. Outcomes that seem reasonable as targets
2. Evidence for each of these:

   a. Relation to reinforcers maintaining symptom
   b. Likelihood of producing additional reinforcers

DOI: 10.4324/9781003141365-12

      c. Feasibility of substitution for jeopardizing symptom (Non-linear Topical Intervention)

      d. Feasibility of establishing other patterns that will depotentiate the disturbing contingency (Systemic Intervention)

      e. Relation to present repertoires

          i. Personal

          ii. Environmental and available Feasibility (costs, resources)

    3. Relation to contingency matrix:
Use a contingency matrix to illustrate the relation of the target patterns to current disturbing patterns and currently available alternatives.

C. Current relevant repertoires

    1. General, for program-recording requirements:

      a. Analytical, types of relations explained

      b. Recording repertoires

    2. For each of targets recommended:

      c. Previous programs

      d. Current relevant repertoires: assay of current resources

      e. Social repertoires

      f. Environmental assets

      g. Maintaining and available consequences; accessibility; symptom as reinforcement indicator

D. Change procedures, programing guides

    1. For program-recording and analysis of each target:

      h. Analytic procedures to be used (texts, manuals, discussions)

      i. Types of records to be kept, graphs

    2. For target areas:

      j. Programs and repertoires in past to be transferred or modeled (How?)

      k. Shaping, modeling, or transfer procedures for changing present repertoires

      l. Getting and shaping program cooperation from others; reinforcing such cooperation

      m. Ways current environmental resources might be used (facilities, possible social models)

      n. Social and other possible support; analysis of symptom as successful operant

E. Maintenance guides

   1. Through program:

      o. Records, graphs, other assignments
      p. Other possibilities
      q. Reliability checks
      r. Extraneous consequences

   2. Thereafter

F. Specific programs

   1. Available specific programs (here or elsewhere)
   2. Staffing
   3. Other suggestions

Note

1 After Goldiamond, 1974

Appendix C

The Smith Case

This appendix is presented to illustrate how cases are conducted within the framework of a constructional approach model. The Smith case involves marital problems and work problems. These are typical problems seen in behaviorally oriented agencies. Although marital crises were present, the program dealt with the husband alone. This is a complete case study featuring all elements of the constructional approach. It occurred prior to the formal manifestation of nonlinear analysis. Of special note is how the reported thoughts and emotions change as the contingencies change. The initial interview was conducted by Israel Goldiamond; the case was carried by Arthur Schwartz; planning and analysis of the case were a joint effort. The case study previously appeared as a chapter in *Social Casework: A Behavioral Approach* by Arthur Schwartz and Israel Goldiamond. It is reproduced here with permission.

Mr. Smith is a middle-aged (44 years old) white lawyer who works in a distinguished law firm. He is in charge of the section on securities and exchange law. This section, though small and not considered as exciting as others in the firm, is central to the firm's business. Mr. Smith also serves as consultant on such problems for clients handled by other lawyers in the firm. He is financially successful and, seemingly to the casual observer, personally fulfilled. However, he reported little personal, marital, or job satisfaction. His marriage was crumbling. He took work home with him, and his family saw little of him. His wife had recently "kicked him out," precipitating the crisis which brought him into therapy.

Mr. Smith's presenting complaint was of a severe and prolonged depression, which was crippling him in his work and marriage. He was able to work, but only at a tremendous cost and without any joy in the work. His appearance reflected his complaint. He spoke in a low voice, with frequent pauses and downcast gazes. The interviewers were shocked to learn his age: he appeared to be in his early sixties. A physical examination revealed that he had no medical problems.

DOI: 10.4324/9781003141365-13

Intake and Initial Interview: The Self-Control Questionnaire

The self-control questionnaire was administered as the initial interview[1] in the program. Its purpose was to obtain information relevant to: 1) terminal repertoire to be established; 2) the current relevant repertoire that could be used to start; 3) programming procedures that were necessary and current programs that were available in the client's repertoire; and 4) natural reinforcers that would maintain progress in programs and their possible sources. An additional purpose of the questionnaire was to communicate to the client both the rationale and the procedures.

1. *Worker: The questions I am going to ask can be grouped into clusters. Before asking you to answer individual questions, let me present the first group, and then we'll go over them one by one. These questions are about why you are coming here. You're coming here because you want certain things to change, you want certain things to be different. Assuming we are successful, the questions are: (a) What would the outcome be like? (b) How would others recognize it? (c) How would it be different from the current state of affairs? (d) Can you give an example? Let's take these one by one. The first question is: If we were successful, what would the outcome be for you?*

2. Client (Slowly, drawn out, voice almost inaudible, manner depressed): Well, I would not be such a mass of tension and such a complete wreck and so scared of people. I would be able to handle the many aspects of things that need handling . . . (pause) considerably better and, uh, my, uh, wife and everybody in my family would be happier and I'd sleep a great deal better, which is a problem. I would just be an altogether relaxed, effective individual.
   (Comment: As is common, client starts with a recitation of what he would not be. He'd be less "pathological." He speaks in very general terms and refers to unobservables both here and when he switches to what he'd like to be. His opening statements are often characterized by reported "inadequacies," since this is typically the "ticket" for admission to psychotherapy. Worker goes on to the second question to get specifics, to start working with the client toward observable problematic and nonproblematic behaviors.)

3. *Worker: A more relaxed, effective individual?*
   (Comment: Worker is responding to one element in the response just given. He is asking for elaboration that can be used to establish positive outcomes.)

4. Client: Yes. More relaxed, more in tune with others.

5. *Worker: (Question 1b) You'd be more relaxed, effective. How would others observe this? What would others see when they looked at you? When they saw you?*
   (Comment: Worker attempts to translate the unobservables given by the client into observable terms, observable by others and to which they respond.)

6. Client: More relaxed in company.
   (Comment: Client has narrowed down what "others" means, but his statement still does not refer to observables. Worker tries to prompt observables.)

7. *Worker: It's kind of difficult to seem "more relaxed in company," in tune, and so forth. What would someone who didn't know you see? What would he observe? How could he tell?*

8. Client: Well, uh, I don't know. If he saw me he wouldn't see anybody who would stand out because of his tenseness.
   (Comment: Again, a definition in terms of negatives and unobservables. Worker is "pushing" the client here.)

9. *Worker: What would he see?*

10. Client: Uh, it's, uh, it's uh very hard, very hard for me to grasp it, to say it.

11. *Worker: Yes, it is often very difficult. (Silence)*

12. Client: He'd see an individual going along, doing his job.
    (Comment: The response is being shaped.)

13. *Worker: What would he see at work?*
    (Comment: The worker moves to an area in which the client will be more likely to be specific and positive.)

14. Client: He'd see a very busy fellow.

15. *Worker: What would he see at home?*

16. Client: He'd see an individual, if we were successful, who, well, who went out more with everybody and took out his wife more. . . *(long pause)*. He would see a man who enjoys his family.
    (Comment: The juxtaposition of enjoyment of family and taking out wife more often suggests possible target area.)

17. *Worker: You mentioned going out with your wife. How often would you be going out with her?*

18. Client: More frequently.
    (Comment: "More" is unobservable.)

19. *Worker: How often?*

20. Client: Two or three times a week.

21. *Worker: How often do you go out with her now?*
    (Comment: This information anticipates the next question but is relevant here.)

22. Client: Not too often. Every several weeks or so. Maybe three times a month. Maybe twice. Certainly no more frequently.

23. *Worker: Is that what your wife would like? Two or three times a week?*

24. Client: Yes. I think she'd like that very much.

25. *Worker: What would you be doing?*
    (Comment: Defines the subrepertoires subsumed by "going out.")

26. Client: Well, going to parties, meeting friends, doing some sports, perhaps golfing—we sometimes used to do that together—swim in the summer. I'd also sleep better.
    (Comment: Sleep better? What does this mean exactly?)

27. *Worker: Sleep better?*
    (Comment: Worker would like this targeted, but he has stated his question too vaguely.)

28. Client: I don't sleep well.
    (Comment: Worker got just what he asked for!)

29. *Worker: How much do you sleep now?*
    (Comment: The question is restated in numerical terms.)

30. Client: Well, actually, I suppose I'd sleep less. What I mean is, I'd stay up later, but get more sleep.
    (Comment: The intent is obvious: sleep would be sounder. However, the program is directed toward making the client's analyses clearer, not those of the worker.)

31. *Worker: I don't understand. How late would you stay up?*

32. Client: Well, I'd stay up until midnight, but when I went to bed I'd sleep soundly, wouldn't toss, turn, dream so much, be more restful in sleep.

33. *Worker: You'd sleep soundly. What time would you get up?*

34. Client: Oh, about 7:00.
    (Comment: Day-to-day behavioral routine is very important for programming purposes.)

35. *Worker: You say you'd be more relaxed and more effective? What do you mean by that?*

36. Client: Well, you would be seeing a man puttering in his garage and with his books at his desk and talking with his children and taking them out and swimming with them and staying around, spending more time with them.
    (Comment: Client has caught on! Excellent.)

37. *Worker: And. . . ?*
    (Comment: Worker reinforces the client's statement by saying "and," which indicates he wants to hear more—a major way of reinforcing speech.)

38. Client: And in more company with others, he is like them, more normal, less hassled, less harried, less of a goddamned feeling that he is on a treadmill, working his ass off and not having a thing to show for it. . . *(long pause)* someone who's organized.

(Comment: The request for "more" turns to the negatives, which are stronger in his repertoire than the positives.)

39. Worker: *Organized?*
   (Comment: Positive area to be established.)
40. Client: Organized, more efficient, knowing what he'll do and what he wants.
41. Worker: *Organized at work? And at home?*
42. Client: At home. More relaxed at home. More efficient at work.
43. Worker: *You mean when he's at work, he's at work, and efficient. And when he is at home, he is relaxed?*
   (Comment: The attempt is now made to define the repertoire involved.)
44. Client: Yeah, that's it. That's it in a nutshell.
45. Worker: *Let's see if I get the picture. A successful outcome would be somebody at work who is a busy person, efficient at his job. At home he is with his family and enjoying it. Taking them out, doing things, spending time with them. He'd go out with his wife two or three times a week. He would stay up till midnight, doing things, then go to sleep, sleep soundly until 7:00, then go to work. After work or on weekends, he'd be puttering in his garage, or with his car, basically an organized person.*
   (Comment: Worker summarizes goals [terminal repertoire]. Some of the client's responses are beginning to define outcomes in observable terms. Emotions, as one can see, are not ignored but viewed as guides to underlying contingencies and not as causes of behavior.)
46. Client: Yes, that sounds like it.
47. Worker: *When he is at work, he is at work. But when he is at home, he is at home.*
48. Client: Yes, that sums it up.
   (Comment: The inference is that when the client is at work, he does not do his job, hence it is carried home. Working at home results in a lack of reinforcement, which adds to the loss of reinforcement on the job. Obviously, to obtain the reinforcements available in each environment, different repertoires are required at work and at home.)
49. Worker: *(Question 1c): How does that differ from the current state of affairs?*
50. Client: Well, I'm very busy at work. *(Long pause)* . . . . I work with inefficiency.
   (Comment: The inference was reasonable, but now requires detailed specification.)
51. Worker: *You're busy at work but inefficient. Tell me about it.*
52. Client: I am tense, disorganized. I just don't seem to have any definite purpose. I don't seem to have any concrete objectives, just disorganization. I am marginal at work.

53. *Worker: What kind of law do you practice?*
54. Client: Security and exchange law. I'm a security and exchange specialist.
55. *Worker: How are you at it?*
56. Client: Well, you may find this hard to believe, looking at this caricature of a human being, but I am one of the top ten experts in the country in this particular area. It's specialized, maybe that's another way of saying that it is dull. It's goddamned dull. Maybe that is why someone like me, without imagination, could go into it and do well, at least financially.
57. *Worker: Do you enjoy any of it?*
58. Client: No. There are no kicks at work. Only pressures.
59. *Worker: You say you don't enjoy it, yet your face lit up. You might even say that you said it with pride. You said you are one of the top ten in the country.*
60. Client: Well, I do all right, that is, as far as meeting my commitments; it just takes a hell of a lot of work and time.
    (Comment: It always did, but something is now different.)
61. *Worker: More time than you feel you should spend to get the work done?*
62. Client: Hell, yes. When things are going well, I spend a lot of time, but then it isn't the pain it is now.
63. *Worker: What things aren't going well that make work such a pain?*
64. Client: Things at home.
65. *Worker: Then the problem is not work, but home?*
66. Client: Yes and no. There is a problem at work, organization and mess sort of thing has always been a problem at work, but *(pause)* recently much worse.
67. *Worker: Is the "recently much worse" due to things at home rather than things at work?*
68. Client: Yes.
69. *Worker: Can you tell me about them?*
70. Client: *(Long pause, sigh.)* Well *(pause)* the story is, well, really, that my wife, my wife kicked me out of the house a couple of weeks ago and put a suit for divorce against me, and I took the children, but I had to put them back after a couple of days. I couldn't take care of them, and uh, she let me back in the house after a few days *(pause).*
71. *Worker: She let you back?*
72. Client: She let me back with the stipulation that, uh, I do this, which uh, is all right because, uh, it's her own good idea, and I, uh, should have done it, oh, a long time ago.
    (Comment: The fact that his wife let him back into the house suggests that the suit for divorce was a drastic operant on her part to force change.)

73. *Worker: She took you back on the condition that you get therapy?*
74. Client: Uh-huh.
75. *Worker: What about the divorce suit?*
76. Client: She dropped it.
77. *Worker: I see. Then the therapy is your wife's idea, not yours?*
    (Comment: This is an attempt to assess the extent to which therapeutic change is more critical to the wife than to the client. If this is the case, a different program and client may be indicated.)
78. Client: No. Not really. I just wouldn't have done it on my own. I wouldn't have had the courage, but now that she sort of forced me—yes, you could say that she forced me into it—I think it is a good idea. I should have done it a long time ago.
    (Comment: Wife's operant [ploy] was extremely successful. She gauged his interest correctly, and she took him back. Likelihood is that she is supportive. This suggests that the situation is not as bleak as described by the husband and that there are strengths to build on.)
79. *Worker: How are things with your wife now?*
80. Client: Perfectly all right. *(Pause)* Hmm. Well, it is not exactly right. We are never perfectly right. But they never will be because—wives being wives, my wife thinks that if I'm gone so many hours a day, that I'm gone some place and when I get home, it's work time. I must have been sleeping some place all that time I was gone. So there is a problem there in, uh, our approach to matters.
81. *Worker: Does she expect you to work, help around the house? (Comment: What are the wife's requirements?)*
82. Client: No. Not really. *(Pause)* She wants me, when I'm home, to spend the time with her and with the children.
    (Comment: The probe was successful in getting the client to talk about his wife's requirements in his own words.)
83. *Worker: You don't?*
84. Client: No.
85. *Worker: (Pause) What keeps you from spending time with your children? [Client remains silent.] Do you take work home with you? (Comment: A prompt.)*
86. Client: *(Sigh)* Yes, I do. I take home work to do.
87. *Worker: I see. And she expects you to spend the time at home with her and the kids?*
    (Comment: His wife has normal expectations. Her deprivation indicates that she likes him and that her efforts to have more of him have resulted in aggression.)
88. Client: Yes.
89. *Worker: Why do you take work home? Can you tell me about that? Is it necessary for your job?*

90. Client: Well, knowing that I am a marginal individual and always have been, knowing that I am not a very bright fellow basically, it occurred to me a long time ago, uh, the only thing that is quite good enough is my absolute maximum effort. Once I start getting sloppy, I fall flat on my face, so I have to look to get a little ahead and have a little margin.

    (Comment: His response is typically deprecatory. An alternative explanation is that situational variables are requiring this high output, which he justifies in personally deprecatory terms. As long as he looks at things this way, he will not change the situational variables. The consultant will move into exploring these.)

91. *Worker: You have to work harder than the next fellow just to get your job done?*

92. Client: I think so, yeah.

93. *Worker: And your wife would like you to spend more time with her?*

94. Client: Yes.

95. *Worker: Do you have the time at the office to read the latest security laws, decisions, and that sort of thing? Is that part of your job? As a lawyer?*

96. Client: No, I don't have the time. It would be ideal if I did, if I could, if I would stay a couple of hours at work, at the end of the day.

    (Comment: A possible program target.)

97. *Worker: You are due at nine?*

98. Client: Yes.

99. *Worker: And what time are you finished?*

100. Client: We are finished when we are finished. We are allowed to go and come as we wish. I am, at least. I don't have as much client contact as the others. I do the looking up, the loopholes, the latest laws, and so forth. Actually, I spend a lot of time seeing various lawyers. That part I like.

    (Comment: Client actually has the opportunity to control much of his environment.)

101. *Worker: So you hold your own with them?*

    (Comment: This is a prompt for a more positive statement about himself. Obviously, other lawyers would not be inviting him to intrude on their time on the regular basis described unless he were competent.)

102. Client: Certainly. I have something they want, and they put up with me. And my personality is such that I intend to have them get it.

    (Comment: Prompt was successful. Client's positive statement will now be reinforced. It should be noted that the reinforcer is a question which extends the discourse.)

103. *Worker: If you were as dull as you are trying so hard to impress on me that you are, do you think that they would keep coming back to you? Don't they pay you rather stiff fees?*

104. Client: I see your point. I guess I must, I must help them. No, they don't pay me fees. I am on salary. They pay the firm.
105. Worker: *Would you make more money, have more independence on your own, in solo practice, or in a firm of your own?*
      (Comment: Probe: Is the high response cost maintained by a monetary reinforcer?)
106. Client: Money? Yes, after a while. Independence, hell, I'd never get anything done, I get uptight about seeing clients.
      (Comment: Apparently, he is an effective lawyer's lawyer.)
107. Worker: *Do you get uptight about seeing their lawyers?*
108. Client: No, generally not, but then it is a lot of technical talk, no bullshit; I'm not good at that kind of bullshit.
      (Comment: Other lawyers reinforce his professional behavior; hence his affect is positive.)
109. Worker: *Have you ever discussed going into solo practice, or your own firm, with your wife?*
      (Comment: Can his wife be recruited here?)
110. Client: From time to time. When things get real bad, and I'm swamped, she says that I really don't have to put up with that sort of thing, that I can get lots of jobs.
      (Comment: His wife apparently does not share his low opinion of himself.)
111. Worker: *Is that true?*
112. Client: God, yes! It is a dull kind of life, but it is specialized, not many in it, and even fewer going into it. No young person wants to spend his time buried in a library.
113. Worker: *Your wife is behind you then, when it comes to decisions at work? (Pause) Is she?*
114. Client: Yes, I'd say that. She thinks I am God Almighty, but only in my work.
      (Comment: The client is inviting derogatory inferences about home. Worker resists "biting" for that. Instead, in order to program patterns, he needs specific information about what actually goes on.)
115. Worker: *Tell me about your daily routine.*
116. Client: I get to work at the office by 9:00, eat lunch at my desk, and sometimes I come home at 5:00. The office gets deserted. Very rarely I stay until 6:00 or 7:00. Not very many evening meetings.
117. Worker: *You get home about 6:00 then?*
118. Client: Yes.
119. Worker: *Then what?*
120. Client: I say hello, have a drink, maybe have a sandwich, and then go into my study.
121. Worker: *How long do you stay there?*

122. Client: Well, again, this is very variable. To say that I go into my study, you are giving me credit for something I don't quite get accomplished. I go in there, and I intend to work, but I often don't.

123. *Worker: But you go there anyhow whether you study there or not? (Comment: Whether anything is accomplished in the study or not, the client puts in his time. This has the effect of separating him from his wife.)*

124. Client: Yes, uh.

125. *Worker: After supper?*

126. Client: After 8:00.

127. *Worker: After 8:00. Tell me what do you do there?*

128. Client: Well, I go in. Sometimes I read new regulations. Sometimes, I check my bank balance. Sometimes I just futz around.

129. *Worker: Until what time?*

130. Client: Maybe 9:00.

131. *Worker: And then?*

132. Client: I go to bed. Sometimes I stay in the study until midnight, but I often go to bed at 9:00.

133. *Worker: And then you get up, go to work. What happens on the weekends?*

134. Client: Conferences in the morning, Saturday morning. Afternoon and Sunday, I am home.

135. *Worker: How much time do you and your wife spend together?*

136. Client: Not much.

137. *Worker: Sounds like she might have some kind of grievance, doesn't it? (Comment: Wife's behavior is rational; the question is designed to shape positive statements about wife as well as himself.)*

138. Client: Yes.

139. *Worker: OK, let's see. First your wife expressed some annoyance with this state of affairs, yes?*
    (Comment: The worker is trying to "pin down" what actually happened to bring the client into therapy.)

140. Client: Yes.

141. *Worker: When she asked you to leave and filed for divorce, what grounds did she give?*

142. Client: Well, there was a blowup, one night, which precipitated things. She had had the flu for two days and was in bed and claims that I didn't pay any attention to her and she had the flu. This is not strictly true. I asked her more than half a dozen times how she was, what could I get for her.

143. *Worker: Did you take time off from work?*

144. Client: No, I didn't.

145. *Worker: Could you have?*

146. Client: Yes.
147. *Worker: Who was at home with her?*
148. Client: Uh-huh. *(Pause)*
149. *Worker: What do you think bothered her?*
150. Client: Well, I took four days to write a brochure, and she heard that I had these four days off and the thing got precipitated so that the four days were wasted. I had the children with me, and the four days were wasted and . . . she, uh . . . there is such a colossal waste in everything . . . but a divorce suit, for example, lawyers, uh . . . very expensive people.
151. *Worker: Let's see, your wife complains that she doesn't see you enough. She says that she doesn't get enough of you, that she wants more of you.*
    (Comment: Designed to shape a positive statement about his wife, and to indicate that there are better relations between them; also to continue shaping positive statements about himself.)
152. Client: Hm-hmm *(pause)*.
153. *Worker: You mentioned waste. What did you mean by that?*
154. Client: The waste is my coming home and I have plans. I may even have a list of things to do when I get home, but instead of getting them done, I, uh, sit and worry about the fact that I am not getting anything done.
155. *Worker: Do you waste time at work?*
    (Comment: The consultant returns to the target of opportunity.)
156. Client: Well, work is a fairly unusual situation. I keep very busy.
157. *Worker: Is there any wasted time there?*
158. Client: There is waste of time there, but I don't know how to get around that part of it. I have to be close by others, to consult with staff clients. You can't get too far away from it.
    (Comment: The "stand-by" implication requires clarification. There are procedures to help with scheduling problem.)
159. *Worker: Do you have your own secretary?*
160. Client: I share one with the pool.
161. *Worker: You are the senior man in your area?*
162. Client: Yes.
163. *Worker: And are you practically a partner in the firm?*
164. Client: Yes.
165. *Worker: Wouldn't it be to your firm's advantage to give you your own secretary, a space of her own, to maximize your efficiency?*
166. Client: Yeah, uh, well, I suppose so.
167. *Worker: And haven't you asked for these things?*
168. Client: No.
    (Comment: Part of the trouble is now evident, and the solution to this part is also evident.)

169. *Worker: I think that this is something that we can work on. Let's go on to some other area, some other material that we need to know.*
(Comment: The fine grain of the work schedule might be difficult to obtain at this time. It should be obtainable from his records. Also, if he gets a good secretary, it may not be necessary for him to acquire the appropriate work schedule. She may do it for him.)

171. *Worker: (Question 2a) Describe the areas that will not be affected by the program.*

172. Client: It is difficult to say, I'll still be a lawyer.
(Comment: Changing his job is not a desired outcome.)

173. *Worker: Yes, you are accomplished at your profession.*

174. Client: And I would still be married to my wife. I don't want to lose her!

175. *Worker: My guess is that she feels the same way. She dropped a divorce suit when she could have gone through with it. She made therapy a condition. She obviously cares enough for you that she wanted you to get help. She has let you know that she doesn't want you buried in the study, but wants to see more of you.*
(Comment: Worker's interpretation contains bases from which to develop further behavior, especially if his wife wants to see more of him. He is a source of reinforcement for behaviors important to his wife.)

176. Client: Uh, yes, that is so; I didn't think of it that way. I thought that she must be getting tired of me. And the children, they wouldn't change; they would remain the same. They wouldn't exactly, they wouldn't by any means, they would get more attention, which is what they need.

177. *Worker: Then that would change.*

178. Client: And my work would change. I would be doing more, but we have been over this.

179. *Worker: Yes, but we shall return to it. Your profession would stay the same, you would be married to the same woman, the children would be the same except that you would feel that you would give them more attention.*

180. Client: Yes.

181. *Worker: (Question 2b) Your work relationships with colleagues would change, your relations with wife and children would change. Is there any other area that would change?*
(Comment: A restatement of the more conventional form of this question, namely, "Are there any other areas which will be affected?")

182. Client: Well, just the stuff we talked about earlier, I'd be happier, more efficient, and more confident, and we would go out a lot more.

183. *Worker: You mentioned earlier that you would get more sleep. Is it just the matter of hours you sleep? Rearranging your schedule?*

184. Client: (*Pause*) No. Not really.

185. *Worker: What is it? Is there something you haven't told me yet? (Comment: Specifics are required.)*

186. Client: No, not really. It is a situation that is not entirely satisfactory. There is a long drive to work, there is an overextended situation. There are six children at home not getting enough attention, and their father arrives home a little crabby. And this is an argument I have with my wife. If I said "yes," it is perfectly true that I need some therapy, I have known this all of my life.

187. *Worker: (Question 3a) You have started to give information about our next area. About attempts to change. The first question is why start now? What are the circumstances?*

188. Client: Well, uh, I am a middle-aged man, uh, it is about time, and uh, my wife insists upon it.

189. *Worker: How old are you?*

190. Client: Forty-four.

191. *Worker: And your wife?*

192. Client: Well, she is thirteen years younger, she is thirty-one.

193. *Worker: Tell me about your wife. What did she do before marriage?*

194. Client: Well, she's from Belgium; she's not so long in this country.

195. *Worker: How long has she been here?*

196. Client: Eight years.

197. *Worker: And you have six children? Fairly close together?*

198. Client: No, no. Only one is by her.

199. *Worker: I see. They are from a previous marriage?*

200. Client: Yes.

201. *Worker: How did the marriage end?*

202. Client: My wife died. I had four children by her. My current wife had one child, and we had one together.

203. *Worker: How old are the children?*

204. Client: Oldest is in high school, she is fourteen, and twin boys twelve, a girl eleven, and my wife's son eleven, and our son two.

205. *Worker: How long were you married the first time?*

206. Client: Eight years. She died of cancer. I was in Seattle at the time. I advertised for a housekeeper, my current wife answered; we married after that, a year later. She was still married when we met, and her divorce hadn't yet gone through.

207. *Worker: What did she do?*

208. Client: She almost got through secretarial school in Belgium, but dropped out when pregnant. Came to America, worked, and answered my ad.

209. *Worker: How is her English?*

(*Comment: This is an area in which programmed instruction exists.*)

210. Client: Oh, she doesn't construct sentences too well; but she is, uh, she gets her messages across. Actually, she doesn't speak English too well.

211. *Worker: How would you describe her?*

212. Client: Not great, but a solid, level-headed person. I guess in answer to your question about starting now, it was her threat of divorce.

213. *Worker: But you had been thinking about doing something about your marital relations. I would say that the way she got you to come here suggests that she is sensitive and understands. (Pause) (Question 3b) How long have you been thinking of some kind of change?* (*Comment: Client in #212 suggested a natural point to introduce this question. The question reads: "3b: For how long or how often have you considered starting?"*)

214. Client: Uh . . . I had not really formulated any plans to seek such help because I know this marginal situation. I know these inadequacies, and I know that such help could be of benefit but I just think, uh, that more in terms of doing well, to make it somehow without, uh, getting into this kind of program.
(*Comment: The client, as was noted, uses vague terms, wherever he can. The next question was introduced to get at the same material in a more specific way.*)

215. *Worker: (Question 3c) When did you first think of getting into this kind of program?*

216. Client: Well, once in law school I went over to a psychiatrist. It was either in the first or second year, I don't remember. I don't recall. I took a battery of tests and took, uh, oh approximately three hours of therapy then, talked to someone.
(*Comment: The specific question produces more specific answers. Questions must be asked very carefully.*)

217. *Worker: What was happening with you?*

218. Client: The conditions were that I was depressed, ineffective. Anyway, I thought that I was in bad shape and at the end of my rope.

219. *Worker: Married then?*

220. Client: Yes, but my problem was not there.

221. *Worker: School?*

222. Client: Well, I was depressed; I felt it was too much effort for what was being accomplished.
(*Comment: A current problem has apparently been encountered before. In the technical terminology of operant behavior, too high a response cost can result in escape, aggression, or other undesirable responses.*)

223. *Worker: You said you went two or three times. What happened? Any results?*

224. Client: Yes, it did a lot of good. I was assigned to a psychiatric resident, and uh, he hardly ever said anything, but listened, he just listened. Which I understood at the time was proper—friends of mine would talk about it and you know how people get kindergarten ideas about, everybody imagines himself a psychiatrist, you know. A cliché in those days was, well, you know, the better the psychiatrist, the less he says. If he says nothing, he must be the world's best.

225. *Worker: Were you satisfied?*
(Comment: The worker channels the discussion away from the client's digression.)

226. Client: Yes. Well, there was improvement. I, uh, suddenly faced things that I've never really thought about.

227. *Worker: Like what?*

228. Client: Oh, the fact that physically I'm not what my mother always admired, I don't have a very strong male identity, and I was raised by a bunch of my mother's sisters, uh, and uh.

229. *Worker: Sounds like the psychiatrist said some things.*

230. Client: No, he didn't. I said all this really, but it. . . . I don't know how it will sound, but after I said them, I bought them.

231. *Worker: With regard to the present situation, what have you done to improve it?*
(Comment: It will be noted that worker brings the discussion back to the present situation and does not respond to the issue of male identity in the family raised by client in #228. By doing so, he could get more information on this subject, and shape the discussion in this direction. This subject is considered important in other forms of therapy, and might supply information necessary for our programming. If the worker finds later that it is important, he will then ask for it, since the effects of the past and of past programs [explicit or implicit] certainly affect relationships to new programs. An operant approach is not necessarily ahistorical, is not necessarily restricted to the here and now. It will be noted that historical data have been obtained all along. However, historical information which is relevant to current programming aims is being sought. These aims are to prevent further deterioration of the client's life situation and to help him to make changes to improve it.)

232. Client: Just what I said. Not much really, till my wife brought the divorce action. It was her idea that I come, but I'm really glad, it's *mine* now. I'm not just saying that; she realized I needed the help, and now I'm glad she made me come.

233. *Worker: If it were indicated, would your wife, come to these sessions too?*

234. Client: Never thought of it. She tries hard in many ways. It never occurred that she might need to come.

235. *Worker: Well, it's too early to tell. Sometimes we see both partners, sometimes we don't. Sometimes it helps speed things up, helps us understand the situation better. It is too early to tell but generally it takes two to make a marital problem. We'll see.*
236. Client: OK.
237. *Worker: (Question 4a) Now let me ask you some questions, some further ones, this time about your strengths. We want to know what we can build on, what strengths you have, and in what related areas, and other things. What strengths would you say you have in areas related to the problem?*
238. Client: My strengths I guess are that I am dependable; I have a certain doggedness.
239. *Worker: And undoubtedly well-placed. What about your wife? What strengths do you have here?*
240. Client: Oh, it's very hard to say.
241. *Worker: She wants you back?*
242. Client: Yeah.
243. *Worker: Anything else?*
244. Client: Well, we have a satisfactory sex life.
245. *Worker: Yes? How often?*
246. Client: More frequently, I would say, than a man my age would average.
247. *Worker: Like?*
248. Client: Oh, say at least three times a week, most likely more.
     (*Comment: An indication that he must be doing something right.*)
249. *Worker: And these relations are satisfactory? Pleasing to you both?*
     (*Comment: The answer seems obvious, but the question is asked to get a specific statement of good relations from the client.*)
250. Client: Yes.
     (*Comment: Note the contrast between the number of words spent on positive statements and the number of words spent on "pathological" statements.*)
251. *Worker: What else in relation to your wife?*
252. Client: Well, I'm an inadequate father, but on the other hand I'm not so bad. She has got the son she brought with her to the marriage. I'm not bad with the boy either.
253. *Worker: Well, we're discussing your strengths. Does he respond to you?*
254. Client: Yes, he does. We do things together. He listens to me.
255. *Worker: He responds to you. The other children?*
256. Client: Yes, they do too. I really don't think I should show any partiality among them.
     (*Comment: The answers describe a home situation considerably at variance with the initial picture of inadequacies presented. He gets*

along well with his wife and children—so well, as a matter of fact, that the family wants more of him.)

257. *Worker: (Question 4b) What strengths do you have in other areas? Besides the problem area?*
258. Client: Until very recently, I kept up with my legal reading better than most people.
259. *Worker: That is awfully hard these days.*
260. Client: Yes.
261. *Worker: OK. Now, leaving aside work and practice and so forth, what strengths would you say you have in other areas? (restatement of Question 4b)*
262. Client: Not very many because uh, oh, I'm a social enough fellow. We have gone out to dinner with friends. We have had a number of cocktail parties at my house on Friday nights since we have been here. In these two years we have had, oh, not a great number, but maybe a dozen.
263. *Worker: You're describing a fairly active social life, for I assume you have also gone to other people's parties. Have you enjoyed these parties?*
264. Client: Yes, very much. As I said before I'd like to enjoy them more.
265. *Worker: (Question 4d) Let me ask you another question. Have there been problems, related problems in the past which you have solved? (Comment: This question seems appropriate at this point. The worker will return to 4c later. Question 4a refers to strengths in the problem area; Question 4d concerns problem-solving strengths. It implies that the client has the solution to the current problems in his repertoire, and it seeks information on these.)*
266. Client: Related problems, in the past?
267. *Worker: Which you have solved, and how you solved them.*
268. Client: With my marginal situation, uh, I would have to say, what relaxes me. Accomplishment does. But since I am not really accomplishing anything, I am a shattered wreck.
269. *Worker: You see yourself on a treadmill? (Comment: The purpose of this question is to define the problem more explicitly.)*
270. Client: Yes.
271. *Worker: Well, in the past, when you were on a treadmill, did you get off, and if so, how? (Comment: The question, not having been answered in its original form, is restated in a manner specific to the client's repertoire.)*
272. Client: Oh, in the past job situations, I'd go on to a steadily better job and end up way out on a limb. (Comment: This answer has two possible branches. If he goes on to a better job, he must have been accomplishing something at the

previous one. He is also reporting inadequacy. Further exploration at this point might involve considerable digression.)

273. Worker: *We'll discuss this in a minute; but have there been other problems you have solved?*

274. Client: I have a problem with my parents. My mother is in bad shape, severe asthmatic. She is also hysterical and always has been.

275. Worker: *Hysterical? In what sense?*

276. Client: In the psychiatric sense. My real judgment would be that she is schizophrenic.

277. Worker: *Where does she live?*
    (*Comment: The specific question steers him away from psychiatric categorization.*)

278. Client: British Columbia. I know what you are going to ask. I only see her about once a year, or less often, and only when I visit her. She doesn't visit me. I am a wreck after the visits, but they only happen that often, so that is not a pressing problem.

279. Worker: *Is your father alive?*

280. Client: Yes, he is alive.

281. Worker: *How do you get along with him?*

282. Client: Well, in a strange way. He is from a small area in a definite society, in a small-town backwoods Ohio environment. He is a strange fellow, too. He has been a construction worker all his life, didn't get through high school, but Mother didn't get to high school either.

283. Worker: *Then college was quite an achievement for you.*
    (*Comment: What the client describes as the poor educational background of his parents suggests an important strength on his part.*)

284. Client: I am told that it is; but if it is, it is nothing an ego will grow on.

285. Worker: *You read, you got good grades in college. What college did you go to?*
    (*Comment: The assumption of good grades is based upon his having been admitted to a law school.*)

286. Client: The University of Wisconsin in Madison.

287. Worker: *You went to U.W., and got good grades! What did you major in?*

288. Client: Economics.

289. Worker: *Then you went on to law school?*

290. Client: I went to the Columbia Law School.

291. Worker: *You went to these schools, passed difficult bar exams, and you call this marginal achievement?*
    (*Comment: The client is being asked to evaluate his assets more realistically.*)

292. Client: Well, I don't really feel it is an achievement.

(Comment: What the client feels about it is also important, for it helps define the reality to him. The fact that he describes it this way suggests that other contingencies are operating. It may, on the other hand, simply be part of a pattern of self-deprecatory behavior. To explore these now would be too much of a digression.)

293. *Worker: I believe you, and no amount of argument is going to change that. This is something that we will have to talk about during our sessions. You got good grades. Who paid for your schooling?*
   (Comment: Obviously, he did not receive a free ride from his parents.)

294. Client: Uh, a combination of things. GI Bill was part of it. Some from my father. A lot of loans.

295. *Worker: GI Bill paid for all of this, plus loans?*
   (Comment: The GI Bill could not pay for both graduate and under-graduate school. The more the worker knows about the specifics, the better job he can do.)

296. Client: It ran out. I had weekend [military] reserve money, which was a little bit. Lots of loans, and some of them from my father.

297. *Worker: Did you work too?*

298. Client: Only summers. I needed every moment I had to study.

299. *Worker: You were in the army? When?*

300. Client: 1944 to 1951.

301. *Worker: You said on your application that you were in the Air Force, right?*

302. Client: Navigator. Captain.
   (Comment: There are obviously highly relevant skills available. These skills have been obscured by the presentation of pathology.)

303. *Worker: With the rank of captain, right out of high school, you went to navigation school, and you obviously did well enough to graduate and navigate. When were you born?*
   (Comment: The purpose of this question will be shortly evident.)

304. Client: September 12, 1927.

305. *Worker: Graduate at seventeen?*

306. Client: Yes.

307. *Worker: Then when you were in the army, with a high school diploma, they sent you to navigation school, where you performed well enough to get your wings and become a captain. You were kept in for seven years, then on the GI Bill went to the University of Wisconsin, got some funds from your father, finished law school, made a pretty good record, for you don't continue in these schools with a mediocre record, and did weekend reserves after studying hard all week. Then you went on to a series of good, or at least from your point of view, pretty high paying jobs. You've had a hard*

life, working all the way through, and you have succeeded against all kinds of odds. You've made it on your own.
(Comment: A statement of achievement.)

308. Client: I guess so, uh, but in the end, where is the success?

309. *Worker: Success is measured partly by where you start from. You have some extraordinary abilities here, which you have not been looking at. What you have been looking at is the problematic side. It seems to me that you have really been working hard and succeeding at it.*

310. Client: Well, it seems also that I've been fooling people all the time.

311. *Worker: How have you been fooling them?*
    (Comment: This may suggest some usable skills. Though "fooling" probably refers to the discrepancy between the obvious esteem with which he is held, and his own reported lack of self-esteem.)

312. Client: Well, I've just barely made it, I'm just. . .

313. *Worker: What do you mean?*

314. Client: I'm a shaky mass of wreckage.

315. *Worker: Well, let's see. You state that you barely made it through navigation school, through college, through law school. You barely made it on these jobs. You know, here I just wonder what is your definition of "barely made it"?*
    (Comment: Nothing wrong with being argumentative or contrary—if this moves the program to help the client along.)

316. Client: Uh . . . I'm saying that I'm the kind of fellow who got, uh, who is mediocre as hell, who somehow got away with it.

317. *Worker: Really, I don't see how you could have "gotten away with it" in so many places for so long.*

318. Client: Well, I don't either.

319. *Worker: Is it quite possible that you haven't been getting away with anything?*

320. Client: Well, it could be.

321. *Worker: You've been with a lot of sharp people. I don't think these people are readily fooled.*

322. Client: Well, if not, then, I still have to repeat again, if there is something there, it is still lacking.

323. *Worker: Well, I see what you are telling me is that you are not really happy.*

324. Client: Nothing any ego will grow on.

325. *Worker: We will have to find out what that means. Are you saying that, in terms of growth, you don't see much of a future in it?*

326. Client: Well, what I am saying is that I think it's uh, the idea of living is to grow, to develop, yet I'm not developing. I, uh, to develop you have to have a certain amount of ego, and I don't have it somehow. Now this is, these are, my own terms.

327. *Worker: You are, well, I get the message. What you are stating is, the idea of living is to grow and develop and you don't see yourself developing. You don't see a purpose in this of the kind that you like. (Comment: Purposive behavior is behavior governed by some definable consequence. A possible outcome target of the program is being considered.)*

328. Client: True enough.

329. *Worker: You don't see yourself going onward and upward; you see a kind of plateau that isn't very happy.*
(Comment: Client may be analyzing events in the terms of the social cliché of someone who has evidently spent a great effort in getting ahead and, now that he is there, does not see the point of it. An alternate explanation is that getting there has been worth it, but something about the current contingencies has disrupted behavior. This suggests another examination of the conditions involved in the situation. The fact that the client has been engaged in extraordinary efforts until now indicates that his behavior has been reinforced by his professional rewards.)

330. Client. True.

331. *Worker: (Question 4c) Let me ask, have there been any conditions under which the present problem hasn't been a problem?*
(Comment: Question provides further clarification and specification.)

332. Client: I can't think of any in my life. The area is too great.

333. *Worker: Are there any conditions right now in which the present problem isn't a problem?*

334. Client: There are times when I'm accomplishing things and I'm getting things done. And I'm putting these things way back and I feel like I am purposeful, or purposive.

335. *Worker: So occasionally when you are accomplishing things, you feel OK? Right now you don't feel you are accomplishing anything? (Comment: See earlier discussion of contingency analysis of emotions. The implied program for changing his depressed affect is to establish those contingencies that reverse the affect.)*

336. Client: Yeah.

337. *Worker: Let me see if I can make a stab at what goes on. During the day, you are supposed to keep up with changes in laws, the state of the market, deal with clients who come in with problems, consult with staff members from other branches of the law, the solutions to whose problems may have implications in your area. You are very efficient and are constantly called upon by others for consultation. (Comment: The worker is attempting to focus this slow-speaking and self-derogatory client in the interests of time, and in order to obtain specific information. The worker is "visualizing" the work*

*situation and trying to check it out, to lead to contingencies which
he infers are competing with the important one the client wants.)*

338. Client: Yeah, that's right, and not only that, but we also have been
getting some law trainees, and I had to devote time to them. They
come in at odd times, and I sympathize with them. They've got a
heavy schedule, and I make time for them at their convenience.
Also, these consultations that I do with other members of the firm
are usually done in their office and when their client is there.

339. *Worker: Well this seems to further complicate your "hamburger"
day. Not only is your time completely chopped up, but the offices
where you spend your time are also chopped up. You run here, run
there, consult this person, talk to that person. If you only could do
something with that time, it would be OK. If you could add it up,
by the end of the day it might add up to something.*

*(Comment: A clear problem is the temporal and spatial arrange-
ments of the client, and a program to rearrange these is highly
feasible. While the client is highly regarded, he does not have an
adequate office; if he had an adequate office, other lawyers would
consult with him there. His secretary could arrange his time, so that
he could do his work at work and not take it home. The client's
depression may be caused by the contingencies that follow the present disarray or by the absence of contingencies, important to him,
eliminated by this disarray.)*

340. Client: Yeah, true, true.

341. *Worker: Then, after a day like that, you come home bucking traffic all the way for one or two hours, your wife isn't too happy, she
hasn't seen you all day, six kids in the house. A woman of thirty-
one years, oldest kid is about seventeen.*

342. Client: Fourteen.

343. *Worker: Fourteen—that's pretty much for a woman who would
like to live and see things. You eat quickly and then you go to your
study and you are unhappy about the day's events, this chopped-
up situation. You sit in your study and it is difficult to sit down
and work, you fritter away up to two hours, feel uneasy and guilty
about having spent your time there. You surface to see your wife at
10 o'clock, 11 o'clock you may have sex and you may not, and then
maybe you fall asleep thereafter and maybe you don't. You toss and
turn in your bed, right? You get a few hours' sleep, and before you
know it there goes the alarm clock and it's another day and another
day and another day.*

*You carry some stuff home with you for the weekend, right? Your
wife makes demands on you and you recognize that these are legitimate. At the same time, there are legitimate demands in regard to
work, but if you could keep them separate, if you could do your*

*work, you could enjoy your wife. You waste time. Then the week
starts. That's the picture, right?*
*(Comment: This picture, which is "finer grain" than that given by
the client, is indeed depressing and may be the "treadmill" which
the client said he is on.)*

344. Client: Yes, that's the picture.
345. *Worker: Well, if that's the picture, I don't see how you can feel
anything but depressed under these circumstances. You wouldn't be
a sensible person if you didn't realize this was fraught with consequences for you as well.*
*(Comment: The client's depression is stated as making sense—indicating
normality rather than pathology.)*
346. Client: Well, if what you say is true, uh, I am much more deeply
disturbed than that.
347. *Worker: What I am saying is that you are giving a very accurate
assessment of what the situation is. Your emotions don't produce
things; your emotions are responsive to events. It is not our depression that makes us work less; it is the fact that we are not doing as
well as we could and not accomplishing what is important for us
that makes us feel depressed. So your emotions are functioning in
a very efficient manner. They are very sensible indicators to what is
going on. And I think you would be in serious trouble if you didn't
feel depressed.*
348. Client: Well, I'm not prepared for that.
349. *Worker: Well, what are you prepared for?*
*(Comment: Rather than "reflecting the feeling" in #348, the worker
changes the sentence from statement of negation [not prepared] to
question about affirmation [are prepared]. Note effect in #350.)*
350. Client: Oh, I suppose I was waiting to cop some, some sort of sick-
ness later, and flee, I want to rest . . . uh . . . a winter something, uh.
*(Comment: Escape via illness or vacation is one way out, but it
would not work in the long run because it would not change the
governing contingencies.)*
351. *Worker: What kind of situation is really going on? Is what I am
saying plausible?*
352. Client: Yes, it is plausible.
353. *Worker: Basically, as I said, you have every reason in the world to
be depressed. Now your wife is miserable, but when she talks about
divorce, she isn't trying to get rid of you, she wants you back. But
what she is saying is, "I am being disappointed. You have certain
things I like, that is what I married you for and I'm not getting
enough of them; I don't see you enough."*
354. Client: Hm-hmm.

355. *Worker: Maybe she doesn't say that when she is angry at you, but I think that is the message; she is willing to take you back. And she says if you undergo psychotherapy, she will take you back.*

356. Client: Then why in the hell does it disturb the hell out of a guy to tell him that he is all right?

357. *Worker: I am not telling him that he is all right, I am telling him that he is in a mess of a situation, and that's why he is disturbed. He is tremendously disturbed. (Pause)*

358. Client: (Client nods his head.)

359. *Worker: Well, let me summarize so far. I think you need help and some guidance to get out of the present kind of situation or this kind of mess. But what I see, I see you in a depression right now, you have these feelings and as I said, you'd be in serious trouble if you didn't have them.*

360. Client: (Client nods his head.)

361. *Worker: (Question 5) Is there anything that we have left out, anything that you consider pertinent that we haven't discussed?*

362. Client: No.

363. *Worker: Anything that you think might have been omitted, or overstressed? Not discussed enough?*
    (Comment: The same question is rephrased—client has required prompting previously.)

364. Client: No.

365. *Worker: (Question 6. Smiles and nods.) Is there any information you may want to know about us, anything we can tell you?*

366. Client: Well . . . not really. Can you help me? What are you going to do?

367. *Worker: The first thing is that we shall set up a regular appointment [discussion follows setting time, etc.]. Then we'd like you to keep some records, a "log" to get a better, clearer picture of your day, your life. Here is a notebook. We'd like you to write in this log for a week, starting when you get up, at least one entry an hour [describes the log].[2] We shall go over this log, analyze it, and try to find out what is happening in very definite terms, what factors played into what problems and also, which is very important, we want to look at those times when there are no problems, when things are going well, and see if we can analyze those and try to understand the difference between the two. I want to stress to you that these logs are very important; they are the raw material that we will be using when we set up a program. When we look at these logs, we'll set a priority of things to work on, and then we will sign a contract. You are used to contracts, being a lawyer. The contract will simply state what we will work on.*

368. Client: OK. It makes a lot of sense. *(Pause)* I want to thank you very much for seeing me, for seeing me so quickly. *(Client turns and goes to the door.)* Tell me, do all your clients leave here feeling so good?
(Comment: The client sees the possibilities of the program, that help is possible and is available.)
End of the initial interview.

Analysis of the Initial Interview

This initial interview can be examined for strengths (current relevant repertoires) upon which a program can be built and that may provide guidelines for a program that will take the client, with this current relevant repertoire, to their terminal (target) repertoire. As often happens, especially in involved situations such as this one (and most situations brought to casework agencies are easily as complicated as this one), the signing of the contract did not take place after the first interview. More detailed information was needed.

Current Relevant Repertoire

This client is vocationally and financially successful, an authority in his field. His job requires continual analysis of possible outcomes, the options available to his clients, and assistance to his clients. It should be possible to program the transfer of these abilities from his professional life to his personal life.[3]

One of his major assets is that he is a valued member of his firm; thus it may be assumed that if he makes reasonable demands on the firm, aimed at increasing his value, they will probably be met. Another asset is the fact that his wife wants the marriage to continue, provided he meets her terms, which are that she and the children get to see more of him. She has also supported him at work. There are *some* pleasures at home. Although it is a complicated family picture (children from previous marriages of each of them in addition to *their* child), they get along well; he enjoys being with them and handles the children well. The family provides *some* pleasure and support for him, but he does not see enough of them. There are *some* mutually enjoyable social activities, and he does report active, probably mutually satisfying, sexual relations.

He claims to be working inefficiently at his profession, but he does have the ability to put in time. There were many other situations in the past that he has handled well (college, and so on). It is possible to formulate a few possible directions that the program might take. For verification, additional information from his logs and from future interviews will be needed.

Tentative Program Direction

Although it is a bit premature to state them other than tentatively, it seems that the following are potential areas for programming. A major element of the program probably should be: (a) the establishment of greater control over his own time at work, so that he can allocate the time necessary to finish his work, as well as complete his professional reading there. If the necessary patterns can be established, he will then be able to spend his time at home with his family. The establishment of appropriate behavioral repertoires at home might not seem to be a problem, for these exist, provided he has the time. His wife also requires some reinforcement from him for her supportive behaviors. His being at home and doing things with her are important to her. His work situation is also important to her, both as it relates to her time with him and to her evaluation of herself in terms of the qualities of the man she married. Other specific outcomes should include: (b) increasing frequency and duration of home-related behaviors; (c) his establishment of patterns of positive presentation of self; and (d) his reinforcement of his wife's behaviors that reinforce him. She may be a strong therapeutic ally, and the program may also include (e) establishment of behaviors on his part which explicitly solicit this.

Ordinarily, the process is to see clients once weekly, although there is no hard and fast rule about this. Sometimes clients need to be seen or contacted more often, and they may be seen less frequently, certainly, at least in the termination process; the process is to "fade out" the therapist. In this case, the second interview was delayed for two weeks because the worker became ill.

The client had continued recording during this time. Generally, recording must be shaped and reinforced, especially in the beginning, on a heavy schedule, every time (CRF). Here, however, it was less important because record-keeping was not only part of his repertoire as an attorney, but it was essential to his making a living. His record-keeping may also have been maintained ("motivated") by hopes generated by the initial interview and the negative reinforcement of his wife's threat to leave him. Regardless of the cause, the records were unusually good for the beginning phase of therapy, and they had confirmed the information obtained in the initial interview.

The Second Interview

The client returned for his second interview on June 10, 1970. While he was still quite depressed, he was nowhere near so downcast as he had been at the first interview. He stated that he had had an "up-and-down week" (a favorite expression of his). He stated that nothing different had happened in the past week.

A contract had not been prepared after the first interview because more information was wanted, as well as a better and clearer picture of the client, his day, and his world. Baseline data were needed, not only to assess the progress or lack of progress of the program, but also to obtain more complete information so that the worker might not intervene prematurely and perhaps upon the wrong problems, and thus extinguish further efforts on the client's part. It has been our experience in the clinic that clients often tend to rush things and attempt to make changes on their own initiative. Sometimes the results have been good, but more often than not the interventions have been premature. This is why the therapist initially takes a greater part in the planning.

Mr. Smith's record-keeping was good and more than adequate for this phase of the process. His days tended to fall into two categories: "bad days" and "less bad days" (his terms). Figures 1a–2b are the records of two days: June 4 was a "bad day," and June 8 a "less bad day."

The client was praised for his excellent logs. These records were then discussed immediately and thoroughly in the session (one of the strongest possible reinforcers a consultant can provide for record-keeping). The therapeutic purpose of the logs is of primary importance; the research purpose is secondary.

The client's days followed a pattern. Whether or not the day started out "well," he arrived at work frazzled by the traffic, and the workday itself was frustrating because he generally did not complete what he perceived to be a good day's work. After a day at work, marred by constant interruptions and fighting with the secretarial pool and characterized by a lack of assertiveness in setting up the conditions that would make his day easier, he would then get into his automobile and buck heavy traffic on the way home. Once there, he would spend a little time with his wife, then he would bury himself in his home office, where he struggled (generally unsuccessfully) to complete his day's work. He would stay in the study until 11:00 or 12:00 at night. On each of these nights his wife would enter the study to get some attention, using the only means she knew, which was essentially an aversive approach. That is, she would interrupt him in his study, demand to know when he was coming out, and an argument would ensue. Negative attention is better than being ignored, and his wife did not want to be ignored. However, on these nights the interaction would end in an argument, and he and his wife either went to bed not talking to each other or, as on June 4, actually sleeping in different rooms. He did not get much work done when he was in his home office because he then brooded about the impending visit of his wife. This pattern occurred in four of the five workdays covered in his records.

One day was an exception. On that day he left work early and, upon arriving home, spent a great deal of time with his wife. He did not work

DATE: JUNE 4

	1	2	3	4	5	6	7
	TIME	ACTIVITY	(setting) WHERE	WHO WAS THERE	WHAT YOU WANTED	(what happened)! WHAT YOU GOT	COMMENTS
T1	7:00 a.m.	Eating breakfast	At home	Wife, 2 yr. old son	A good day. Peace at home. Things back to normal.	Good breakfast. Was patient with son, conversed with wife.	A good start. I'm optimistic—feel good today.
T2	8:00 a.m.	Driving	Highway	Self	To get to work	Slow, jams, got there	Damn traffic, but there's nothing I can do about it.
T3	9:00 a.m.	Mail	At desk	Mr. X. (next desk)	To get mail out of way	Chatter and demands for advice from this young ambitious man	Complied with his request, but seething inside
T4	10:00 a.m.	Work	Desk, on telephone	Constant interruption	Get work done. Get important papers typed.	Delay as no one free in secretarial pool	Frustrated—depressed—work fell off
T5	11:00 a.m.	Same	Same	Same	Same	Same	Just sat at desk shuffling paper.
T6	12:00–1:00 p.m.	Lunch	Cafe	Was alone	Relax—have drink	Nothing	Didn't help. Still depressed.

Figure 1a Daily Events Log for June 4

DATE: JUNE 4

	1	2	3	4	5	6	7
	TIME	ACTIVITY	(setting)! WHERE	WHO WAS THERE	WHAT YOU WANTED	(what happened) WHAT YOU GOT	COMMENTS
T7	1:00–5:00 p.m.	Work	Desk, other offices	Co-workers	Get work done.	Some of work done	Will have to take work home to catch up.
T8	6:30 p.m.	Finally get home	Highway	Self	Get home, relax, catch up on work	Angry at traffic	Finally got home, worn out—had sandwich, spoke with wife, went into office
T9	10:00 p.m.	At desk	Home office	Alone	Get some work done—catch up and possibly be ahead for tomorrow.	Nothing. Sat, shuffled papers—had several drinks	Really discouraged, depressed
T10	10:15 p.m.	Desk	Home office	Wife	To be on good terms with wife	Argument. She wanted to know when I was coming out.	Upset
T11	11:30 p.m.	Tried to sleep	Bed	Alone; wife in spare bedroom	Wife—good relations, good feeling	Tossed and turned—slept poorly, restlessly	A typical night after my wife and I have had a fight.

Figure 1b Daily Events Log for June 4

DATE: JUNE 8

	1	2	3	4	5	6	7
	TIME	ACTIVITY	(setting) WHERE	WHO WAS THERE	WHAT YOU WANTED	(what happened) WHAT YOU GOT	COMMENTS
M1	7:00 a.m.	Breakfast	Kitchen	Wife, 2 yr. old son	Eat, leave on good terms	Very nice breakfast. Talked with wife.	A good start—hope things go well after a so-so weekend.
M2	8:00 a.m.	Driving	Highway	Self	To get to work	Same	Frustrated
M3	9:00 a.m. —12	Work	Office	Self, others	Get work done	Same—did much less than I wanted to.	Same goddamned feeling of depression, uselessness. If I were more adequate, I'd get more done.
M4	12:00–1:00 p.m.	Lunch	Cafe	Alone	Eat	Nothing—had a drink	Don't know which I like less—eating alone or eating with co-worker discussing shop.

Figure 2a Daily Events Log for June 8

DATE: JUNE 8

	1	2	3	4	5	6	7
	TIME	ACTIVITY	(setting) WHERE	WHO WAS THERE	WHAT YOU WANTED	(what happened) WHAT YOU GOT	COMMENTS
M5	1:30–4:00 p.m.	Work	Desk	Same	Same—get things done	Same—only got part of work done.	Got disgusted—left early—let them fire me if they don't like it.
M6	4:00 p.m.	Driving	Highway	Alone	Get home	Got home quickly—beat the rush.	Came home not feeling frustrated for a change.
M7	4:40 —! 6:00 p.m.	Playing with kids, eating	House, back yard, kitchen	Family	Eat, good relations—and then go to home office and get work.	Ate—had good time—figured "to hell with work."	Change. Good evening so far—I want it to continue.
M8	7:00 p.m.—1:00 a.m.	Sitting outside, talking, eating, and drinking	House, back yard	First kids and wife then wife alone	A good evening—good relations with wife and kids	Got just that—talked with wife, went together to bed—had sex.	Why can't all my evenings, and all my relations be like today?

Figure 2b Daily Events Log for June 8

in the evening, but played with his children and, having a good time, decided not to work that evening. He and his wife spent the evening talking and drinking out on the patio. The evening was a very "good" evening (as can be seen in the logs), and that evening he and his wife went to bed happy with each other and had sexual relations.

The difference in pattern between the two days was discussed with the client. He stated that the usual pattern was the day when he buried himself in his home library, although there were occasions such as Monday when he took the evening off. However, he had never realized the relationship between the behavior and the consequences. That is, he had not seen the startling contrast as pointed out during this interview. Technically, his activities were not under proper stimulus control. His office should have been a discriminative stimulus for working; home should have been a discriminative stimulus for enjoying his family and not for doing his office work. This "lack of stimulus control" is an example of the "scrambled eggs" effect. It is common in a great number of behavioral problems.

A familiar example of such "scrambling" is the student who goes to the library to study. After sitting down and depositing his books, he divides his time, generally unequally, between looking at his book and gossiping with his neighbor. He then goes out to the lounge for refreshments and more talk. If the student's behavior were under different stimulus control, he would both study and gossip, but study only when in the library and gossip only when in the lounge; the two activities would be separated.

For both the student and the lawyer client, despite the different topographies of the behaviors, the consequences are the same. Behavior that is not under proper stimulus control soon begins to function as a kind of escape and avoidance behavior for what are perceived by the "actor" to be aversive situations. In the case of the student, the aversive behavior is, obviously, studying. While the immediately reinforcing qualities of escaping studies are tempting, the ultimate aversive consequences (flunking examinations) are enormous.

With this client, his home situation was marked by quarreling and fighting with his wife. Burying himself in the library had the immediate consequence of escaping aversive contacts with her. However, resultant consequences were even more aversive, escalating into a circular effect that damaged his marriage and lessened his performance at work.

It seemed clear that the immediate choice of intervention, the tactic that seemed to promise the greatest and most immediate relief, was to try to establish, as quickly as possible, stimulus control over each of the behaviors and to assist the client to heighten his stimulus discrimination. This became the goal of the program to establish appropriate (to him) stimulus control over work and home behaviors, separating the office as the place for work from the home as the place for relaxing with his family. Improving the quality of the relationships at both places would be a later agenda item, but for the time being the immediate intervention was to establish this stimulus control.

When the worker applied a similar contingency analysis to his work situation, the recordings in the logs, typified by June 4 and June 8, confirmed the information elicited during the intake interview. Regardless of how well the day started for this client, he soon encountered a series of extinction trials. In operant terms, he was engaging in behavior, often a great deal of behavior, that had no payoff for him. The accompanying lack of payoff often lowered the behavior, but was accompanied by a feeling of depression. Whether the depression caused the extinction or the extinction caused the depression is a moot point. For purposes of intervention programming, they went together; they covaried.

Mr. Smith had to take work home because continual interruptions from the telephone and from his colleagues' "chatter and demands for advice" kept him from completing his work. He did not have a secretary who could serve as a filter. As a result, he reported frustration and depression, resentment, and inability to work.

This interpretation is stated in barest outline. The therapist in this case actually went through a "fine-grain" analysis of the contingencies. For example, he examined the transaction of the intrusion from the point of view of other reasons for the colleagues' "intrusive" behavior (possibly a way of being "social") and what was maintaining it (client's reinforcement) and why (the desire to be considered friendly and sociable, as well as following a norm in his firm of giving advice to younger colleagues).

The therapist also went through a process of weighing other solutions. He examined the client's emotional responses of rage in contrast to reported feelings of anger, in terms of whether or not the client was discriminating properly.

Programming is often very complicated, and good programming requires a great deal of skill and knowledge of human behavior, as well as the behavior of a particular client. There is much more depth to behavior analysis than is usually understood or acknowledged.

Setting the Contract

A two-week baseline had been collected, and record-keeping was being shaped. The information received in the initial interview was collated, and a program assessment for Mr. Smith and his family and work situation had been formulated. It was now time to discuss and set the contract with Mr. Smith.

There are priorities in intervention. Situations of immediate importance should be worked on first, but a high priority should also be to provide a situation in which the client can have an immediate success experience. Fortunately, in this case, the immediate target of intervention, the establishment of stimulus control over work and home, fulfilled the requirements of both priorities.

Since therapeutic contracts may be revised, the contract (at this stage) was considered tentative, although this one turned out to be the final contract. The contract had three general target areas (stated nonbehaviorally): 1) to "make work more rewarding"; 2) to improve upon and enjoy a happy home life; and 3) to develop procedures, related to 1 and 2 to achieve these goals. In other words, goals 1 and 2 are terminal repertoires for the client's life; goal 3 is a constellation of program goals that he needed to master in order to achieve goals 1 and 2. The specifics of the contract were as follows:

I. Terminal Repertoires

The two major target areas agreed upon by the client and the worker were the following (statements actually written into the contract are italicized):

1a. *Work:* Work is to be made more rewarding; that is, the reinforcers that have maintained the client's behavior up to now are to be continued, but the response cost in obtaining them is to be reduced, so that there is time during the 9 to 5 office day to do the work currently brought home. Events that compete with the behaviors appropriate to these goals are to be brought under control. The following specific items are to be included in the contract:

1b. *Specified: Your work situation is to be rearranged so that you will be able to complete your daily work during the working day, including the work you now take home. Further, it will be more enjoyable. Specifically, you will do the following:*

    (i) You are to obtain your own secretary rather than working through a pool. Your schedule is to be arranged through her.
    (ii) You are to obtain a larger office.

2a. *Home:* The client is to devote more time to his wife and family. Currently, the problem is not the nature of his interactions during the few hours he spends with them but the fact that he spends too few hours with them. The following specific items are to be included in the contract:

2b. *Specified: Your evenings and weekends are to be free for you to spend with your family. Specifically, you will do the following:*

    (i) You are to spend at least one hour an evening with your wife, giving her your exclusive attention.
    (ii) You are to spend at least one hour each night with your children, giving them your exclusive attention during this hour.

> *(iii) You are to go out with your wife, without the children, at least two times a week.*

3a. *Programming Targets: In order to establish these patterns, records will be required as the basis for their specification: You are to observe and note events and relations in those areas which you can harness to maintain and extend Targets 1 and 2.*

The client stated goals initially either in such negative terms as "not being a mass of tensions" and "not being scared of people," or in such vague positive terms as being able to handle "aspects of things," "enjoy family," and "improve marital relations." The contract is not concerned with eliminating depression, eliminating work problems, or eliminating marital tensions, and so on. Rather, the contract is stated in terms of constructing or putting together repertoires which already exist and which are to be maintained by the natural reinforcers in the environment. The absence of such reinforcers produces the presenting problems. The client will have to develop or reinstate a variety of patterns which will have cumulative effects, as, for example, speaking to his employers to get a secretary, notifying his colleagues that he is to be on call less frequently and at regular times, and discussing his program with his family. Communication with all concerned should have manifold effects in his relations with them. Each of the patterns will also have to be discussed and programmed. The two sets of target goals are deceptive in that, as stated, they seem simple and narrow.

Two further considerations influence the choice of these targets. They are attainable, and they vary in closeness to present repertoires. This closeness indicates ease of establishment or reinstatement, thus providing fast relief. Accordingly, among them are patterns which can be *(a)* considered as steps in a program and *(b)* attained rapidly, thereby reinforcing such programming behaviors as keeping logs, analyzing the data, and meeting appointments. Stated otherwise, the client should rapidly begin to experience success. This should relieve his depression somewhat, and the effects of the depression on his family and colleagues. Note that success would be attained in patterns which are *clearly target-relevant*, hence the importance of consideration *(a)*. The current relevant repertoire, and suggestions for steps in between, will be considered under "current relevant repertoire" and "program notes" respectively.

II. Current Relevant Repertoires (Entry Patterns)

Reinforcers maintain progression through the program to the outcome. Accordingly, the current repertoires must be keyed to the outcome. These repertoires are discussed with the client and recorded on the program worksheets whenever the target outcomes are programmed.

1a. *Background:* Client is a valued member of the firm, and his secretarial and space requirements are necessary for his usefulness to the firm. If this is not already evident to his firm, he should be able to make it so. A question here is: Where do we start? *1b. Specified:* Client is making extensive use of secretaries in the pool. He has the "ear" of the head of the firm, who relies on him. One of the tasks is to transfer stimulus control of those *assertive behaviors*, which exist elsewhere in his repertoire, to the situations where they are lacking. Such behaviors are in his repertoire; he could not have come this far without them. The pattern of apparently good-natured acceptance of outrageous conditions (inadequate office, no assigned secretary) may have served a function in getting him "up in the world." This pattern is still reinforced, but he is now also being punished by its high response cost and the withdrawal of reinforcers associated with his taking work home, among other consequences.

2a. *Background:* His wife's expulsion of her husband has been interpreted as an operant of desperation on her part, which produced the desired consequence: he went into treatment, which she felt might make him more available to her. Obviously, she still wants him as a husband. The task is to bring them together more. The reinforcers are available.

2b. *Specified:* Client spends some time with his wife and children. He goes out with his wife when they are invited out. They invite others to their home. He and the children do things together and enjoy each other (mutual reinforcement of behavior), as do he and his wife.

3a. *Strategy:* He has the ability to analyze relations, as evidenced by the pathology-oriented analyses of his parents' behaviors and of his own inadequacies. These analytic repertoires can be converted into (or supplemented by) analyses which suggest plans for action toward constructional outcomes. Such constructional analyses are already in his repertoire as a successful lawyer, along with the necessary record-keeping system. It is not necessary to establish new repertoires or even to reinstate old ones. Therefore, the task is to transfer these repertoires to the problem areas.

3b. *Specified:* He analyzes and observes his own behaviors and those of others. He notes consequences and their effects on behavior. As a lawyer, he analyzes cases and laws. He also keeps meticulous records and refers to them.

The outlook is optimistic.

III. Change Procedures

The worker has indicated where he hopes to go and what resources he will utilize or possibly develop on the way. These are apparent at the outset;

undoubtedly, the client will develop new ones, or they may be suggested in transit. The procedures are guides which are subject to change.

1. *Work program:* If it becomes necessary to convince the firm that he should have his own secretary and office, he can draw up a cost-benefit analysis in advance; as a securities expert, he is familiar with these.

He can discuss these ideas with his wife and colleagues. By discussing the problem with them, he (a) familiarizes them with the problem (they probably think the changes are long overdue); (b) makes it their cause; (c) gets their understanding and possible support (he has social skills); (d) increases communication with them; and (e) lays groundwork for changes.

Assuming that he gets a secretary and office, he should then work out the scheduling of his time through her. She should keep his appointment log, and he should not be as available as he has been.

He should discuss these changes with the office staff and solicit their advice. He is to instruct his future secretary to block out for him an inviolable period of time in which to read his law journals and to do what he now does at home. No one should interrupt during those periods, all callers are to be told he is in conference, and she is to take messages.

2. *Home program:* He is to discuss scheduling of time with wife and children; they will want the family to stay together and will want to help him. Perhaps he should see the children while his wife is washing the dishes. Perhaps he might help clear the table and wash the dishes with his wife. Perhaps the children should join in. In all events, the discussions should be a family issue. The conferences should signal a new turn.

In a highly visible place, he is to set up a chart for scheduling time. In the event that the requirements are not met one night, owing to some emergency, he is to discuss make-up time with whoever was involved. The family is to monitor this chart. It may come in handy later. (When the children start dating and staying out late, they can keep charts.)

When there are to be exceptions to the schedule, such as, for example, possible Saturday conferences at work, these are to be programmed at least three days in advance.

3. *Programming procedures:* He should write out each of the contract items on a legal-sized pad. Each is to be on a different page, and each is to be in a different folder. (These behaviors are in his repertoire.) He might write at the beginning the type of campaign he might institute

in each of these areas, and when he might institute them. Any notions he has are to be recorded on the pad. In a separate folder, he can record which of the various folders will have priority, which will be worked on simultaneously, etc. He should bring these materials into sessions for discussion, along with his logs and worksheets.

The client, as a lawyer, is familiar with the fact that favorable outcomes are not obtained immediately and often come stage-by-stage, in a sequence. This repertoire can be used in the program.

The items proposed may sound artificial and contrived. People should *want* to go out with their wives spontaneously. They should not have to plan it on paper. These criticisms overlook the difference between well-established repertoires and those which have to be established (or reinstated or transferred). People walk spontaneously and go up stairs, alternating their legs without thinking. The patterns are well-established, or what the psychologist calls "overlearned." However, if you watch a child learning to walk you will see him first switch from moving one foot up a step to meet the other, and later struggle to alternate legs. If driving a car is now spontaneous, try to recall the explicit instructions you were given or developed for yourself.

IV. Environmental Resources and Reinforcers

When the reinforcers required for a program are lacking or are not readily available, special reinforcers may have to be devised or applied, such as points, tokens, words of praise, money, candies, or other special "treats" or "rewards." In such cases, an artificial economy or ecology may have to be constructed. A system should be justified, however, not because it lacks artificiality, but because it has advantages over the alternative contingency systems available. Given the resources and reinforcers readily available to this client, "artificial" contingencies do not seem to be needed here. Early success in attaining some of the steps toward the terminal outcome may be all that is necessary to get this program moving.

1.   Work resources and reinforcers

The opportunity to engage in his professional behavior has maintained progression through an extensive academic curriculum and is even maintaining his homework at present. The homework, however, as was already noted, generates problems. The task is to help him eliminate the homework and "unscramble the eggs" into work behaviors at work and home behaviors at home. The programmer should probably not encourage him to manipulate the professional reinforcers. He can, however, very profitably try to alter the setting of the journal reading.

His superiors and colleagues provide other reinforcers, which might be manipulated indirectly. His supervisors, for example, will probably reinforce assertive behaviors of the types discussed by readily granting them.

2.   Home resources and reinforcers

The family has the economic means to enjoy family living, and they also treasure the client's presence. His wife has encouraged him, in the past, to get him to assert himself. She is supportive, and an important resource. Her cooperation is critical to the success of the program.

His wife should be enlisted immediately. Her husband is probably the best person to get her involved in this task, by discussing programming aims and developments with her. It is strategic to change the order of the targets in the actual contract, which she may see. She is tired of his consideration of work ahead of everything else. Accordingly, the contract order might be: 1) home repertoires; 2) work repertoires; and 3) program repertoires. The success of a program can rest upon such seemingly insignificant procedural details.

3.   Program resources and reinforcers

Advancement in the program is the reinforcer available from the program consultant. It is generally sufficient, if the program is well-conceived, well-designed, and well-executed.

Intervention Procedures

By the end of the second interview there emerged a fairly clear picture of Mr. Smith's life and the ecology of contingencies that were controlling him and it. There was enough information for baseline purposes. Therefore, the contract was proposed, and intervention was initiated with this interview. The weekly worksheet was used (the client worksheet, described in Chapter 4). This form states, in concise, visual presentation, the subgoals for the next week, the repertoires upon which these can be based, and the change procedures whereby the client can progress from his current relevant repertoire to the subgoals for the week. These increasingly approach the terminal repertoire. The following form lists a subgoal on the right, to be accomplished during the coming week, and a strength the client now has upon which he can draw to accomplish this goal, the current relevant repertoire for this particular subgoal. At the bottom is the specific programming aid or assistance to help and guide the client toward the achievement of this goal. The weekly worksheet looked like what is shown in Figure 3.

Name: John Smith	Date: June 17
Current Relevant Repertoire: Session 2	Subgoals:
1. Has ability to conceptualize and some organizational skills, many legal skills. 2. Can enjoy wife and children if not hassled by work, distractions. 3. Go out with wife at least one time this week. 4. Has control over certain contingencies, e.g., can set own hours. 5. Is keeping current record exceptionally well.	1. Arrange schedule so that work done 9–5. Leave materials at work, leave briefcase at work. 2. At home, spend at least 30 minutes with children (if they wish) and at least one hour with wife alone. 3. Enjoy each other's company on the occasions that they go out or have time alone. 4. Analyze work situation and bring in lists of changes that would facilitate goal #1. 5. Keep new records.

Program Notes:
1. Start out day by initiating chat with office mate. Take him into your confidence, tell him you're going to try to complete your work at office. Enlist his cooperation.
2. and 3. Tell kids and wife of resolution; ask for their help.
4. Use legal pads; separate pages for categories.
5. Refer to past records for guides.

Figure 3   Program Worksheet June 17

One of Mr. Smith's strengths is that he has the ability to conceptualize, and he has some organizational and much legal skill. He is conscientious about work. The first goal is to apply these skills and arrange his schedule so that work can be done from 9 to 5. The specific suggestion was offered that he leave his briefcase at work. If he did not finish his work on one day, then it was to be done on the next—at the office. This goal is a first step, albeit a large step, to establish stimulus control over work.

The second goal, which was closely linked to the third goal, had to do with relationships at home. It was obvious that he could enjoy the company of his wife and his children under certain conditions. This appeared from his log on Monday, from the conversations during the second interview, and from the data obtained during the initial interview. Therefore "current strength #2" was that he could enjoy the company of his wife and children if the conditions were "right." Therefore, the second subgoal was to spend at least 30 minutes with the children (if they wished and were undistracted by other activities) and at least one hour with his wife alone. This was linked to the third strength, his enjoyment of his wife's company; the subgoal here, for the week, was to go out alone with his wife at least one time without the children.

The fourth strength was the recognition that he could control certain contingencies at work. For example, he could set his own hours. Therefore, the subgoal for this week (#4) was to analyze his work situation and bring in lists of changes that could facilitate goal #1.

The client was very receptive to the worksheet, especially the Program Guide, in which he himself initiated procedures to stop the daily "waste of time."

In the program notes, the second and third entries are related to the terminal goals of "happy marriage" and "happy home life." The fourth explicitly reiterates his professional skills and is designed to have him realize that he is a skilled person in much demand and much more in control than he has realized. The purpose is to make concrete proposals and to try to program toward them.

The next week Mr. Smith brought in further logs. He continued to use the form that is illustrated for June 4 and for June 8, for these provided the client and the worker with enough information to proceed. Going over the written logs, plus any other items the client wishes to talk about, forms the process of the interview. The content of the interview is not restricted to reading and discussion of the logs. Logs are used as a springboard, a starting point for discussions that will further the client's progress. The client started the interview with, "Well, let's see how well I did" and reported the following progress:

Goal #1. The client was partially successful in the first goal. He kept his work at the office on three of the five workdays. He did take work home on the weekend.

The goal of five days was too high—the step was too large. Making steps that are too large is a common programming error. Shaping should be gradual. All things being equal, it is usually better to make the steps too small, so that they can be achieved, rather than too large, when they will be failed (produce ratio strain). However, the error here was by far overshadowed by the client's apparent delight in achieving the goal on three of the days. He regarded this as a really great achievement, which was seconded by the worker and commented upon most enthusiastically.

Goal #2. This was met on four days. On the days he came home without his work he exceeded the criterion; that is, he spent more than 30 minutes with the children, and more than one hour with his wife. On the two days that he brought home his office work, and on the weekend days, he repeated the pattern of being in the home office. His partial progress was praised and encouraged, and the next step was planned.

Name: John Smith	Date: June 24
Current Relevant Repertoire: Session 3	**Subgoals:**
1. Was successful on three days. Worked at home on weekend. 2. Successful in time with children and wife on four days; on days home without work, exceeded expectations. 3. Went out Saturday night to movies. 4. Made a list of changes at work. 5. Keeping excellent records.	1. (a) Try procedure on all workdays. (b) No work on Sundays. 2. Try to meet criterion (30 minutes with children and one hour with wife) on all weekdays. Spend all day Sunday with children and wife. 3. Repeat on Saturday p.m. and do one thing together on weekdays. 4. Ask for larger office. 5. Continue, and soon we'll have graphs as a visible reinforcer.

Program Notes:
1. Tell office mate you made it last week on three days and want to shoot for more this week. Also ask him how he'd feel if he had present office all to him-self, and explain.
2. and 3. Discuss notion of chart with family.
4. Try to approach head of firm; good list; we'll try them one by one.
5. Try to figure out what to graph on yourself.

Figure 4 Program Worksheet June 24

Goal #3. Met. He went out to the movies Saturday night with his wife, and they both had an excellent time. He reported her conversation as animated, and the evening culminated in sexual relations.

Goal #4. Met. The client made a list of changes at work. Client and worker agreed to focus on one, namely, asking for a larger office. This would have immediate consequences in terms of facilitating work.

Goal #5. Met. Excellent records were kept.

The program worksheet made out that week is shown in Figure 4. It can be seen that the progress made in meeting last week's subgoals was continued, and that the goals achieved are *now* part of the current relevant repertoire.

A comparison of this week's current relevant repertoire with the goals of the preceding week provides an immediate assessment of outcome and program effectiveness. For the next week, he maintained the goals achieved but slowed the "keep work at work" segment down. The worker suggested keeping only Sunday work-free (as compared to last week's goal of the entire weekend). The goal with the children was repeated and was extended to Sundays by mutual agreement. On goal #3, time with wife, the results were so positive that the behavioral requirement was increased to include a "date" during the week. He was asked to consider graphing his behavior—a technique not appropriate for all clients.

Fifth Interview: July 1

The logs indicated that Mr. Smith succeeded completely in meeting most of the target requirements, as indicated in the program worksheet drawn up that day. The worksheet is shown in Figure 5. Mr. Smith succeeded in the goal of not bringing home any work on any weekday and in spending Sunday at home. It was decided to continue this requirement, repeat this task, in order to make it a permanent part of the current relevant repertoire, and to consolidate the gains. The importance of not moving the program too fast cannot be overemphasized.

The client also met the criteria for spending time with his family and achieved the goal of going out alone with his wife two times. They went out to a cocktail party Tuesday night and, although they did not go to the movies Saturday, they went out for a long walk, bought ice cream, and talked. Both found this activity mutually gratifying ("a lot of fun"). It was decided to repeat all three activities the next week (again, to consolidate gains).

Name: John Smith	Date: July 1
Current Relevant Repertoire: Session 4	Subgoals:
1. No work taken home on any weekday. Sunday spent at home with family. 2. Criterion met on all workdays and Sunday. 3. Went to cocktail party Tuesday night; long walk and ice cream Saturday night. 4. Had discussions with head of firm, but on matters other than office. 5. Excellent records.	1. Continue to do all work at work, and reserve time at home for family. 2. Continue to devote stipulated (?) time to wife and children. 3. Continue to go out with wife at least twice a week. 4. Ask for assigned secretary three days a week. Try to figure out ways to get office. 5. Continue records. Start keeping client worksheet.
Program Notes: 1. 2. See preceding weeks. 3. 4. Step too great. Let's substitute smaller step as indicated, try to figure out what can be broadened easily and safely. 5. New worksheet is a chance to display your analytic skills, take over programming. [Note: Therapist missed next session because of illness.]	

Figure 5 Program Worksheet July 1

IBSW

1. Statement of Subgoals	2. Your Understanding of How Stated Subgoals Relate to Contracted Goals	3. Programming Variables: Manner and Extent to Which Subgoals Were Reached	4. Comments and Subgoals/ Program
1) No work taken home weekdays. 2) 30 min. with children and 1hr. with wife daily. All day Sunday. 3) Go out 2 times a week with wife. 4) Ask for assigned secretary. 5) Start keeping this sheet.	1) and 2) Unscramble "scrambled eggs." 3) Better relations with wife 4) Easier work situation. 5) Help me program. Make less dependent on analyst.	1) and 2) No problems about time. Problems about children. Sometimes want to be off by selves. 3) Planned a play, but couldn't get ticket—went to two movies in neighborhood. 4) Surprisingly easy. 5) All right. Sheet is more work.	1) and 2) Feeling much less depressed; in fact, sometimes almost happy! This subgoal easy (so far). 3) Wife and I will join theater guild this fall. Will start going to golf driving range. 4) Will ask for larger office. 5) None

5a. Tentative Next Step(s) for Program: Your Suggestions	5b. Justification: Relation to Contracted Goals	6. Tentative Agenda for Coming Session: Your Suggestions	
1) See comment on theater guild and golf range. 2) Try manipulating working hours. Get in at 8:00 leave at 4:00. 3) Wife and I will join theater guild in fall. 4) Ask for bigger office.	1) Better relationship 2) Scrambled eggs. Also avoid agitation of driving delays, and help work and home. 3) Planning activities. 4) Bigger office will make work easier.	1) Home going better, but wife still not one in. Can we talk about involving her? 2) Ask for bigger office; discuss more work-related items 3) Discuss cutting down on amount of record keeping.	

Figure 6 In-Between Session Worksheet (IBSW)

He did not meet the fourth task of asking for a larger office. He was afraid of the possible repercussions. It was obvious that in this part of the program the steps were too large. Also, the program was moving satisfactorily on several fronts. It may have been unrealistic to expect movement on *all* targets at the same high pace. However, the feeling of achievement even for a partial success can transfer to other aspects of the program.

Success in one area "breeds" success in another area as Mr. Smith had verbalized it the preceding week.

By mutual agreement it was decided to hold off with regard to the office and to switch the target. Mr. Smith was being assigned secretaries on a random basis from a secretarial pool. He agreed that the next step would be to ask for a definite, assigned secretary three days a week, as a starter.

Mr. Smith's records were excellent, and he also agreed that he might start to transfer programming to himself by completing the client worksheet.

Seventh Interview: July 15

The July 8 session was canceled by agreement, since the worker was ill. Mr. Smith had been asked to fill out a client worksheet for the week of July 1–July 8 and did so. The result follows. The client quickly grasped the manifest purpose of transferring the programming function (control) to himself. He stated the subgoals accurately in his own words; they are not direct copies of targets from program worksheets. While goal #1 had been stated positively by the worker, "Do all work at work, and reserve home time for family," the client typically made this into the negative: "No work taken home weekdays." While they amount to the same, there is a difference in emphasis and explicitness: the goal of "no work at home" can also be fulfilled by not doing it at office. This can lead to difficulties.

The relations to contracted goals are well stated. Column 3, row 3 is interesting (see Figure 6). He could not get tickets to a play he and his wife wanted to attend, and so, as shown in column 4, row 3, he made a decision to avert such problems in the future. All independent programming by clients should be heartily applauded, especially programming that may avoid (prevent) future problems.

The request for a secretary was met; it was "surprisingly easy." Reinforcement of this assertive behavior increased its strength and led to the revival of the goal, "Will ask for larger office" (column 5, row 4). In column 2, row 5, the negative note again: the worksheet will "make [one] less dependent on analyst" rather than "make [one] more self-reliant."

In the next steps (columns 5a and 5b) the client is making very sensible suggestions for the program and future agenda (therapy) topics (#6).

For his coming agenda he wanted to talk about specifics to make his program easier. It will be noted that the client himself began to ask that the amount of record-keeping be cut down. This was a realistic request. While such requests can be interpreted in a variety of ways, they are often a sign that the client is thinking of termination. Indeed, from the success of the program, it was not too early to consider termination.

The logs suggested that he had the office work very well under stimulus control, that he had met the criteria of time with his children and had gone out three times with his wife. He was given a secretary not for three but for five days! He was told that this was simpler for the personnel office.

Some program changes were made. Mr. Smith was to spend ten minutes alone with each of the children, talking about one of the child's particular interests; if necessary, he was to plan something in advance if this could not be done spontaneously. Even though he was going out three times a week with his wife, this was lowered to two, and one of these times was to be with another couple. He was also to ask for a larger office. Client and worker began to change the emphasis from *frequency* of interactions to changing the quality of his relationships with his family and at work. Working hours were to be rearranged from the original 9 to 5, to 8 to 4. This change would enable him to eliminate the rush-hour traffic in both directions. The particular nature of his law practice made this innovation quite acceptable to his employer, and this was put into effect. The immediate result was alleviation of the hassle of the traffic situation. This might seem to be unusual, but in a surprising number of cases, especially those involving middle-class professionals, manipulation of hours is possible. Most of us are too entrenched in the 9-to-5 mentality.

The logs were simplified. In the Social Interaction Log, he was to record time, place, audience, what he said, what other people said, and then comment.

The program worksheet made out during that session follows. The first and second procedures are not combined, as the client has pretty much attained stimulus control over work. The programming notes are very general and nonspecific, for the client knows the details, and he is being encouraged to program on his own.

When he appeared for his next appointment, he had attained all of his subgoals, and the subgoals of the previous week were now the current relevant repertoire. He *had* raised the question of his need for a larger office. He was surprised that the firm had been aware of his needs, but shuffling people around would take some time; he would get a new office the first time someone left or was transferred. Actually, he never *did* get the office, for he left the firm (see follow-up), but in the case of this client, the assertive behavior of asking for the office was almost as great a therapeutic triumph as getting the office itself would have been (see Figure 7).

Name: John Smith	Date:
Current Relevant Repertoire	*Subgoals: Subterminal Repertoire!*
1. No work at home in p.m. or on Sundays. 2. Met criteria of time with children and wife two weeks in a row. 3. Went out three times with wife. 4. Asked for assigned secretary three days; got full time! Terrific! 5. Records fine.	1. Try procedures 1 (office work), 2 (family) a third week. 2. Spend at least 10 minutes alone with each child this week, talking about one of their interests (play with youngest). 3. Go out at least two times; one of times with another couple. 4. Ask for bigger office. Change recording procedures, as below.*
Program Notes: 1., 2., and 3. Improve quality of interaction with children, wife unscrambling the "scrambled eggs" beautifully. Let's keep practicing to be sure. 5. Do social interaction record at home. 5a*. Time Place With Whom What I Said What They Said What I Said Comments	

Figure 7 Post-IBSW Program Worksheet

In order to improve the quality as well as the numerical frequency of the interactions, the worker asked the client to change his logs to a simplified social interaction type. The new log proved to be useful in ferreting out remaining problems in his social relations. The following sample "interaction" logs illustrate this type and its utility in this case. The first (depicted in Figure 8) was with his wife and the second (depicted in Figure 9) with a fellow worker.

The first interaction was described by the client as a typical interaction. His wife apparently had one thing on her mind (she wanted to talk), and he had another on his mind (he wanted to work). The interaction ended in an argument. It should be noted that the log is deliberately set up in a form that starts and ends with the speech of the client rather than that of the significant other. The intention is for the client to learn both to initiate and to terminate interactions in a positive way (Goldiamond, 1974). In many angry interactions, one partner portrays the other as starting a conversation with a negative remark, himself answering positively, and the partner ending on a negative note. Here the interaction was begun and ended by the other person, and the conversation *did* end on an angry note. One therapeutic injunction is to get the client, if he does not initiate the interaction, at least to end it positively, or not contribute to the heat by a further angry comment (which produces another, and so on).

INTERACTION LOG: JOHN SMITH

Time	1 Place	2 With Whom	3 What I Said	4 What They Said	5 What I Said	6 Comments	7 Therapist's Comments
10:15 a.m.	Home	Wife		1. Will you clean the garage today?	2. Later. I want to read a brief first.	I was busier than hell and had no time to spare.	Wife disappointed. She ended interaction. You end it in future on a positive note.
				3. (Angrily) You weren't going to bring work home any more.	4. (Angrily) I have to get it done; I'll do it later.		
				5. The hell with you (slamming door).		Did not speak with each other for several hours.	
3:00 p.m.	Home	Wife	1. Let's go get ice cream.	2. I have dishes to do.	3. Do them later.	We got ice cream. Did dishes later. Worked out OK.	Fine. You began and ended on a positive note. Also, showed her you would share with her.
				4. I want to do them now.	5. Leave them for later, and I'll help you with them.	I wonder if she believed me.	

Figure 8 Interaction Log: Home

INTERACTION LOG: JOHN SMITH

	1	2	3	4	5	6	7
Time	Place	With Whom	What I Said	What They Said	What I Said	Comments	Therapist's Comments
9:20 a.m.	Work	Mr. Johnson		1. Can you spare a minute?	2. Yes.	I was busier than hell and had no time to spare.	Don't say "yes" when you mean "no." Related to consequences of wrong SD to Mr. Johnson.
				3. He gave a long story about a case, without interruption.	4. I'm busy now; I don't have time to talk.		
				5. Why the hell didn't you say so before I told you about the case?	6. Nothing.	He's right. I should have said something. He went away angry.	He ended the interchange on a sour note. End (your control) on a positive note.
10:30 a.m.	Work	Mr. Johnson	1. I am sorry I didn't make myself clearer earlier. I'd like to hear about the case now.	2. Told me about the case.	3. Gave my opinion and advice.	Delay as no one free in secretarial pool	Frustrated—depressed—work fell off.
				4. Thanks a lot.	5. It's my pleasure. Ask me again.	I wonder if he believed me.	Act as if he did. You ended the conversation on a good note.

Figure 9 Interaction Log: Work

The client described both interactions as typical. He had postponed cleaning the garage, a chore he had promised his wife he would do and chose to read some work that he had brought home. The interaction took place on a Saturday, a day on which work at his house office was permitted (on Sunday, he was to do no work). He took the work home that Saturday—a kind of "slippage." This was later resolved by including the home on Saturdays as a nonwork site; work on Saturdays was to be explicitly restricted to the office.

However, in keeping with the general therapeutic policy to reinforce positive interactions, the consultant's comment on this interaction was linked with the conversation that took place at two in the afternoon of the same day, when Mr. Smith initiated an interaction with his wife. She reacted as he had in the morning, stating that she had work to do. He persisted and she persisted, but this time he proposed the alternative solution of leaving the dishes until later, when they could cooperate in doing this unpleasant chore. They went out and bought ice cream, talked, and later did the dishes together. The therapist praised both the analysis of the problem and the immediate programming of an alternative solution.

The analysis of the second interaction, that of the interview with a colleague at work, is self-apparent.

Eighth to Thirteenth Interviews: July 29– September 3 (Intervention Concluded)

Mr. Smith came for a total of 13 visits. The remainder of the contacts focused on the details and quality of interaction at home and in the office. At home, the interaction was at first scheduled, then later replaced by spontaneous activity with wife and children, in both planned and unplanned activities. Stimulus control, separating work activity from home activity, was maintained throughout these contacts.

A further problem area remained. Mr. Smith had reported that he was extremely awkward in his interaction with personnel at the office. Therefore, a program was developed to increase interaction with his colleagues. The contract was amended to add "improved relations with others at work." Modeling procedures were used. Mr. Smith was to observe and record how others in the office interacted with one another around the water cooler and during coffee breaks. He recorded how others approached one another for coffee breaks and invitations to lunch. He continued this observation of others when he lunched in the restaurant where others were lunching. These "small-talk" behaviors (his term) had not been in his repertoire under these conditions, nor did they exist with regard to clients, hence his preference for dealing with lawyers, with whom he could get down to business immediately. However, they were in his repertoire when he was with his wife.

The worker and client together discovered that what was lacking in the client's repertoire was the skill to *initiate* interactions—the kind of introductory small talk which begins interactions, keeps interactions going, and which is topographically different for different groups (baseball in some, political indignation in others, and so on).

The second step for Mr. Smith was to continue to observe and analyze the procedures others used to initiate, maintain, and terminate social interaction, and then to begin to use them himself. The program consisted of his beginning short, work-related conversations with other individuals at *their* desks. Much of this was already within his repertoire: others were eager to share his professional knowledge. If the conversation became burdensome or negative, he could terminate by returning to his own desk.

A third step was for him to begin short, nonwork-related conversations, which were to be no more than two or three minutes long and were to be terminated by Mr. Smith. As a fourth step he began to invite people to take coffee breaks with him and to discuss some business during those breaks. The next step was coffee breaks interspersed with nonwork-related conversations.

In a short time, Mr. Smith began to invite others to lunch, and the invitations were reciprocated. By the end of treatment, he was lunching with his colleagues two or three times a week. He regarded this as satisfactory, and he could increase the frequency if he felt the need to do so.

He and his wife had set their vacation to begin in mid-September (their suburban schools started in early October), and termination was scheduled for September 3.

The office situation was under control. He had a secretary of his own, who filtered his contacts. He was next in line for a new office. Most important, he was able to do his office work at work. He socialized with others—on his terms. At home, things went equally well. Mr. Smith was steady, more content, and confident. He had encountered his problems and had overcome them.

Follow-Up

A follow-up six months later, in March, revealed that Mr. Smith had left the firm to become a senior partner in one of his own. The new job not only paid more money but also was closer to his home. Needless to say, he has his own secretary and a large office of his own. Members of his family occasionally drop in, and he shows them off.

Mrs. Smith never did become directly involved in the therapy. However, she did begin to attend evening classes in English. The increasing demands of an enlarging social life (which she found indeed to be quite pleasant) made this a necessity. Relations with the children continued to be on a very high level. In further conversations, first in person and later on the telephone, Mr. Smith reported that he no longer felt so depressed. There were occasional periods of depression, which he was able to analyze and relate to specific contingencies at home or at work. He then tried to program events that altered these contingencies and was hoping to set up others that would prevent their occurrence. At the last follow-up, he reported that things were going well.

Notes

1 The interview has been edited, disguised, and shortened for purposes of presentation.
2 The log referred to is a slightly modified form of the Daily Events Log (Goldiamond, 1974).
3 The fact that the client is a lawyer does not make the task of behavior analysis simpler than if he were engaged in some other occupation, such as teaching, business, medicine, housewife. Consequences and contingencies are involved in behavior in general. The fact that he is a lawyer, and an efficient one at that, suggests that he be approached with the repertoire that is most familiar to him, namely, law. In addition to his skills in legal analysis, he has considerable skills in record-keeping, spending hours on cases, taxes, and so on. Actually, the client is already "analyzing" his situation, but in terms of pathology, not constructive actions; in psychiatric jargon, not specific, observable, and remediable terms.

The Behavioral Contingency Analysis Paradigm

A Brief Tutorial

The assessment and analysis of consequential contingencies is based on a formal model that organizes what we have learned about some important determinants of behavior from a long tradition of controlled laboratory experiments. These have revealed how a number of environmental variables can influence behavior in particular ways and have aptly demonstrated that these variables indeed function in natural settings in the same ways they do in the laboratory. This model comprises the "scoresheet" we will use for understanding behavior.

In Chapter 3 we explicitly define consequential contingency. As noted earlier, it is our Rosetta Stone for analyzing and understanding behavior in context. We shall now further describe the elements that comprise and influence a consequential contingency.

Stimuli: Before and After

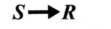

$$S \longrightarrow R$$

The word *stimulus* is one of the most familiar terms in all of psychology. It is familiar to professionals and laypeople alike and is often equally misunderstood or misused by both. This term comes from the Latin, *stimulus (n.)*, which means "a goad" or prod, like the herder's pole that is used for poking cattle in their behinds to get them to move forward. The sense in which the term is used most commonly in psychology preserves this meaning, of a goad—the stimulus event is thought to goad a reaction out of the organism. This meaning is so pervasive that it is often the only one people think of when they hear (or use) the term *stimulus*. That is why it is almost always paired with another term, *response*. In fact, *stimulus-response* may be one of the few concepts most students remember from their first courses in psychology, and it is probably the one given most often by people who have not taken any courses in psychology at all.

DOI: 10.4324/9781003141365-14

> *Light* ⟶ *Action potential in visual receptor cell*
> *Sound* ⟶ *Action potential in auditory hair cell*

As a form of causality, the stimulus-response paradigm, diagramed above, best fits physiological events, like reflexes and reactions to sensory events. The stimulus is a form of energy (say, light, or a disturbance of air waves) that impinges on a sense organ (eye or ear). The energy is transduced into neural events (nerve impulses) sent along axons to the primary visual or auditory areas of the brain. Light and sound are stimuli, and the receptor-cell action potentials are the sensory organs' responses.

On a more gross level, when a physician shines a light into a patient's eye, the iris constricts and limits the amount of light entering the eye (a protective reflex). Or a tap on the patellar tendon (percussive stimulus delivered just below the kneecap) elicits a contraction of muscles that kick the lower leg forward (the "knee-jerk reflex"). Other examples abound: the Babinski, Moro, Plantar, and sucking reflexes; withdrawal of the hand from a painful stimulus; the gag reflex; release of cholecystokinin (CCK) into the duodenum when fatty material enters from the stomach; salivation in response to a bolus of food entering the mouth, and so on.

The S→R model is a special case of the more general paradigm of linear causality, "cause-and-effect" (Cause→Effect), which we have used to great advantage since ancient times. It pervades our descriptions of physical events (codified in such statements as, "For every action, there is an opposite and equal reaction") and has become commonplace in various areas of psychology as well. The condition-action pairs discussed in cognitive psychology take the familiar form: a specific word is presented→an associated word is evoked. Pain and "frustration" are said to cause aggressive responses (Pain→Aggression, Frustration→Aggression). Thoughts are said to cause overt actions (Thought→Performance of some action).

Using this model of linear causality, the first experimental psychologists studied simple perceptual responses to sensory stimuli (in the area known as psychophysics). Following the lead of the physical sciences, psychophysicists presented highly controlled visual or acoustical stimuli to human subjects and measured simple, unambiguous perceptual responses to these challenges ("Yes/No" indicator responses, subjects' adjustments of presented stimuli to match standards or to differ from them, etc.). Later, Pavlov[1] discovered that physiological reflexes could be extended to include stimuli that by themselves did not elicit particular responses: when certain "neutral" stimuli were paired repeatedly with other stimuli that elicited reflexive responses, the neutral stimuli would eventually elicit the same response when presented alone (a process called "conditioning"). This discovery heralded the birth of psychology's focus on "associative-learning" and served as nearly the sole basis for Soviet psychology through most of the 20th century. Conditional reflexes were thought to explain all variety of psychological phenomena, from the "gut-reactions" people experience in vaguely threatening situations, phobias, and whole memories evoked by partial presentation of suggestive stimuli, to more complex repertoires like understanding speech, solving quadratic equations, and reading *War and Peace*. And while there is a certain appeal to the simplicity (or parsimony) of this form of psychological explanation, it has proven to be of relatively little use in relation to the more complex forms of action that generate our greatest and most significant interests in psychology.

At the same time, biology had relied for centuries on this form of explanation. The concept of linear causality led biologists to posit that organisms had the characteristics of their respective species because they contained "entelechy," a form of species-defining energy that drove embryonic development forward along a specific trajectory leading to the adult forms of given species. These "entelechies" were simply present and immutable in the different species (ostensibly from their original creation). Darwin's concept of natural selection changed that view and eventually revolutionized biological thought. In his model, observed historical changes in species were driven, not by the perfection of "entelechies" in some unexplained manner, but by the selective effects of environmental contingencies upon the reproductive success of certain variations in natural populations of organisms. Stated differently, the environment into which organisms were born favored some forms over others. Hence, the reproductive consequences of having some characteristics rather than others resulted in structural changes within breeding populations of organisms. This concept of "selection by consequences" has important and just as revolutionary implications for the way we explain behavior as well.

Control by Contingent Consequences

Let us return to the truth table we discussed in Chapter 3. You will recall we substitute for the variables X, Y, and Z, the terms *occasion*, *behavior*, and *consequence*. Our truth table now looks like this:

X	Y	Z
Occasion	Behavior	Consequence
0	0	0
1	0	0
0	1	0
1	1	0
1	1	1

To review, the same rules apply as before: the event we are calling a consequence *can* occur only if the behavior has occurred on the appropriate occasion. We say the consequence *can* occur rather than *will* or *does* occur, because sometimes behavior occurs on the given occasion, but the consequent event does not follow (as shown in Row 4 of the table). Under these circumstances, then, we say the consequence is contingent upon the occurrence of the behavior on a given occasion but is not dependent upon it. (A *dependency* relation would include the "if (and only if)" part of the contingency rule, but Row 4 of our table would not be true—this means that, in a dependency, whenever the behavior occurs on the right occasion, the consequence always follows.)

We have now defined the consequential contingency in terms of three variables—occasion (Ocn), behavior (Behv) and consequence (Csq)—which may be diagramed as follows:

$$\boxed{Ocn \bullet Bhv \longrightarrow Csq}$$

Compare this to the standard depiction of S→R relations, and there are two notable differences: 1) in our contingency model, the causal arrow goes from the behavior to the consequence, rather than from a stimulus to a response; and 2) there is no causal arrow between the antecedent stimulus (i.e., the occasion) and the behavior—instead, we use the logical symbol for "and," because a contingency relation only requires that the behavior occurs when the right occasion arises (the behavior is not thought to be a simple response to antecedent stimuli).

This three-term contingency serves as the core relationship for our approach to defining various "real-world" factors by their specific influences over behavior.

In our earlier discussion of "stimulus," we classified stimuli as basically sensory events. We may also consider stimuli in terms of their effects on behavior, beyond simple sensation. Skinner in 1938 defined stimulus as a "specified part, or change in a part, of the environment correlated in an orderly manner with the occurrence of a specified response." This is the definition we will adhere to for the remainder of the discussion.

Our three-term contingency includes the two sets of events that are considered stimuli, namely, the occasions (antecedent to the behavior) and the consequences that follow behavior. Let's consider the consequence term first.

In the context of our three-term contingency, we are interested in assessing what effect (if any) the consequence has on the behavior. To do this, we must first examine how likely the behavior is before the contingent consequence has had a chance to exert any influence. This baseline probability of behavior is referred to as its "operant level"—how often the behavior occurs in the absence of an influential consequence. This baseline condition is explicated in the following table:

Occasion	Behavior	Consequence
0	0	0
1	0	0
0	1	0
1	1	0

Note that this is essentially the same as our table of contingency, described earlier, except that Row 5 is now missing (where X=1, Y=1, and Z=1). Thus, during our "no consequence" baseline, we observe the behavior throughout a period when the occasion is sometimes present and other times absent—and the behavior is free to occur at any time. Once we have so characterized the operant level, we are ready to define a consequence in terms of its behavioral function (if it actually has one—remember, this is considered an empirical question).

We now arrange conditions under which we allow the consequent event to follow behavior when it occurs on the right occasions (we restore Row 5 to our table of possibilities). The probability of the behavior (pB) during the baseline condition (let us call this Time One, t1) is compared to its probability once the consequence is allowed to occur (Time Two, t2). That is, we compare pB_{t1} and pB_{t2}. If we observe that the probability of the behavior in fact increases once it is followed by the consequence we have arranged (i.e., $pB_{t2} > pB_{t1}$), then we can define that consequence as a "reinforcing consequence," a "reinforcing stimulus," or just a plain "reinforcer." This is a functional definition of the consequence, based upon its effect on behavior. Because the behavior becomes more likely when followed by particular consequences under the specific occasioning conditions, it is said that the consequence *strengthens* the behavior (hence the metaphorical term, *reinforcer*—as when we pour concrete into the foundation or walls of a building and reinforce the concrete by embedding iron bars for added strength). Simply calling events "reinforcers" does not define them, nor can they be defined simply as "things that are pleasant" for the individual (this was the approach Thorndike took in defining his "Law of Effect"), though they may often be experienced that way subjectively. As noted, reinforcing consequences are defined solely by their effects on behavior. They are events whose arrangement as contingent consequences of behavior increases the likelihood that the behavior under certain conditions will occur again.

In testing our contingency model in the manner described earlier, we consider the Consequence to be the *independent variable* (z, the one we manipulate), and joint occurrence of the Occasion-and-Behavior (Ocn•Bhv) to be the *dependent variable* (x•y, the one we observe). We can now state that the probability of behavior on certain occasions is a function of the consequences that follow the behavior in those particular circumstances, or $p(\text{Ocn•Bhv})=f(\text{Csq})_{\text{under } c}$. This is a specific case of the more general statement of functional relation given in the expression, $y=f(x)_{\text{under } c}$.

To the extent that the value of a dependent variable is controlled or determined by the independent variable to which it is functionally related, then we may say that behavior is controlled or determined by its consequences under certain circumstances.

Reinforcers: Contingent Consequences That Increase or Maintain the Frequency of Behavior

We have functionally defined reinforcing stimuli as events that 1) follow behavior and 2) increase or maintain the likelihood that it will occur again. The most familiar examples of reinforcing events involve new stimuli that are *presented* once the behavior has occurred—stimuli that were simply absent before then. These might include the taste of foods when we eat, the laughter of children when we tickle them, the light that goes on when we flip the switches on lamps, and so on. Stimulus presentations like these may be depicted in the following manner:

In a contingency relation, when a reinforcing stimulus presentation is the consequence of behavior, we can now depict this in a similar diagram:

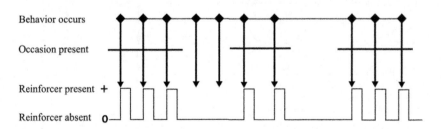

Note that reinforcer presentations occur only after behavior in the presence of the occasioning stimuli, but not when the occasion is absent.

In those instances where the behavior is followed by the contingent presentation of a reinforcing stimulus (S^r+), we define this as *positive reinforcement*—positive in the sense that the reinforcer is presented or added to the situation after the behavior has occurred.

Sometimes, behavior results in the removal or elimination of a stimulus that is already present when the behavior occurs. Stimulus removal may be depicted as follows:

Stimulus present o

Stimulus absent —

In this figure, the baseline condition is the presence of the given stimulus (stimulus present = 0), but occasionally the stimulus is removed (stimulus absent = -).

Just as in those situations when the presentation of certain stimuli can function as reinforcers (i.e., they increase the likelihood of behavior that results in their presentation), so can the contingent removal or postponement of other stimuli. We are all familiar with circumstances in which we take action to remove painful stimuli, as when we remove slivers that pierce our skins, or put on scarves to shield our necks from freezing winds. Desert animals crawl under rocks to escape direct exposure to the burning sun. People often avert their eyes from looking at the victims of gruesome accidents. In all these examples, the behavior results in the removal or elimination of stimuli already present when the behavior occurs, and these kinds of events can also have reinforcing functions.

A relation in which behavior results in the contingent removal of stimuli can be depicted as follows:

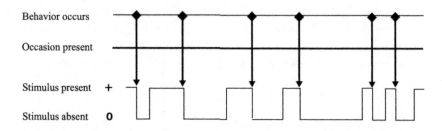

Behavior occurs

Occasion present

Stimulus present +

Stimulus absent o

Here, a stimulus is already present when the behavior occurs, and each instance of the behavior is followed by the brief removal of the stimulus (stimulus absent = -). If the removal of a stimulus increases the likelihood that the behavior will occur again, then we can define the stimulus removal as a *negative reinforcer* (S^r-). The stimulus itself can be functionally defined as an *aversive stimulus* (S^a)(from the Latin root, *avolare*, meaning "to flee or fly away from"). Negative reinforcement, then, involves the contingent <u>removal</u>, subtraction, or avoidance of an aversive stimulus present before the behavior occurs.

Both kinds of contingencies abound in the environment (involving positive and negative reinforcement), some of them quite subtle or complex. Part of our approach to behavioral contingency analysis, then, will be to identify exactly what stimulus events function as reinforcers of the behavior we observe and to define troublesome behavior in functional terms as a means of finding less troublesome, but functionally equivalent, target behaviors.

A brief note on terminology

Behavior whose probability is determined by its consequences is often called *operant behavior*, or simply, *an operant*, because it operates on the environment. An older descriptive term for this kind of activity is *instrumental behavior*, which suggests that it is somehow a tool for reaching a goal, but this implies that the control comes from some internal mental agent who picks the tools the organism works with. Therefore, throughout this text, we use the terms *operant behavior* or *operant* in discussing behavior whose probability is determined by its consequences.

Occasioning Stimuli: *Stimulus Control*

In our definition of the consequential contingency relation, we stated that the behavior can only produce a consequence on particular occasions, or in the presence of particular stimuli. The unit that is strengthened by reinforcement, though, is not the behavior itself, or we would see it occur with higher probability at all times, not just when it mattered. We know this is not the case.

Behavior is exquisitely fine-tuned to the details of the circumstances in which it takes place. The words we read aloud from a text are not simply words we have read in the past—our oral reading is intimately connected point-to-point with the signs and symbols on the pages before us. You don't step on the brakes of your car every time you reach a corner (though that has often paid off in the past)—but you usually stop at corners when the traffic lights facing you are red. Unquestionably, you speak to your professor or employer very differently from the way you talk to your friends (or at least, you should). Children have tantrums in the presence of one parent but not the other, or not when the parents are wearing certain facial expressions.

All these familiar examples reveal the fine-grained control that specific elements of certain occasions seem to exert over behavior. As noted above, the effect of reinforcing consequences is to make behavior more likely in the presence of exactly those stimuli that are required in the definition of the contingency—those specific stimuli in whose presence the behavior can be reinforced (element Z in our truth table). This is not a typical S→R relation, but the result of reinforcement, making the behavior's probability higher in the presence of the occasioning stimuli than in their absence. The reliable increase in the probability of a given behavior in the presence of its occasioning stimuli is referred to as *stimulus control*, and the specific Ocn•Bhv relation whose probability is affected by reinforcement is called a *stimulus control topography*.[2] It is worth noting here that the Ocn•Bhv relation is formally quite similar to what is referred to in cognitive psychology as a "condition-action pair." As such, it is one of several points of entry for behavioral approaches to analyzing so-called cognitive phenomena. Most of education is not about teaching new behaviors, though that is certainly a part of it; rather, a vast majority of instructional programs are concerned with establishing important and useful stimulus control relations that fall under the rubric of cognition.

Stimulus control is *inferred* from the influence certain stimuli exert over behavior—the more probable the behavior is when its occasioning stimuli are present, the stronger or better we consider that stimulus control to be. We can test for such stimulus control by alternately presenting or removing specific stimuli from the environment, and then observing any correlated changes in behavior. When one behavior occurs reliably in the presence of a given stimulus, but not in its absence, we infer that the behavior is under the control of that particular stimulus.

The exact stimulus that we arrange as an occasion for the behavior of interest is defined in terms of the contingency relation we establish. It is precisely that stimulus element whose presence is required for the behavior to be reinforced. To the extent that the contingent consequences of a particular behavior are different in the presence and absence of the precisely defined occasioning stimulus, we call that stimulus a *discriminative stimulus* (S^D). And while stimulus control is inferred from whether or not a particular behavior occurs in its presence, the S^D itself is defined by the contingency, not by its effects on behavior.

$$S^D / S^\Delta$$

This point is important because, in most naturally occurring situations, the S^D is embedded among many other stimuli, all with a variety of attributes of their own. When behavior occurs and is reinforced in those situations, it may often be unclear to us exactly what element of the stimulating environment has gained control over the behavior—this is particularly true in applied settings. In the laboratory or in educational settings, we can try to restrict what specific elements of the environment gain control over behavior through carefully designed establishing procedures, but we are not assured of such control in applied settings unless we actually test for it.

The discriminative stimulus (S^D) is so named because the consequences of behavior differ in its presence or absence. In the absence of S^D, there are still various other unspecified stimuli present. To distinguish this circumstance from S^D, the absence of S^D is referred to as S-delta (S^Δ). Thus, the simplest form of stimulus control may be described as S^D/S^Δ discrimination: in the presence of S^D, the behavior occurs with high probability, but in the presence of S^Δ (i.e., the absence of S^D) it does not. This kind of discrimination is exemplified by the pigeon who pecks a plastic disc on the wall (and obtains food) whenever the disc is illuminated, but not when the disc is dark. Or the case of a child with autism who remains calm as long as he is allowed to clutch a fragment of baby blanket he has had since infancy but throws tantrums if a parent or circumstances separate him from it. The behavior changes as its discriminative stimuli are changed.

In other instances, S^D/S^Δ discrimination involves a more specific S^Δ than simple absence of S^D. For example, the pigeon can be trained to peck a red key (S^D) rather than a green one (S^Δ). A child is taught to distinguish between the letters *b* and *d*, or between the numbers 6 and 9. People will eat bananas that are yellow but not green or black. In other words, some discriminations are between specific S^Ds and specific S^Δs. The precise procedural distinctions between contingencies that make up different kinds of discriminations affect behavior in specific ways that have been characterized in detail in the laboratory.[3]

The Contingency Context: *Satellite Variables*

So far, we have discussed the consequential contingency in terms of the three variables that formally define it—the occasion, behavior, and consequences. And while this is sometimes sufficient for describing behavior in tightly controlled laboratory settings, contingency control in the natural ecology is often complicated by a variety of other variables that can strongly influence behavior. Probably the most substantial difference is that, at any given moment, the natural environment offers myriad alternative opportunities for behavior to occur—and not just the behaviors that interest us, or contingencies we have arranged.

These alternative contingencies vie for control over ongoing behavior, affecting the probability not only of behaviors directly influenced by the available alternatives, but also of unrelated behaviors. The most obvious of these effects is that, often, engaging in one behavior preempts doing something else. Moreover, these alternative contingencies interact in such a way that variables related to one contingency in a specific manner may play a different role in another contingency.

We will refer to these as "satellite variables" because they may be considered as offshoots and "revolve" around the main contingency elements (i.e., Ocn, Bhv, and Csq). They include, as already noted, schedules of consequences, instructional and abstractional stimuli, stimulus props, potentiating variables, available alternative contingencies related to critical consequences, concurrent costs and benefits, contingency-induced patterns, and the history or program leading to the current behavior. For the purpose of organizing our classification of variables, we will distinguish between *intracontingency relations*, those involving variables within a given contingency, and *intercontingency relations*, involving interactions among variables between alternative contingencies.

Intracontingency Relations: The "Referent Contingency"

When we identify behavior problems, we begin by first describing the behavior of interest and its immediate context—the contingency in which it is embedded. Our initial analysis refers specifically to the occasion for and consequences of the problem behavior; hence we will call this our "referent contingency" (the one to which the analysis refers), and we begin by considering the satellite variables associated directly with this relation.

Reinforcement Schedule: The "Contingency Rule"

One of the earliest topics of specific interest in the effects of reinforcement was the so-called partial-reinforcement effect, or "intermittent reinforcement." The question was: "What happens to the strength of behavior when some instances are not followed by the reinforcer?" This issue had theoretical importance related historically to the way behavior itself was regulated "internally." But it also has practical significance because behavior in the natural environment often is not followed by any discernible reinforcing consequences. We have all experienced cases when some mechanical device did not immediately respond to our actions: the car that wouldn't start on our first attempts; vending machines that immediately spit our money back into the coin return slot when we tried to purchase snacks or drinks; computer desktop icons that did not immediately open the files we wanted the first time we double-clicked on them; and lamps that failed to turn on when we flipped their switches. Or, in a social setting: people who aren't heard the first time they ask questions and then have to repeat their questions again before getting answers; parents who tell their children to do something and get no satisfactory response; or standup comedians who tell what they think are their best jokes but are met with deafening quiet from the audience.

When the usual result does not follow a given behavior, does the behavior simply stop, or does it persist in a weakened (or possibly strengthened) state? There is a familiar adage, "If at first you don't succeed, try, and try again." The implication of this advice is that some further attempt is likely to pay off. It reflects common experience with real-life contingencies, and it functions as a "rule" in the sense that it accurately describes the way consequential contingencies actually work. But people don't always follow rules, although their actions often fit those rules. So how does this come about?

Early in the history of research on operant behavior, Skinner, as a graduate student, sought to make his life in the laboratory a little easier.[4] He had been spending a lot of time making tiny, carefully shaped food pellets that could be dispensed by an automated feeder to the rats he was working with. The pellet manufacturing process was tedious and time-consuming, and forced him to spend more effort on pellet-making than he wanted to devote. He reasoned that if he changed his equipment such that, instead of every press on the lever being followed by food, now only every other press was, he could make his pellets last twice as long and he could cut in half the tedium of making pellets. And if he reduced the ration even further to every third or every fifth press on the lever, he could cut his manufacturing time by 60–80%. To his surprise, he found that the rats compensated for the reduced food deliveries by rattling off quick successions of lever-presses that rapidly met the new requirements of two, three, or more presses. This accidental discovery (serendipity!) led eventually to a systematic program of research on the effects of so-called "schedules of reinforcement" on behavior.[5] In our diagram of the contingency, the schedule requirement is inserted as follows:

$$\text{Occasion} \cdot \text{Behavior} \xrightarrow{\text{Schedule}} \text{Consequence}$$

The schedule may be thought of as a "rule" that explicitly describes the relation between the behavior and its consequences in the contingency—how many times the behavior must occur for a consequence to follow, at what point in time an instance of behavior is required, or whether any discriminative stimuli change when the requirements change. And like the general effects of the contingencies themselves, the schedule exerts its characteristic influence whether or not the person is aware of the particular schedule's requirements. Hence, in the natural environment, schedules are typically *descriptive* rules rather than prescriptive (though, our old adage, "If at first you don't succeed. . .," is an example of a loose *prescriptive* rule—it prescribes an action required for eventual reinforcement).

In the laboratory, different reinforcement schedules are procedurally defined by using *counters* (producing so-called ratio schedules, requiring a certain ratio of instances of behavior to reinforcers), *timers* (resulting in so-called interval schedules, where instances of behavior are reinforced only after certain periods of time had passed since the previous reinforcements), and *combinations of these and other occasioning variables*. Extensive laboratory research has demonstrated that such schedules powerfully modify both the short-term and the long-term effects of contingency relations, and it has led to substantial progress in our understanding of how reinforcing consequences affect behavior, not only in the lab, but in the natural ecology as well.

Each of the procedural arrangements defining specific schedules was found to produce *characteristic patterns of behavior that reflect changing probability of behavior over time*. Moreover, each arrangement also resulted in *characteristic patterns of "extinction" of the behavior* (reduced probability of behavior) once the established contingency relation between the behavior and its usual consequences was terminated—different schedules of reinforcement seemed to produce different kinds and degrees of persistence once the contingency relation was broken.

Another of the major experimental findings about schedule effects was that when the requirements for reinforcement were varied from one opportunity to the next (in other words, when the contingency requirements were "variable," or changed after each reinforcer), the probability of the behavior remained relatively constant over long periods of time, with almost no pausing after reinforcements. Conversely, when the requirements remained constant (or "fixed") from one opportunity to the next, there were pauses in behavior right after each episode of reinforcement, followed by either an immediate high rate of behavior that remained constant until the next reinforcement (in those cases when the contingency requirement was defined by a fixed number of times the behavior had to occur for each reinforcer), or a gradually increasing rate of behavior until the next reinforcer delivery (when a fixed time-interval had to pass before the next instance of behavior would be reinforced). These basic relations between schedule requirements and patterns of behavior over time are summarized in the following table:

Requirements	Counter-defined	Timer-defined
Constant ("fixed")	Constant, high rates of behavior, with pauses after each Rf	Gradually increasing rates of behavior, with relatively constant pauses after each Rf
Changing ("variable")	Constant, high rates of behavior, with no pauses after Rf	Moderate rates of behavior, with no pauses after Rf

There are a number of other important variations on these four basic schedules of reinforcement: some involve contingency requirements that alternate with and without changes in explicit discriminative stimuli (called "mixed" and "multiple schedules," respectively); others require that behavior cannot occur again for a given period after reinforcement (called "differential reinforcement of low rates"); and still others comprising choices between two or more requirements presented at the same time for different behaviors (called "concurrent schedules").

These various complex schedule arrangements yield specific and now well-understood patterns of control over behavior. They are important because they approximate the kinds of complicated contingencies we see commonly in the natural environment. Although a thorough acquaintance with the effects of schedules of reinforcement can be useful in understanding complex natural contingencies, further discussion here is beyond the scope of this text. For more complete and detailed treatments of schedule control over behavior, see Ferster and Skinner,[6] and Schoenfeld.[7]

"Packages" of Consequences: *Costs* and *Benefits*

In the natural environment, the reinforcing consequences of behavior are rarely purely beneficial.[8] Whatever reinforcers may follow behavior, they usually do not come without some costs—whether those costs are concurrent aversive stimuli (as suggested by the expression, "No pain, no gain," for people seeking the benefits of rigorous exercise), or lost opportunities for obtaining other benefits that are preempted when we engage in one choice rather than another (sometimes called "opportunity cost," as when studying for an upcoming test causes a student to miss a fashionable party).

We can think of the joint consequences (concurrent costs and benefits) of a given contingency as being "bundled" together and having composite effects on behavior. The relative "payoffs" of available alternative contingencies make up the choices we undertake every moment we are behaving.

$$\text{Occasion} \cdot \text{Behavior} \xrightarrow{\text{Schedule}} \text{Csq (Costs/Benefits)}$$

Sometimes, the reinforcing consequences of one contingency will be the same as those of an alternative, but the costs associated with the first will be greater than those of the second: in such cases, the behavior will often be controlled by the less costly alternative (in decision theory, this choice would represent a "minimax strategy,"[9] *mini*mizing the *max*imum cost of the choice). For example, a student could (a) study hard for an exam, get a passing grade, but miss a good party; or (b) go to the party, later cheat on the exam, and get the same passing grade. With a choice like this, students often engage in the behavior that costs less (passing grades are often relatively weak reinforcers, so missing a good party is worse than the low risk of getting caught cheating).

In other instances, the costs of two alternatives will be the same, but their benefits will be different: here, the behavior often will be controlled by the contingency with the highest payoff (called a "maximin strategy," *maxi*mizing the *min*imum gain). On the way to a party, a student goes to a liquor store and is confronted by a choice between two bottles of wine—one is a liter of good Chilean red wine, and the other is a gallon of muscatel for the same price. Our reveler buys the latter.

Other combinations of costs and benefits result in other "strategies." In behavioral ecology, common strategies include "optimization," "melioration," and various mixed approaches.

Hence, the relative costs and benefits of alternative contingencies are important determinants of which specific behavior will occur in a given situation. In subsequent discussions, we will assess these "bundled" consequences in terms of a "payoff matrix," for comparing the relative costs and benefits of the alternative contingencies. This payoff matrix is crucial to our understanding of why certain patterns of disturbing behavior occur and how we might best approach treatment.

Instructional and *Abstractional* Stimuli

Discriminative stimuli control behavior in very precise ways—not only whether the behavior occurs in the first place, but also what exact form of the behavior occurs and with what specific aspect of the discriminative stimulus the behavior is correlated. The written letters, C, A, and T, when combined, control the spoken word "cat," not "dog" or "bird," but they might also evoke the words, "animal" or "pet," depending on the specific instructions given. A red traffic light leads us to step on the brake, not on the gas pedal. But when the same traffic signal turns green, releasing the brakes and stepping on the gas is appropriate. The color of the signal is the specific aspect of the traffic light that influences our behavior.

$$S^D_a \qquad S^D_i$$

Occasion • Behavior $\xrightarrow{\text{Schedule}}$ Csq (Costs/Benefits)

Instructional stimuli (S^D_i) comprise elements of the occasion that specify *how* we behave with respect to the discriminative stimulus. For example, a history teacher points to the date, "1066" (the S^D) and asks the student, "What important event happened in this year?" (the S^D_i). The student says, "The Battle of Hastings." The teacher says, "Right," points again to the date (same S^D), but now asks the student, "What historical person is associated with this event?" (a different S^D_i). The student now answers, "William the Conqueror." *How* the student responds to the date is altered by the instructional stimulus (S^D_i) presented with the date (S^D). (The date 1066 may also be considered the dimensional S^D (or S^D_d) and represents *what* is occasioning our response [see Goldiamond, 1966; Layng, Sota, & Leon, 2011].)

Not all instructional stimuli are made up of words, like the ones our teacher presented to the student here. Under most circumstances, people's facial expressions (S^D_i) can similarly affect what we say to them—whether we give them bad news, ask them for favors, reveal our secrets to them, or lie to them about certain matters—their facial expressions can change what we say or how we otherwise behave toward them in a variety of situations. Tellingly, utterances by a person with Autism Spectrum Disorder may not be effectively controlled by their listeners' facial expressions.

Other aspects of the occasion can function differently. When our teacher pointed to the date written on the blackboard, the pointer actually touched the space next to the date, not the date itself. Yet the student responded to the date. Why was the behavior controlled by the text near the tip of the pointer rather than by the blank green or black space[10] the pointer actually touched? In the past, student's answers were reinforced only when nearby text, rather than other aspects of the blackboard controlled them. Children learning to name colors are often presented objects or shapes that are the same except for their colors; when they name the correct colors of objects, they are told, "Correct, that's red!" or given some other confirmation. Specific attributes of the discriminative stimulus (like color, size, shape, orientation, and so on, for visual stimuli, or pitch, loudness, and tone, for auditory stimuli) gain control when behavior in their presence is reinforced differentially. This kind of control that emerges by direct interaction with discriminative contingencies is referred to as "abstractional control," and the stimulus attributes are called "abstractional stimuli" (S^D_a).

Although control by specific attributes of the discriminative stimulus may arise by direct interaction with the contingencies (establishing S^D_a), these same patterns of abstractional control may be brought subsequently under control of instructional stimuli (S^D_i). This is evident when parents present, say, a toy fire truck to their children, and ask, "What is this kind of truck called?" or "What color is this truck?" "What is this truck used for?" "What sound does it make?" These questions will come to evoke appropriate answers when the child's responses to each attribute of the truck are reinforced following presentations of each of the particular instructional stimuli.

Stimuli in the Background: *Stimulus Props*

The great actor, Sir Richard Burton, once staged Shakespeare's play, *Hamlet*, on a dark set, with the actors speaking their lines while sitting on stools facing each other under a single spotlight throughout the play—no Elsinor Castle in the background, no throne-room, no ramparts, no graveyard, no swords or vials of poison. Yet, even without props or any movements off their seats, the actors' performances were superb, and the audience was left with the distinct impression they had actually seen the castle, sword fights, and the rest. The missing props turned out to be unnecessary for the actors' doing the play effectively.

Suppose we have another staging of the same play at a local high school, this time with the usual props in the background. Everything goes well during rehearsals, yet when opening night arrives, in the middle of the first act, one of the prop castle walls tips over during the ghost's entrance—the actors who had performed flawlessly during rehearsals now flub their lines and seem to be lost for a moment. Though normally static props are not crucial to the action, now, when they change unexpectedly, they disrupt the previously stable performances of the actors.

Whenever behavior occurs, there are always stimuli in the background that are irrelevant to the prevailing contingencies. We call these "stimulus props." Like the props in the background of a play onstage, these stimuli are not absolutely necessary to the action (though they may help "set the mood"). Nevertheless, changes in these background stimuli can momentarily disrupt behavior in the contingency.

Several common ways of describing these familiar disruptive effects include words like *distraction*, *diversion*, and *interruption*, while changes in the stimulus props themselves (abbreviated SS^P) might be referred to as "background noise."

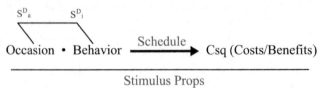

Stimulus Props

A classic study by Azrin (1958) on some behavioral effects of "noise"[11] revealed: 1) a change in background stimuli ("white noise" in an otherwise quiet experimental space) would immediately disrupt well-established ongoing behavior; 2) the disruption was only temporary—when the noise occurred repeatedly, its disruptive effects diminished until eventually it produced no demonstrable effects (this process is called "habituation"); and 3) once background noise was made constant and no longer disrupted behavior, the momentary *elimination* of that noise *would*. Moreover, when noise (or its absence) is correlated with the opportunity for reinforcement in a contingency relation, the noise (or its absence) will function as a discriminative stimulus. Finally, at higher intensities, noise functioned as an aversive stimulus—the subjects would work to escape from or avoid the noise, and its delivery contingent on instances of behavior had punishing effects.

There are several ways in which changes in stimulus props and the momentary disruption they cause can be important in the assessment and modification of behavior. One way has to do with the contingency analysis of behavioral deficits and the incidence of problem behaviors that fill in the gaps.

People often learn or practice new skills in settings that differ from the places where they will need to use those skills. For example, students typically will study for final exams in their university courses, for Graduate Record Exams (GREs) or Medical College Admission Tests (MCATs), in quiet, private environments, like their dorm rooms or isolated library carrels. When they actually take these exams, they are usually seated in large, crowded rooms with unfamiliar sounds and many other new background stimuli SS^P) that may now distract them. In the end, many of these students will feel they did not perform as well as they thought they might, given their careful preparation for the exams. They simply couldn't remember some of the materials they felt confidently about going into the exams.

This problem pervades nearly all applied programs that seek to establish useful skills and repertoires for their clients, whether in educational, clinical, rehabilitative, or preventative settings: how to ensure that clients will be able to use new skills effectively in their natural environments once they have left the training setting. Most basic textbooks on behavior modification address the issue in chapters on "programming for generalization,"[12] which describe strategies for varying background stimuli during training in such a way that the conditions under which a new behavior is learned resemble the final natural environment in which the behavior will be used, to facilitate the transfer of skills from training to target settings.

The background stimuli that function as SS^P are not necessarily restricted to the external environment—they may also involve physiological variables that act as interoceptive stimuli. There is an entire area of behavioral pharmacology (or psychopharmacology) devoted to "state-dependent learning" (see e.g., Overton, 1984). In this area of research, subjects are trained typically to engage in specific new behaviors while under the influence of drugs that have strong physiological effects. Throughout their training, the drugs remain in their systems, but subsequently the subjects are tested without the drugs, and the new behavior ceases to occur, as though it had never been learned in the first place. Once the drugs are administered again, the behavior recovers immediately. A prototypic drug used in this line of research was methamphetamine ("speed"), often used by students while they study for exams. How many students who have used the drug while studying have found that, when they later took their exams without the drug in their systems, they could not recall material they had studied extensively? Another instance involves patients who, medicated while in psychiatric hospital programs, learn to engage in new coping behaviors, but upon discharge, stop taking their medications and fail to continue using their new skills. These examples demonstrate some *simple* disruptive effects of changes in stimulus props on well-established behavior, but more complicated problems can arise in some other cases, which we will discuss in the section on the influence of alternative contingencies.

Altering the Effectiveness of Contingency Elements: *Potentiating Variables*

So far, we have been concerned first with defining behavior itself, and then those elements of the contingency comprising straightforward stimulus events—antecedent stimuli (S^D, S^D_i, and S^D_a), background stimuli (SS^P), consequential stimuli (S^{r+}, and S^r, costs and benefits), and rules describing the occurrence of consequences in relation to instances of behavior (schedules of consequences). We now turn to another set of variables that subsumes what traditionally would be thought of as "motivational" phenomena, but also includes other arrangements whose classification together is based solely on their common influences over other elements of the contingency.

People are sometimes moved (or "motivated") to seek out food or water, and at other times not. Low ambient temperatures make them seek out warmth (by getting closer to a nice fire or by putting on thick sweaters or coats), while high temperatures lead them to cool off (by shedding as many of their clothes as modesty allows or by jumping into a cold shower or swimming pool). Perhaps the most familiar type of explanation in such cases is that we seek out food because we feel hungry, water because we are thirsty, and so on. Accordingly, hunger and thirst have been considered to be "internal drive states" or physiological "motivational forces" that push out the behavior appropriate to reducing their particular effects.[13] In this approach, people are said to eat or drink in order to reduce their hunger or thirst drives—in other words, hunger and thirst function behaviorally as aversive stimuli, and eating and drinking under these circumstances are negatively reinforced (by reduction of these apparently aversive drive states).

We often hear these kinds of familiar explanations for a variety of behaviors and situations. People are said to behave aggressively because they feel angry. Others cry because they feel sad. Children get into mischief because they have curiosity. Some psychologists have posited almost as many drives as there are behaviors in the human repertoire and have arranged these drives in hierarchies that are said to reflect their relative strengths.[14] Hunger and thirst drives are higher on the list than, say, curiosity or the need for friends, and so on.

But what have we really said with explanations like these? People eat because they are hungry. How do we know they're hungry? Because they are looking for something to eat, or talking a lot about eating, or putting objects like pens and paperclips in their mouths. Sometimes, we infer that they must be hungry because they haven't eaten anything in the past six hours. But usually, the drive is inferred from particular behaviors we see occurring. Aside from being circular, this kind of inference also begs the question, "Can we find any physiological manifestation of this kind of drive?" The answer, after more than 60 years of research in physiological psychology, has been a disappointing "No." Numerous studies on hunger, thirst, and aggression have revealed curiously contradictory evidence about how eating, drinking, and aggressing are regulated physiologically, none of which supports any simple drive theories.

But let us go back to our passing comment about inferring hunger from the observation that somebody has not eaten for hours and folk wisdom reflected by such statements as "Absence makes the heart grow fonder." Psychologists often refer to food, water, or any other kind of deprivation as "drive operations," because they purportedly increase the hunger, thirst, or other drives, respectively. Nevertheless, what we actually observe in these instances is that when people are deprived of these commodities, they are likelier to engage in behavior that has been reinforced by acquiring them. In other words, deprivation makes certain reinforcers momentarily more potent. In accord with this, we will call such operations (or procedures) *potentiating variables*,[15] because they increase the potency of certain consequences of behavior (like obtaining food after being deprived of it for a time or obtaining water after hiking in the desert for an hour without water).

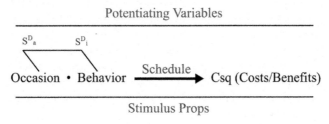

Another term used to refer to such arrangements targeting behavioral consequences is *establishing operation*, suggested first by Jack Michael— these are procedures that establish given events as reinforcers. The term was later changed to *motivating operation*.[16]

Any arrangement or procedure that increases the potency (or power) of certain consequences to control behavior in a contingency relation is a potentiating variable. This formulation has the virtue of defining the effects of such procedures in terms of their observed effects on behavior, and not on any unobservable drive states that may or may not be present. We do not need a hypothetical intervening physiological drive to explain the observed relation, and physiologists are free to study how the operations materially affect the organism, whether or not such a drive eventually presents itself.

Deprivation is but one kind of potentiating variable for increasing the strength of reinforcers. The old adage about being able to lead a horse to water but not making him drink grossly overstates the case. Take the horse past a salt lick beforehand, and when he finally reaches the water, he'll likely drink. Bartenders know this trick quite explicitly: they put out free peanuts, nachos, beef jerky, and other salty treats; kick up the temperature in the bar; or dehumidify the air in the room; all done to increase the likelihood that patrons will order more drinks. Anyone who has given blood at the local blood bank, or bled profusely from a wound, experiences a strong craving for something to drink afterward. Eating cheese or other colloidal foods will increase the probability the person will also seek out water. There are several different ways in which obtaining water can be made a powerful reinforcer of behavior, and each of these has quite different physiological mechanisms associated with it.

This holds true for all kinds of reinforcers. For example, money can be made more potent by giving people a greater variety of worthwhile goods or services to purchase[17] or less potent by other arrangements. Consider the following: Your professor asks you to help paint her garage over the weekend, and she says will pay you $50 to do so (it's a small garage, so you think this is a good deal); on Monday, after you have been paid, you find out that one of your classmates was paid $100 to paint an even smaller area in the professor's basement; suddenly, the $50 you earned doesn't seem so great, and you feel angry about what you now think was a bad bargain. The potency of reinforcers can be altered by many different means.

Another arrangement that can change the potency of reinforcers involves restricting behavioral alternatives. By withholding the opportunity to engage in a certain high probability behavior (a form of deprivation), we can make it potent as a reinforcer by making it contingent upon other available alternatives that, by comparison, are less likely to occur (an application of the so-called Premack Principle). Restricting access to a good ski hill by charging hefty lift fees makes it likelier someone will work at a menial job during the week to earn enough money to ski on the weekends (if, because of their histories, they are strongly inclined to ski).

Elements of the contingency other than the consequences may also be made potent by specific procedures. For example, discriminative stimuli may be rendered more effective by enlarging them or otherwise making them more noticeable (as when big, bright red letters are used for "Exit" signs, important words in a text are underlined, or certain advertising signs are lighted and rendered in bright colors rather than dark and printed in black and white).

Contingency-Induced Behaviors

When currently occurring behaviors are interrupted by changes in stimulus props, punishment, extinction, physical restraint, or by any other means, different behaviors will occur in their absence. These patterns are called contingency-induced behaviors.

Sometimes, these emergent behaviors may create new problems in their own right. Very commonly, they involve emotion-related behaviors, particularly troublesome aggressive behaviors, or other previously successful disturbing patterns that had subsided with the therapeutic establishment of the now-disrupted behavior (a phenomenon often called "regression"). Sometimes, novel behaviors (usually variations or new combinations of older patterns) will occur. And once a recently established behavior is interrupted and older behavior it was meant to replace recurs, or a novel pattern appears, that emergent behavior itself may be reinforced and become persistent as a new problem. These patterns may be considered as adjunctive[18] to those that are part of the contingency. Historically reinforced behavior may reoccur when current behavior decreasing in frequency or if reinforcement is terminated, a process called resurgence.[19]

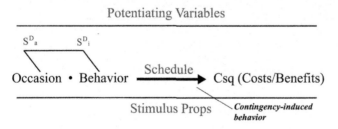

Programing and History

An important variable in our analysis is that of the program. A program is a sequence of contingencies with changing criteria that leads to an outcome. Simple shaping by successive approximations is one type of program. Reinforcing behavior in the presence of one stimulus and not another until the behavior occurs only in the presence of one stimulus is a program. Carefully arranging stimulus sequences such that a stimulus comes to control a behavior with almost no errors is a program. Escalating aggressive behavior until one prevails is a program. Ignoring more and more nagging before giving in is a program. Recognizing better and better drawings is a program. In essence all our behavior is a function of a program. But all programs are not the same and can have a variety of different effects even though the outcomes are similar. Discriminations between stimuli programed with trial and error procedures and those programed with errorless procedures may have similar outcomes, responding to S^D but not S^Δ. However, when stimuli that have values between S^D and S^Δ train to respond to red but not to yellow, and then present orange, those trained with the standard S^D, S^Δ procedure respond to orange, but not as strongly as red; those trained errorlessly do not. In a study conducted by Gordon L. Paul and colleagues,[20] psychotropic medication was shown to have different effects given different treatment programs. Layng et al.[21] were able to program a range of complex component repertoires that culminated in learners achieving a remarkable degree of reading comprehension.

When we consider behavioral history, we are engaging in a *retrospective* attempt to reconstruct possible past programs—contingency sequences. When we develop a program, we are attempting to *prospectively* specify a sequence of contingencies. We can represent these as follows:

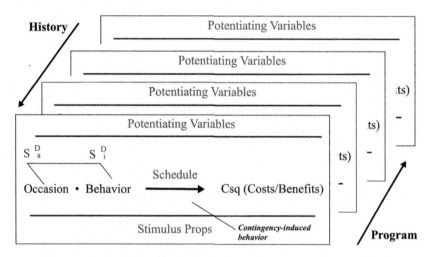

Intercontingency Relations: *Alternative Contingencies*

Throughout this book we have stressed that looking at a single contingency is inadequate. We may hear such terms as *approach/avoidance behavior*, *approach/approach conflicts*, and *behavior allocation,* among others. Each of these terms describes the effects of multiple contingencies on our behavior. Stimuli we may want to escape or run away from may have to be encountered in order to obtain a consequence critical to us. We may feel we want to both run away and go forward. We may have to decide between equally appealing universities, or we may find ourselves doing one thing for a while and then switching and doing something else. There are many ways in which contingencies combine to determine behavior, and to overlook them only provides an incomplete account. This book has emphasized the importance of a nonlinear analysis in understanding the matrices these alternative contingencies create and their importance to clinical practice.

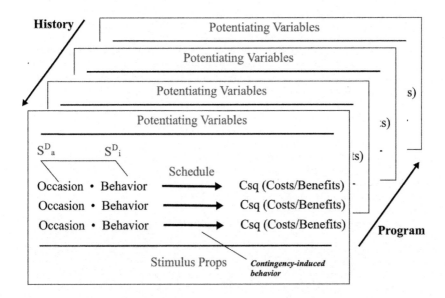

Notes

1 1927
2 The term, stimulus control topography, is meant to refer to the exact form of stimulus control at play when behavior occurs—exactly what occasioning stimuli and what behavior are involved, after Ray & Sidman, 1970
3 See Goldiamond & Thompson, 1967/2004
4 Skinner, 1956, A Case Study in Scientific Method
5 Ferster & Skinner, 1957
6 1957
7 1970
8 This is also true of behavior studied in the laboratory, but there, we typically arrange the experimental environment so that costs are minimized and the benefits of certain choices by our subjects strongly outweigh all other alternatives (in a sense, we actually leave them "no choice" but to behave as we arrange for them to do).

9 Like the "rules" arranged in schedules of reinforcement, these decision "strategies" may be *descriptive* (describing an economic rationale for an observed choice, *as though* the behavior followed the strategy), or *prescriptive* (specifying which choice *should be made* for the behavior to be considered economically rational).
10 Some "blackboards" are really green.
11 Here, "noise" refers specifically to changes in previously static background stimuli, not to noxious or potentially dangerous sound levels (like jet engines and live rock concerts produce) that can damage one's hearing.
12 The use of the term *generalization* here should not be confused with the classic phenomenon of "stimulus generalization."
13 Physiological models refer to these kinds of drives under the general heading of "homeostasis," a tendency of physiological systems to adjust back to some optimal level if they deviate from a previously set point (oddly enough, actually called a "set-point").
14 For example, Maslow (1943) constructed a "needs hierarchy" to organize empirical observations about the relative importance of various motivational variables (needs) in relation to human behavior. Various homeostatic theories have been offered to explain these hierarchic motivational forces (e.g., Stagner, 1977, cf. P. T. Young, 1959), though none is yet in accord with physiological findings. Nevertheless, the methodology of hedonic scaling is widely used in industrial research into factors that influence consumer product preferences.
15 see Goldiamond & Thompson, 1967/2004; Brady, 1968; Goldiamond & Dyrud, 1968
16 1983; for a later treatment, see Langthorne & McGill, 2009
17 see Cohen & Filipczak, 1971
18 Falk, 1977
19 Epstein & Skinner, 1980; Layng et al., 1999
20 Paul, Tobias, & Holly, 1972
21 2011, also see Sota, Leon, and Layng (2011); Leon, Layng, and Sota (2011)

Comparison of Topical Direct, Topical Functional, Topical Nonlinear, and Systemic Nonlinear Interventions

Key: DP = Disturbing Pattern; AAP = Available Alternative Patterns; TP = Target Pattern

Topical: Direct*	Topical: Functional*	Topical: Nonlinear*	Systemic: Nonlinear*
Approaches include: Reward and punishment programs, specified activity monitoring and feedback (SuperBetter, StickK, etc.).	Approaches include: Motivational Interviewing, Acceptance and Commitment Therapy, Functional Analytic Psychotherapy.	Approaches include: Constructional Clinical Behavior Analysis, some forms of Behavioral Economics.	Approaches include: Constructional Systemic Clinical Behavior Analysis, some forms of Behavioral Economics.
DP = f (maintaining variables)	DP = f (maintaining variables)	DP = f (matrix resolution)	DP = f (matrix resolution)
DP considered maladaptive.	DP considered maladaptive or inflexible.	DP considered a rational choice given the available alternatives.	DP considered a rational choice given the available alternatives.
Consequences maintaining DP typically not considered.	Consequences maintaining DP considered.	Consequences contingent on DP considered, consequences contingent on AAP considered.	Consequences contingent on DP considered, consequences contingent on AAP considered, interaction between matrices (sets of alternatives) and their consequence considered.

DOI: 10.4324/9781003141365-15

Key: DP = Disturbing Pattern; AAP = Available Alternative Patterns; TP = Target Pattern			
Topical: Direct*	**Topical: Functional***	**Topical: Nonlinear***	**Systemic: Nonlinear***
DP focus of intervention, eliminative procedures, or train or reinforce incompatible or other behaviors, TP.	DP focus of intervention. May try to substitute alternative behaviors, TP, that produce the same consequence. May attempt to alter the function of certain (often private, DP) aversive stimuli. Other patterns may be encouraged that provide additional benefits (reinforcers).	Matrix in which both DP and AAP occur is the focus of intervention. May try to substitute alternative behaviors, or reduce costs for available alternatives. TP are patterns that resolve the matrix by providing the same or other benefits at lower cost.	DP typically not the focus of intervention. TP are patterns that resolve the matrices by providing the same or other benefits at lower cost. Consequences may be different from those maintaining DP. Benefits of TP often depotentiate consequences of DP in the matrix: DP typically drops out with no direct attention.
Thoughts are considered negative or positive. Positive thoughts practiced, negative to be reframed.	Thoughts are may be categorized as negative or positive. Certain practices, e.g. diffusion, may be used to change thoughts. Thoughts are to be experienced without judgment, examined and accepted.	Thoughts are seen as private experiences that are a product of matrix relations, and are used as indicators of where one needs to intervene. No attempt is made to directly change thoughts. Thoughts change as contingencies change.	Thoughts are seen as private experiences that are a product of matrix relations, and are used as indicators of where one needs to intervene. No attempt is made to directly change thoughts. Thoughts change as contingencies change.

Key: DP = Disturbing Pattern; AAP = Available Alternative Patterns;
TP = Target Pattern

Topical: Direct*	Topical: Functional*	Topical: Nonlinear*	Systemic: Nonlinear*
Emotions are often ignored or treated as by-products, or as respondent (Pavlovian) responses: strategies may be provided to try and directly change them.	Emotional events (which are often private) are to be changed as to their function. Instead of feelings to be avoided, they are to be experienced and accepted. More proactive goal directed behavior encouraged despite experienced emotions.	Private emotions seen as indicating matrix relations. Sensitivity to them is trained as indicators of what is happening and needing change. Expressed emotions (emotional behavior) may be patterns that have their own benefits.	Private emotions seen as indicating matrix relations (including interacting matrices). Sensitivity to them is trained as indicators of what is happening and needing change. Expressed emotions (emotional behavior) may be patterns that have their own benefits.
Intervention often involves reducing DP or increasing TP; regimens feature self-monitoring, feedback, reward or punishment (tangible or social): direct contingency management.	Intervention involves finding what maintains DP and finding less costly substitutes for DP, or changing the function of often "covert' stimuli. May involve becoming more focused on the "now" and how one responds (mindfulness). Goal setting based on personal consequences (values) often a component.	Intervention involves resolving a consequential matrix, or building new patterns that once attained, result in the DP no longer being required. Individuals become very sensitive to the world around them, using thoughts and feelings as guides to analyzing environmental events and making changes.	Intervention involves resolving consequential matrices, or building new patterns that once attained, result in the DP no longer being required. Individuals become very sensitive to the world around them, using thoughts and feelings as guides to analyzing environmental events and making changes.

References

Andronis, P. T., Layng, T. V. J., & Goldiamond, I. (1997). Contingency adduction of "symbolic aggression" by pigeons. *The Analysis of Verbal Behavior*, *14*, 5–17.

Azrin, N. H. (1958). Some effects of noise on human behavior. *Journal of the Experimental Analysis of Behavior*, *1*(2), 183.

Azrin, N. H., Holz, W., & Goldiamond, I. (1961). Response bias in questionnaire reports. *Journal of Consulting Psychology*, *25*, 324–326.

Bem, D. J. (1972). Self-perception theory. In L. Berkowitz (Ed.), *Advances in experimental social psychology* (Vol. 6, pp. 1–62). New York, NY: Academic Press.

Brady, J. V. (1968). The biology of drive: A report on NRP work session. *Neurosciences Research Program Bulletin*, *6*(1), 19–21.

Cardinali de Fernandes, R., & Dittrich, A. (2018). Expanding the behavior-analytic meanings of "freedom": The contributions of Israel Goldiamond. *Behavior and Social Issues*, *27*, 4–19.

Cohen, H. L., & Filipczak, J. (1971). *The authors cooperative behavior analysis series. A new learning environment: A case for learning*. Authors Cooperative.

Cohen-Mansfield, J., Marx, M. S., & Rosenthal, A. S. (1989). A description of agitation in a nursing home. *Journal of Gerontology: Medical Sciences*, *44*, M77–M84. http://dx.doi.org/10.1093/geronj/44.3.M77

Cummings, J. L., Mega, M., Gray, K., Rosenberg-Thompson, S., Carusi, D. A., & Gornbein, J. (1994). The neuropsychiatric inventory: Comprehensive assessment of psychopathology in dementia. *Neurology*, *44*(12), 2308. http://dx.doi.org/10.1212/WNL.44.12.2308

Drossel, C., & Trahan, T. A. (2015, June). Behavioral interventions are first-line treatments for managing changes associated with cognitive decline. *The Behavior Therapist*, 126–131.

Dyrud, J. (1971). Treatment of anxiety states. *Archives of General Psychiatry*, *25*, 298–305.

Epstein, R., & Skinner, B. F. (1980). Resurgence of responding after the cessation of response-independent reinforcement. *Proceedings of the National Academies of Science*, *77*(10), 6251–6253.

Falk, J. L. (1977). The origin and functions of adjunctive behavior. *Animal Learning & Behavior*, *5*(4), 325–335.

Farber, B. A., Blanchard, M., & Love, M. (2019). Secrets and lies in psychotherapy. *American Psychological Association*. https://doi.org/10.1037/0000128-000

Farber, M., & Blanchard, B. (2015). Lying in psychotherapy: Why and what clients don't tell their therapist about therapy and their relationship. *Counselling Psychology Quarterly*, *29*(1), 1–23.

Ferster, C. B., & Skinner, B. F. (1957). *Schedules of reinforcement*. New York: Appleton-Century-Crofts.

Flanagan, B., Goldiamond, I., & Azrin, N. H. (1958). Operant stuttering: The control of stuttering behavior through response contingent consequences. *Journal of the Experimental Analysis of Behavior*, *1*, 173–177.

Flanagan, B., Goldiamond, I., & Azrin, N. H. (1959). Instatement of stuttering in normally fluent individuals through operant procedures. *Science*, *130*(3381), 979–981.

Gambrill, E. (2012). *Social work practice: A critical thinker's guide*. London: Oxford University Press.

Gambrill, E. (2015). Birds of a feather: Applied behavior analysis and quality of life. *Research on Social Work Practice*, *23*(2), 121–140.

Gimenez, L. S., Layng, T. V. J., & Andronis, P. T. (2003). Contribuições de Israel Goldia- mond para o desenvolvimento da análise do comportamento [Contributions of Israel Goldiamond to the development of the analysis of behavior.]. In M. Brando, et al. (Eds.), *Sobre comportamento e cognicao* (Vol. 11, pp. 34–46). Santo Andre, Brazil: ESETec Editores Associados.

Goldiamond, I. (1962). Perception. In A. J. Bachrach (Ed.), *The experimental foundations of clinical psychology* (pp. 280–340). New York: Basic Books.

Goldiamond, I. (1964). Response bias in perceptual communication. *Disorders of Communication. Research Publications of the Association for Research in Nervous and Mental Diseases*, *42*, Chapter 23.

Goldiamond, I. (1965a). Self-control procedures in personal behavior problems. *Psychological Reports*, *17*, 851–868. Monograph Supplement 3-V 17 (Reprinted in R. W. Ulrich, T. J. Stachnik, & J. H. Mabry (Eds.), *The control of human behavior* (pp. 115–122). Chicago: Scott Foresman.).

Goldiamond, I. (1965b). Stuttering and fluency as manipulatable operant response classes. In L. Krasner & L. P. Ullman (Eds.), *Research in behavior modification* (pp. 106–156). New York: Holt, Rinehart, & Winston.

Goldiamond, I. (1965c). Justified and unjustified alarm over behavioral control. In O. Milton (Ed.), *Behavior disorders: Perspectives and trends* (pp. 237–261). New York: J. B. Lipincott.

Goldiamond, I. (1966). Perception, language, and conceptualization rules. In B. Kleinmuntz (Ed.), *Problem solving* (pp. 183–224). New York: John Wiley.

Goldiamond, I. (1969). Applications of operant conditioning. In C. A. Thomas (Ed.), *Current trends in army medical service psychology* (pp. 198–231). Aurora, CO: Department of the Army, Fitzsimmons General Hospital.

Goldiamond, I. (1970). Human control over human behavior. In M. Wertheimer (Ed.), *Confrontation: Psychology and the problems of today* (pp. 254–406). Glenview, IL: Scott Foresman.

Goldiamond, I. (1974). Toward a constructional approach to social problems: Ethical and constitutional issues raised by applied behavior analysis. *Behaviorism*, *2*, 1–84.

Goldiamond, I. (1975a). Alternative sets as a framework for behavioral formulations and research. *Behaviorism*, *3*, 49–85.

Goldiamond, I. (1975b). A constructional approach to self-control. In A. Schwartz & I. Goldiamond (Eds.), *Social casework: A behavioral approach* (pp. 67–130). New York: Columbia University.

Goldiamond, I. (1975c). Singling out behavior modification for legal regulation: Some effects on patient care, psychotherapy, and research in general. *Arizona Law Review*, 17, 105–126.

Goldiamond, I. (1976a). Protection of human subjects and patients: A social contingency analysis of distinctions between research and practice, and its implications. *Behaviorism*, 4(1), 1–41.

Goldiamond, I. (1976b). Singling out self-administered behavior therapies for professional overview. *American Psychologist*, 31, 142–147.

Goldiamond, I. (1976c). Coping and adaptive behaviors of the disabled. In G. L. Albrecht (Ed.), *The sociology of physical disability and rehabilitation* (pp. 97–138). Pittsburgh: University of Pittsburgh.

Goldiamond, I. (1977). Insider-outsider problems: A constructional approach. *Rehabilitation Psychology*, 22, 103–116.

Goldiamond, I. (1978). *A programming contingency analysis of mental health (MABA Presidential Speech, revised and expanded 1983)*. Israel Goldiamond Papers, Accession No. 2005–59, University of Chicago Library Special Collections Research Center Archives and Manuscripts.

Goldiamond, I. (1979a). Behavioral approaches and liaison psychiatry. *Psychiatric Clinics of North America*, 2, 379–401.

Goldiamond, I. (1979b). Emotions and emotional behavior: A consequential analysis and treatment. In *Audiotape, association for the advancement of behavior therapy*. New York: BMA Audio Cassettes Publisher.

Goldiamond, I. (1984). Training parents and ethicists in nonlinear behavior analysis. In R. F. Dangel & R. A. Polster (Eds.), *Parent training: Foundations of research and practice* (pp. 504–546). New York: Guilford.

Goldiamond, I., & Dyrud, J. (1968). Some applications and implications of behavioral analysis for psychotherapy. In J. M. Shlien (Ed.), *Research in psychotherapy* (Vol. 3, pp. 54–89). Washington, DC: American Psychological Association.

Goldiamond, I., Dyrud, J., & Miller, M. (1965). Practice as research in professional psychology. *Canadian Psychologist*, 6, 110–128.

Goldiamond, I., & Hawkins, W. F. (1958). Vexierversuch: The log relationship between word-frequency and recognition obtained in the absence of stimulus words. *Journal of Experimental Psychology*, 56, 457–463.

Goldiamond, I., & Schwartz, A. (1975). The Smith case. In A. Schwartz & I. Goldiamond (Eds.), *Social casework: A behavioral approach* (pp. 131–192). New York: Columbia University.

Goldiamond, I., & Thompson, D. (1967/2004). *The blue books: Goldiamond & Thompson's the functional analysis of behavior* (P. T. Andronis, Ed.). Cambridge, MA: Cambridge Center for Behavioral Studies.

Grant, P. M., Bredemeier, K., & Beck, A. T. (2017). Six-month follow-up of recovery-oriented cognitive therapy for low-functioning individuals with schizophrenia. *Psychiatric Services*, 68, 997–1002.

Isaacs, W., Thomas, J., & Goldiamond, I. (1960). Application of operant conditioning procedures to reinstate verbal behavior in psychotics. *Journal of Speech and Hearing Disorders*, 25, 8–12.

Langthorne, P., & McGill, P. (2009). A tutorial on the concept of the motivating operation and its importance to application. *Behavior Analysis in Practice*, 2(2), 22–31.

Layng, R. (2016). *Need results fast? Use your imagination.* Paper presentation, the 42nd Annual Conference of the Association for Behavior Analysis, Chicago, IL.

Layng, T. V. J. (2006). Emotions and emotional behavior: A constructional approach to understanding some social benefits of aggression. *Brazilian Journal of Behavior Analysis*, 2(2), 155–170.

Layng, T. V. J. (2009). The search for an effective clinical behavior analysis: The nonlinear thinking of Israel Goldiamond. *The Behavior Analyst, 32*(1), 163–184.

Layng, T. V. J. (2017). Private emotions as contingency descriptors: Emotions, emotional behavior, and their evolution. *European Journal of Behavior Analysis, 18*(2), 168–179. http://dx.doi.org/10.1080/15021149.2017.1304875

Layng, T. V. J., & Andronis, P. T. (1984). Toward a functional analysis of delusional speech and hallucinatory behavior. *The Behavior Analyst, 7*, 139–156.

Layng, T. V. J., Andronis, P. T., & Goldiamond, I. (1999). Animal models of psychopathology: The establishment, maintenance, attenuation, and persistence of head- banging by pigeons. *Journal of Behavior Therapy and Experimental Psychiatry, 30*, 45–61.

Layng, T. V. J., Merley, S., Cohen, J., Andronis, P. T., & Layng, M. (1976). Programmed instruction, self-control, and in-patient psychiatry. *Educational Resource Clearinghouse (ERIC)*, Document Listing No. 142 886.

Layng, T. V. J., Sota, M., & Leon, M. (2011). Thinking through text comprehension I: Foundation and guiding relations. *The Behavior Analyst Today, 12*, 1–10.

Leon, M., Layng, T. V. J., & Sota, M. (2011). Thinking through text comprehension III: The programing of verbal and investigative repertoires. *The Behavior Analyst Today, 12*, 11–20.

Maslow, A. H. (1943). A theory of human motivation. *Psychological Review, 50*(4), 370–396.

Merley, S., & Layng, T. V. J. (1976). In-patient psychiatry and programed instruction: Application and research in constructional theory. *Improving Human Performance Quarterly, 5*, 35–46.

Michael, J. (1983). Evocative and repertoire-altering effects of an environmental event. *The Analysis of Verbal Behavior, 2*(1), 19–21.

Overton, D. A. (1984). State dependent learning and drug discriminations. In L. L. Iversen, S. D. Iversen, & S. H. Snyder (Eds.), *Drugs, neurotransmitters, and behavior.* Boston, MA: Springer. https://doi.org/10.1007/978-1-4615-7178-0_2

Paul, G. L., Tobias, L. L., & Holly, B. L. (1972). Maintenance psychotropic drugs in the presence of active treatment programs: A triple-blind withdrawal study with long-term mental patients. *Archives of General Psychiatry, 27*(1), 106–115.

Pavlov, I. P. (1927). *Conditioned reflexes* (G. V. Anrep, Trans.). London: Oxford University Press.

Ray, B. A., & Sidman, M. (1970). Reinforcement schedules and stimulus control. In W. N. Schoenfeld (Ed.), *The theory of reinforcement schedules* (pp. 187–214). New York: Appleton-Century-Crofts.

Robbins, J. K., Layng, T. V. J., & Karp, H. J. (1995). Ambiguity and the abstract tact: A signal detection analysis. *Analysis of Verbal Behavior, 12*, 1–11.

Schoenfeld, W. N. (Ed.). (1970). *The theory of reinforcement schedules.* New York, NY: Appleton-Century-Crofts.

Schwartz, A., & Goldiamond, I. (1975). *Social casework: A behavioral approach.* New York: Columbia University.

Skinner, B. F. (1953). *Science and human behavior.* New York, NY: McMillan.

Skinner, B. F. (1956). A case history in scientific method. *American Psychologist, 11*, 221–233.

Skinner, B. F. (1957). *Verbal behavior.* Englewood Cliffs, NJ: Prentice-Hall.

Sota, M., Leon, M., & Layng, T. V. J. (2011). Thinking through text comprehension II: Analysis of verbal and investigative repertoires. *The Behavior Analyst Today, 12*, 21–33.

Stagner, R. (1977). Homeostasis, discrepancy, dissonance. *Motivation and Emotion, 1*, 103–138.

Trahan, M. A., Donaldson, J. M., McNabney, M. K., & Kahng, S. (2014). The influence of antecedents and consequences on the occurrence of bizarre speech in individuals with dementia. *Behavioral Interventions, 29*(4), 286–303. doi:10.1002/bin.1393

Travis, M. (1982). *Matching client entry repertoires and professional programming repertoires in a nutrition program.* Unpublished doctoral dissertation, University of Chicago.

Twyman, J. S., Layng, T. V. J., Stikeleather, G., & Hobbins, K. (2004). A Nonlinear approach to curriculum design: The role of behavior analysis in building an effective reading program. In W. L. Heward, T. E. Heron, N. A. Neef, S. M. peterson, D. M. Sainato, G. Y. Cartledge, et al. (Eds.), *Focus on behavior analysis in education: Achievements, challenges, and opportunities* (pp. 55–68). Upper Saddle River, NJ: Prentice Hall.

Wetherington, C. L. (1982). Is adjunctive behavior a third class of behavior? *Neuroscience and Biobehavioral Reviews, 6*(3), 329–350.

Whitehead, W. E., Renault, P. F., & Goldiamond, I. (1975). Modification of human gastric acid secretion with operant-conditioning procedures. *Journal of Applied Behavior Analysis, 8*, 147–156.

Young, P. T. (1959). The role of affective processes in learning and motivation. *Psychological Review, 66*(2), 104–125.

Index